DESIGN
MATTERS

ROCKPORT

© 2012 ROCKPORT PUBLISHERS, INC.

First published in the United States of America in 2012 by
Rockport Publishers, a member of
Quayside Publishing Group
100 Cummings Center
Suite 406-L
Beverly, Massachusetts 01915-6101
Telephone: (978) 282-9590
Fax: (978) 283-2742
www.rockpub.com

10 9 8 7 6 5 4 3 2 1

ISBN-13: 978-1-59253-738-9

This publication is comprised of excerpted material previously published in *Design Matters //
Brochures 01, Design Matters // Logos 01, Design Matters // Packaging 01,* and *Design
Matters // Portfolios 01,* © Rockport Publishers

Digital edition published in 2012
ISBN-13: 978-1-61058-1-622

Library of Congress Cataloging-in-Publication Data available

Design: CAPUSLE
Layout: Rockport Publishers

Printed in Singapore

DESIGN MATTERS

AN ESSENTIAL PRIMER

MAURA KELLER   MICHELLE TAUTE   CAPSULE

BEVERLY MASSACHUSETTS

ROCKPORT PUBLISHERS

Contents

EVERYTHING IN SIGHT.

THE WALLPAPER OF SPANISH CAVEMEN, THE HIEROGLYPH-RIDDEN OBELISKS OF ANCIENT EGYPT—MODERN DESIGN HAS DESCENDED FROM A PRIMEVAL TRADITION OF ICONOGRAPHY, EMBODYING THE SAME SIMPLICITY, DIRECTNESS, AND PREOCCUPATION WITH VISUAL CODIFICATION HUMANS EMBRACED LONG, LONG AGO.

What Is a Logo?

Just as ancient ancestors communicated through visual icons, modern graphics speak to customers through imagery and text to impress values, functions, and hierarchies on millions of people. You have the responsibility and opportunity to make a lasting global impression.

Visual icons communicate basically and directly—which is perfect for branding, when the goal is to convey a message with minimum time or strain on the audience. This is not to say words aren't important, especially for more-evolved forms of communication, such as, say, novels or inauguration speeches. These benefit greatly from well-bred vocabularies.

This book aspires to inform anyone who has joined or wants to join the great tradition of long-gone cave men and Egyptians. It's for designers hoping to make a unique mark on the canvas of time, presenting theories, process, examples, and methods from design professionals around the world. It's structured to guide readers through the defined stages of process: planning, creating, and implementing. *Design Matters* delves into the abstract, emotional, and instinctual elements that are so critical to creativity of any kind.

PLANNI

- BROCHURES
- LOGOS
- PACKAGING
- PORTFOLIOS

NG

"COME AT THESE PROJECTS FROM THE STANDPOINT OF BEING AN ADVOCATE AND A PARTNER—NOT AN AUTHORITY. YOU DON'T EVER WANT TO TALK DOWN TO YOUR CLIENT." —CHRISTIAN HELMS, A PARTNER AT THE DECODER RING

IT'S TEMPTING TO HEAD STRAIGHT FOR
THE COMPUTER OR SKETCHBOOK WHEN A
BROCHURE PROJECT HITS YOUR RADAR SCREEN.
BUT JUMPING AHEAD TO THE PIECE'S LOOK AND
FEEL BEFORE YOU TRULY UNDERSTAND THE
PROBLEM—AND HOW BEST TO SOLVE IT—ONLY
MAKES MORE WORK IN THE LONG RUN.

Building a Foundation

"The visual part is fun," says Thomas Hull, a principal at Rigsby Hull in Houston. "You want to cut right to the chase quickly." Taking the time to plan, however, is one of the most crucial stages of any successful project. Without knowing exactly what you're trying to achieve, it's nearly impossible to come up with an appropriate solution. So, where do you start if it's not at the keyboard? Ben Graham, a principal at Turnstyle in Seattle, believes there are three things you need to understand right away:

1. The client: do you know who the company really is and what challenges it faces?

2. The target audience: whom does your client want to reach and what will this group find compelling?

3. The relationship between the two: what will be believable to the audience?

These three knowledge points provide the foundation for working on any project, and if you want to truly understand each one, you'll need to spend some quality time getting to know your client. When Tim Hartford, president of Hartford Design in Chicago works with a new company, his team sits down with the key players and goes through a list of important questions. They'll ask about the business, target audience, and competition. Most clients can provide fairly detailed information about all three. Also, asking for samples of the company's existing materials offers further insight.

RbK

women

a few simple beliefs

▲ ► *Understanding the audience is a key part of planning any brochure. This piece, for example, was created to communicate with several groups: department-store buyers, fashion experts, and internal Reebok staff. "Overall, I think the feeling is somewhat soft and feminine," says Ben Graham, a principal at Turnstyle. "But it's not floral or dainty."*

We **believe** in a thousand shades of strong.

For women, strength comes in many forms. Not just the might and muscle kind of strong. Or the in-your-face kind of strong. But the kind of strong that's quiet. That's personal. That starts inside and works its way out. Above all, we believe in strength defined by courage—whether it's athletic courage, mental courage, or simply the courage of our convictions.

We believe in the brand called you.

Some brands need to own the spotlight. They command you to do it, be it, reach it—or else. Which begs the question: whose brand are we talking about anyway? We believe women care about brands, but they don't necessarily want to be a billboard for corporate aspirations. At Reebok, we're honored to play a supporting role in the starring attraction called you.

It also helps to conduct a little initial research of your own—even if it's just visiting the company's website—so you can ask more educated questions. "Try to learn as much as you can about the client and what their needs are," Hartford says. "That may even change what is delivered. They may have a preconceived notion that they need a website, but one of your questions may find that a direct-mail campaign really makes more sense."

Hartford recommends heading into the first client meeting with a blank slate and a willingness to listen. As the discussion progresses, try to hit all the essential questions. What differentiates the company from the competition? What messages would the client like to convey? Where would the company like to be in three to five years? What kinds of messages resonate with its audiences? Once you start to achieve a clearer picture of the company and audience, you can start to pare down the information. Hartford sums it up with this question: "If someone just walked away with one key message, what would it be?"

Eventually, the conversation should turn back to the project at hand. "What is it we want people to do as a result of that piece?" Graham

says. "Or is it just something they want them to think or feel about the company?" It's also crucial to know how the brochure will be used. Is it going to be given out on sales calls? Or mailed? Hull's firm takes the time to create a written summary—roughly a third of a page—outlining the message, who it's from, and who's going to receive it. "Once you have that clear in your mind, the content informs how it's going to look," he says.

▲◄ *It's important to know what a brochure needs to achieve. In this piece, Hartford Design helped position the Metaphase Design Group as the leader in handheld product research, ergonomics, and design. One way they accomplished this was by making the piece tactile. The push button on the cover, for example, is embossed.*

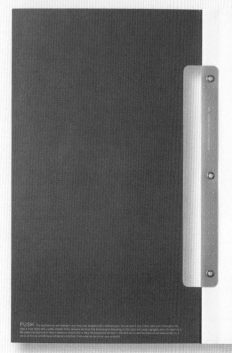

PULL
TWIST
GRIP
PINCH
MOVE
STEER
HOLD
SQUEEZE
TURN
TOUCH
LIFT
SLIDE
TIGHTEN
TAP
BEND
OPEN

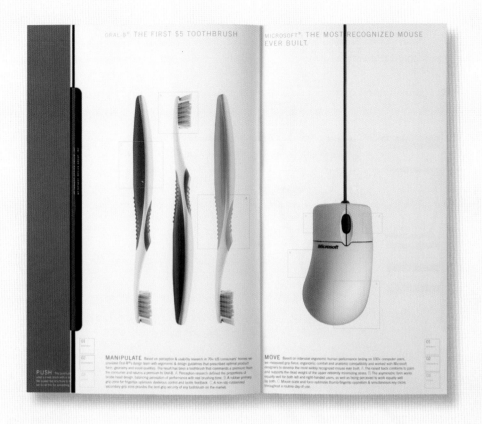

Communicating with Visual Cues

The team at Hahn Smith Design in Toronto approaches these early stages as an opportunity to build relationships and truly partner with clients. To foster better communication, they sometimes use visual cues. "Words like bold, or beautiful, or elegant, or modern—everyone has a very different interpretation of what they mean," says Nigel Smith, a principal at the firm. In order to get everyone on the same page, they might ask clients to bring actual objects they like or dislike to a meeting.

By helping designers get a handle on style preferences, this visual shorthand can move the conversation forward better than vague descriptors. One client, for example, presented Hahn Smith with a collection of items ranging from an architecture book and note cards to photos and artwork. "The client was saying, 'I want my stationery to fit in with this group of other things,'" Smith says. "It was a very proactive way of communicating." In the retail world, Hahn Smith might ask clients extremely direct questions such as, do you like the Gap logo or the Macy's logo? The responses provide them with feedback on style, color, and type, and help build the relationship.

Hands-on Research

Though talking with clients typically unearths a wealth of information, there's also something to be said for hands-on research. When Hahn Smith started working with the flatware company Gourmet Settings, for example, they did a lot of deliberate exploration into the context in which the product was sold. The team organized what they refer to as a "Happy Tour," renting a van and driving to Buffalo, New York, with the president of Gourmet Settings. The group spent the day visiting retailers and taking a look at how silverware is sold on store shelves.

▲► Hahn Smith created this identical brochure in two sizes; the larger one goes to buyers, while the smaller version is included in every box of silverware. The woman holding the heart inside the front cover is actually Gourmet Setting's president. Since Hahn Smith has such a friendly relationship with her, they're truly able to partner on projects.

It's what Alison Hahn, a principal at the design firm, refers to as a trends-based approach to differentiation. After taking a hard look at silverware packaging, it became apparent that "conventions were rampant." This insight guided the team to work with Gourmet Settings to create a distinctive brand voice—one that extends from packaging to brochures. If you take your own retail tour, be sure to watch how consumers interact with the products on the shelf and snap a few pictures of the environment.

Smith warns, however, that small stores may not be happy about your snapping photos.

Anything you can do to become more familiar with a client's products or services will make the problem-solving process more effective. Hahn, for example, went for an eye exam and consultation when she worked on a brochure for a laser-eye surgery company. Though she couldn't see for a few hours after, it gave her firsthand knowledge of the client's

high standards for care and meticulous attention to detail. "Laser eye surgery is very competitive," she says. "We really needed to communicate the commitment and quality." Other information-gathering efforts are less time intensive. For example, the firm had the office administrator send a letter from home requesting a catalog from a client's competitor.

Visual freedom is possible.
What are you waiting for?

►▼ *As part of her research for this brochure, Alison Hahn, principal of Hahn Smith Design, visited the Herzig Eye Institute for a consultation and eye exam. "The free consultations are key to what they do," she says. Since many competitors' materials are cluttered, Hahn Smith worked with the client to hit key points and keep this piece simple.*

Our goal is 100% patient satisfaction. No gimmicks, and no surprises.

Be confident.
Imagine feeling assured about your appearance, and more importantly, being in control, less vulnerable to the annoying dependence on glasses and contacts. It's about being the best you can be. Why wait?

The Herzig Difference. At the Herzig Eye Institute our commitment is to provide each patient with their best possible vision correction, superior surgical treatments, and the highest level of patient care.

Medical Excellence. You have high expectations. We have the highest standards of medical excellence at the Herzig Eye Institute. Our team of renowned surgeons has been selected for their outstanding microsurgical experience in custom vision correction. Thanks to our superb track record, doctors across North America regularly and confidently refer their more difficult cases to us.

The Best Option for You. Your eyes are complex and precious. There is no one-size-fits-all solution. The Herzig Eye Institute specializes in precisely matching the appropriate treatment to a patient's unique needs to achieve their best possible vision. Your treatment may involve Laser Vision Correction or one of our other customized treatments. At the Herzig Eye Institute we utilize only the most advanced and proven vision correction technology to ensure we offer the best and safest option to you.

Excellence in Patient Care. We are committed to providing a full continuum of quality care from start to solution. From your thorough eye examination and personal consultation with your surgeon, to ensuring a comfortable and relaxed surgical procedure, to the very finest follow-up care during your recovery. Your care is our priority. We are also committed to keeping you fully informed. No question is too simple, no concern is too trivial. After all, the more you understand, the more confident you'll be in making the right decision. This unyielding passion for excellence in patient care is why the Herzig Eye Institute has been awarded the prestigious ISO 9001 certification.

The Herzig Lifetime Commitment. Our goal is 100% patient satisfaction. No gimmicks, and no surprises. Though infrequent, our surgeons will recommend a retreatment to further enhance your primary vision correction treatment if necessary, which of course we will do at no additional cost. At the Herzig Eye Institute our commitment is to provide you with your best possible vision. It's that simple.

www.herzig-eye.com

The Right Message

"Content is king," Hull says. Before his firm sits down to work out a design, they decide what they want to say. For a brochure for a rug dealer, for example, the firm met in the client's shop and listened to her stories about the background and origin of different rugs. Then the team came across a picture of Sigmund Freud's couch with a rug draped across it and discovered that the famous psychologist had written about rugs.

Stories seemed like the perfect way to help this client expand awareness about her business beyond the South. The resulting piece—Eight Rugs, Eight Stories—pairs gorgeous, original product shots with short literary excerpts about rugs. These hail from writers ranging from F. Scott Fitzgerald to Charles Dickens. First, the design team picked the stories, then the client helped pair each one with the most appropriate type of rug. They pulled it all together with a clean, classic feel.

In fact, it isn't uncommon to come up with the perfect concept after carefully listening to how your clients talk about their products. Hahn Smith, for example, based the concept for a Gourmet Settings brochure called "This is just a fork" on the way the company's president discussed the silverware. Designers sat in on sales meetings, met with suppliers, and heard the president talk about the products and company goals quite informally. This helped define the brochure's casual, friendly tone.

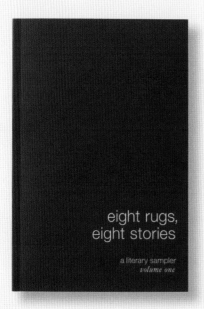

▼ Though they sketched out the shots for this photo shoot in advance, Rigsby Hull made some changes based on the props available on-site. The shoot took place at a private home.

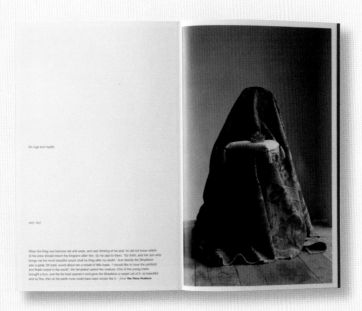

This is just a fork.

◀▼ *This brochure's content and tone was inspired by the way Gourmet Setting's president talks about her company and products. Hahn Smith used the piece to articulate the difference between this flatware company and its competitors.*

We know that. But we're obsessed. Forks (and knives and spoons) are what we're all about. Gourmet Settings really cares about flatware — in fact we're obsessed with it. This is our entire world.

It's just a fork — but it means everything to us.

It's personal. **We'll replace it. We'll improve it. We'll find a new fork for the one you lost** — even if it means that our president will go and find one for you. Personally.

We do a lot to earn your business — but we do even more to keep it.

Design Specifics

Page planning is another powerful tool in your brochure-design arsenal. Create a table of contents. Figure out the best way to unfold the story page by page. Think about pacing. Take a hard look at the text. "Don't tell the whole story on the cover," Hartford says. "Evolve the story over a series of pages."

As you decide what to include in a brochure, you may need to educate your client about the value of being concise. "They think of the printed page as real estate," Hartford says. "They want to build a high-rise when maybe they should be leaving a little bit of grass." Work with your client to edit down information to the essential points and talk with them about the value of making the piece more inviting to read. Focus on the most important information rather than trying to cram more on the page.

Sometimes, though, there's just no way to get around designing a text-heavy brochure—either because all that information is truly necessary, or the client insists on sticking with the extended copy. But this scenario doesn't mean a brochure has to be overwhelming for readers to navigate. Here are some ideas for making all that copy more manageable:

- Look for ways to break up the copy. Partner with the client or a copywriter to insert some catchy subheads where it's appropriate. Are there paragraphs that can be pulled out into sidebars or made into bullet points?

- Try varying the shape and size of the text block. It helps make the piece more approachable if there isn't the same square of copy staring out at readers from every page.

- Think about information architecture. Is it immediately clear what the most important message is on each page? And the second? As a rule of thumb, stick with no more than three levels of information on a given spread—a headline, deck, and body copy.

- Consider using pull quotes to break up blocks of copy. These can help draw readers into the text and make the amount of copy seem less intimidating.

- Mix things up with color. You might try making the body type, or perhaps just the subheads, a different shade. Sometimes even a colored paper can help brighten up a brochure with lots of text.

There are a lot of bases to cover before you start designing, but careful planning is the only way to make sure you're getting the right message across. As Hahn says, "It can be the most beautiful piece in the world, but if it doesn't communicate, it's a failure."

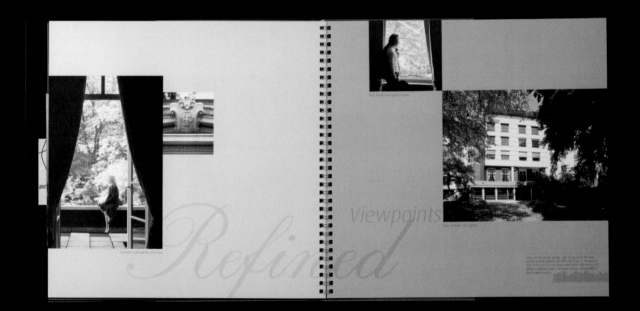

▲► *Since this historic property is located on a canal, reflections became a theme for the piece. The concept is reinforced through the photography, which depicts actual reflections in the water as well as people reflecting in thought.*

ORGANIZING AN INTERNATIONAL PHOTO SHOOT

It can seem like there are a hundred things to worry about before a photo shoot, but when you're coordinating one in another country, it becomes even more critical to pay attention to every detail. This was the situation facing Jason & Jason, a design firm based in Israel, after they were tapped to produce a high-end brochure to promote a commercial property in Amsterdam. Since the images needed to convey exclusivity, the design team decided to direct the shoot in person rather than rely on an unsupervised photographer. Jonathan Jason, executive creative director, walks us through the process he used to make the shoot successful—one that might work just as well for a photo session across town.

- **SCOUT THE LOCATION.** On Jason's first trip to Amsterdam, he checked out the building that would be featured in the brochure. "We use a simple pocket digital camera and shoot as many images as we can," he says.

- **SUBMIT SKETCHES TO THE CLIENT.** The design team uses the initial images to create sketches that show how the photo session will unfold. They try to include as many details as possible, such as how the models will be dressed, to keep the client informed.

- **HIRE AND BRIEF THE PHOTOGRAPHER.** Once the client approves the sketches, the firm locates a photographer and sends along the sketches. Then they discuss these ideas through email and phone conversations. On this shoot, the photographer was responsible for finding models, locating a stylist, arranging for props, and organizing the location.

- **BRING THE CLIENT TO THE SHOOT.** When possible, Jason recommends bringing a client representative to a shoot to authorize critical decisions. This makes it easy to get quick approval on a given shot. On this shoot, the client signed a waiver that gave creative authority to the design firm.

- **CHECK THE WEATHER FORECAST.** Since part of this photo shoot took place outside, the design team needed to build flexibility into their trip dates and the shoot schedule once they were in Amsterdam. "We had to cancel our trip plans twice because of weather," he says.

HERENGRACHT 458
AMSTERDAM

IDENTITY GUIDELINES ARE ONE OF THE ULTIMATE PLANNING TOOLS FOR GRAPHIC DESIGNERS. LIKE A WELL-WRITTEN BUSINESS PLAN, THEY PROVIDE A CONCRETE ROADMAP FOR THE FUTURE. THEY DEFINE WHAT A BRAND STANDS FOR AND HOW IT'S GOING TO BE PRESENTED VISUALLY—WHETHER YOU'RE WORKING ON A BUSINESS CARD OR A TEN-PAGE BROCHURE. THESE BRAND RULES MIGHT DEFINE EVERYTHING FROM CORRECT LOGO USAGE TO ACCEPTED COLOR PALETTES.

Working with Identity Guidelines

At Cincinnati Children's Hospital, a 43-page book helps make sure every project that passes through the hospital's marketing and communications department accurately reflects the brand. "These guidelines set the stage," says Andrea McCorkle, senior art director. "They're the foundation of any communication we do." The hospital's identity guidelines have evolved over time, but the current set emerged from a brand refresh.

During this rebranding process, the department conducted focus groups with different target audiences, including parents and referring physicians. This research helped refine the current visual identity. Parents, for instance, responded well to the hospital's bright, energetic color palette, but there was a need for something slightly more sophisticated when targeting doctors. This insight helped define the brand's secondary color palette, which features a wider range of choices.

The identity book also covers everything from how to use the logo on promotional items, such as T-shirts, hats, and mugs, to the hospital's photography style. Each section includes clear takeaway points for any designer working on the brand. Photos used for the hospital's materials, for example, should be editorial in style and shot with natural light when possible. In addition, the photography guidelines include benchmarks for composition, models, and model direction. This creates a cohesive look across a wide range of projects.

◄ *Cincinnati Children's Hospital identity guidelines come as part of a larger branding kit that includes editorial guidelines, paper samples, and a poster summarizing the brand. These materials keep the hospital's visual identity consistent across a range of materials created by both in-house and external designers.*

► *The target audience for this brochure was referring physicians nationwide, so it needed to have an added level of sophistication. To accomplish this, it uses colors from the brand's secondary palette, which is specifically designed to communicate sophistication and innovation.*

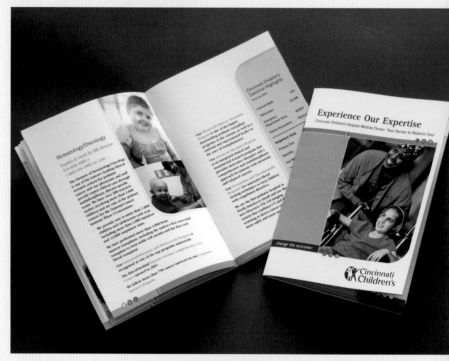

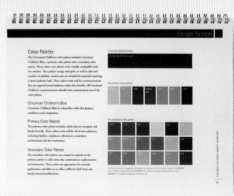

These rules and strategies pay off in countless ways, especially when it comes to maintaining the hospital's brand. "Our company is growing quickly, so more people are becoming heavier users of the brand who aren't in our department," McCorkle says. She uses the identity guidelines, for example, as a starting point when she out sources design work. It gives external graphic designers a crash course in the hospital's visual look and provides a great starting point to talk about specific projects.

All this upfront planning has also helped strengthen communication with the hospital's internal staff. "Sometimes a client will come in with a predetermined idea of what the piece will look like," she says. "We can use the ID guidelines to talk with them." In essence, the book provides an easy way to educate other departments about the hospital's brand. And though you might not find McCorkle flipping through the book at her computer—she knows the guidelines by heart—its content informs design decisions in all her work.

No matter how good the identity guidelines, there's still a lot of planning that needs to take place before you start working on a layout. McCorkle tends to kick off projects by meeting with the marketing representative—similar to an account rep at an agency. They'll talk about the audience and the challenges at hand. She also makes sure to ask a lot of questions. For a piece about an outpatient MRI facility, she made sure to address differentiation: What makes us different from the competition? Why would someone choose this facility or service over other available options? What makes it better? Discussing these points helped her flesh out the creative aspects of the piece.

▲ This brochure kicks off with colorful grids on the front and back covers, a design element outlined in the hospital's branding guidelines. Every new patient at the hospital's outpatient locations receives this guide. It covers topics ranging from insurance to financial aid and provides information in an easily accessible format.

McCorkle recommends some of these same techniques for other designers, whether you're with an agency or working in-house. Start by asking a client whether they have guidelines and requesting samples of previous brochures and communications materials. Then prompt the company to identify the projects they considered successful and, if they're willing, ones they didn't think were up to par. Talking about these past efforts helps build a relationship and provides a framework as you move forward. Another good tactic: ask the client to identify a competitor who they feel may be marketing themselves better.

Once you've nailed all the hard questions, you can move back to those identity guidelines—assuming you're lucky enough to have them. They won't do the hard work for you, but they'll keep you on the same page as the rest of the brand.

▲ Like any good set of identity guidelines, Cincinnati Children's Hospital includes enough flexibility to encompass a range of projects and goals. This mailer, for example, is printed on a metallic paper to give it a special feel. There's a coupon for a free bike helmet inside, so designers wanted to differentiate it from other mailers.

above & beyond

A PICTURE OF PROGRAMS THAT BENEFIT THE COMMUNITY

Cincinnati Children's

change the outcome®

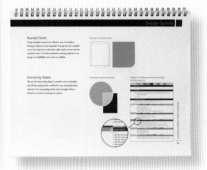

◄▼ *This brochure discusses how the hospital's programs benefit the community. The rounded corner on the photo caption represents a design element from the identity guidelines and helps pull attention to this spot on the spread.*

No Time to Wait
College Hill Campus Addresses a Critical Need

In 1995 the Emergency Department at Cincinnati Children's treated 800 children and adolescents with mental illness. In 2000 that number jumped to more than 2,000 — a 150 percent increase.

With outbacks to state and federal funding and limited insurance reimbursement, families were forced to seek emergency solutions for chronic behavioral health illnesses or send their children out of the Tristate for longer-term, residential services. Where else could families turn?

Cincinnati Children's responded to this crisis by opening the College Hill Campus, a 60-bed psychiatric treatment center for children and adolescents requiring inpatient hospitalization for acute psychiatric care, residential treatment for chronic mental illness and outpatient psychiatric services.

Meeting the Need
"Before we opened the College Hill Campus, kids were leaving the area

and going to other states to get help for mental illness. We decided we needed to bring kids back," says Mike Sherlton, RN, PhD, senior clinical director of the Division of Child and Adolescent Psychiatry. "If we can meet them here, then as a community we can take care of our kids."

Paying the Price
From the beginning it was understood the cost to open and operate the College Hill Campus would be substantial. In fiscal year 2005 Cincinnati Children's lost more than $6 million on outpatient and residential mental health services at the medical center and the College Hill Campus. But the cost of not providing care to those suffering from conditions such as schizophrenia, bipolar disorder, major depressive disorder and obsessive-compulsive disorder would be far greater.

Without treatment those with mental illness face unnecessary disability, unemployment, substance abuse, homelessness, inappropriate incarceration and suicide. The National Alliance on Mental Illness estimates that the economic cost of untreated mental illness is more than $100 billion each year in the United States.

"We offer high-quality care to a population with desperate needs. The children we see often struggle with a major mental illness like bipolar disorder or severe depression, a history of abuse and neglect or exposure to violence, and cognitive impairment that challenges traditional methods of treatment," says Michael Sorter, MD, director of the Division of Child and Adolescent Psychiatry. Despite these realities, "Our outcomes demonstrate that mental health treatment works."

Family-Centered Care in Action
Having a child with mental illness can be difficult for all family members. Treatment plans take a multidisciplinary approach that includes family involvement. Parents and guardians are encouraged to visit their sons or daughters daily, take part in therapy sessions and talk with medical providers. Families learn about the roles of medication and therapy so treatment can continue successfully after a child leaves the campus. As their understanding of mental illness deepens, parents and guardians become equipped to manage their child's illness in ways that benefit the entire family.

Having a child with mental illness can be difficult for all family members. Treatment plans take a multidisciplinary approach that includes family involvement.

Measuring the Outcome
Since 2003, when residential treatment began at the College Hill Campus, more than 200 individuals have been through the program. Offering intensive treatment with an emphasis on family-centered care has significantly reduced the amount of time children are in treatment. The average length of stay for children in the residential program at the College Hill Campus is 99 days, compared to six months to a year in other residential treatment facilities across the country.

The treatment of mental illness comes in many forms. Recreational therapist Jill Forest has teenagers from College Hill Campus make weekly visits to a nearby nursing home to assist with activities, take walks and have conversations with the elderly residents.

"We give our kids a chance to do something for someone else," Jill says. "Making a difference in another person's life can improve physical and mental health, particularly for those who struggle with depression and mental illness." ●

The College Hill Campus is a 60-bed psychiatric inpatient center for children and adolescents requiring inpatient hospitalization for acute psychiatric care, residential treatment for chronic mental illness and outpatient psychiatric services.

Pet therapy is one of the recreational therapies at the College Hill Campus.

BY THE TIME THEY SOUGHT OUT A DESIGN FIRM, THE OUTFIT MEDIA GROUP ALREADY KNEW WHAT THEY WANTED: A LOGO AND A SIMPLE BROCHURE. THE HOLLYWOOD PRODUCTION COMPANY HAD RECENTLY BROKEN OFF FROM ANOTHER GROUP AND NEEDED TO PROMOTE ITS CAPABILITIES TO POTENTIAL CLIENTS. LUCKILY, THE COMPANY TURNED TO THE DECODER RING FOR HELP—AN AUSTIN-BASED DESIGN FIRM THAT ISN'T AFRAID TO ASK QUESTIONS.

DESIGN MATTERS // PLANNING | BROCHURES

Is a Brochure the Right Solution?

The design team took the time to understand the company's goals before they jumped into producing a brochure. What was Outfit Media Group trying to achieve? How is it different from the competition? It quickly became clear that a one-sheet—a simple brochure commonly used in this industry—wasn't going to grab attention. Designers also learned a key selling point for Outfit Media Group: the relatively small company could handle projects from start to finish.

This insight led to the idea for the logo, a one-eyed octopus with many legs. It represents a company with multiple capabilities (the legs) and a singular creative identity (the eye). Designers also decided a brochure wasn't the best way to promote Outfit Media to potential clients. "These one sheets either get thrown out or the best-case scenario is they get put into a file folder," says Christian Helms, a partner at The Decoder Ring. "We made it our goal to defy the file folder and the trash can."

The client liked the idea of a poster that recipients could hang on the wall, but designers decided to take things one step further and think of other ways this piece could work around the office. After a little brainstorming, they came up with a host of functional items to feature on the back of the poster, ranging from an air freshener and capabilities sheet to a DVD sleeve. These are things people might actually tear out and use, giving more promotional mileage to Outfit Media.

Think your clients would never go for such an offbeat solution? Try Helms' tips for working collaboratively and championing big ideas:

- Think past the physical object. "Work harder and don't accept what you're told," Helms says. "Don't be a service bureau. If they say they want a logo, ask them why they want a logo. Ask what the goal is."

- Listen and ask questions. Start with your initial contact, then move on to key decision-makers and even the secretary. "You never know where that insight is going to come from," Helms says. Rank and file employees often have a unique—and sometimes more realistic—perspective compared to their superiors.

- Explain your process. "We show examples of other projects and talk about how they evolved," Helms says. You can't count on every client to know what designers do, so make the extra effort to illustrate your working methods and capabilities.

- Work hard to build trust and strong relationships. "Come at these projects from the standpoint of being an advocate and a partner—not an authority," Helms says. "You don't ever want to talk down to your client." Nor should you approach a client as an adversary.

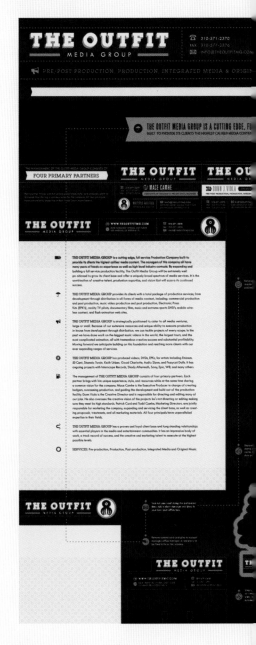

▲ Though the client originally wanted a brochure, The Decoder Ring worked with them to uncover a better solution—this 18 x 24–inch (45.7 x 61–cm) poster. It gave the Hollywood production company more face time with potential clients and turned into a conversation piece in many offices. People passing through asked who the Outfit Media Group was and what they did. The back features a host of items for people to tear out and use, ranging from an air freshener to a capabilities sheet.

MAPS COME IN ALL FORMS. DIGITAL NAVIGATION SPEAKS TO DRIVERS. OLD PHOTOS AND SCRAPS OF PAPER ILLUMINATE THE PATH TO DEEPLY HIDDEN MEMORIES. SETTING STRATEGY IS A PROCESS OF SKETCHING THE MAP, WHETHER YOU BASE ITS CREATION ON LOGIC OR INSTINCT. THE REALLY GOOD ONES LEAD TO TREASURE.

Setting Strategy

Setting strategy is all about understanding what you have to say and to whom you have to say it. If a company wants to base strategy on price, it should say it is the best value, and it should say it to people for whom value is the most important selling point. Storewide sales can be a profitable selling tool for these companies, especially in generic product categories.

Of course, another strategy is to emphasize unique qualities that make a brand desirable, regardless of price. This way, the brand can attract consumers without having to cut into profit. Classic brand strategy engages the consumer thought process by designing emotional benefits into brands. By tying emotion to the brand, brand strategy meets the consumer's emotional requirements while leaving price, availability, purpose, and other features and benefits to satisfy rational needs.

Logos are an important part of this equation. Logos help consumers make decisions by embodying the meaning of the brand, spreading the most desirable attributes in front of the consumer and making the decision identifiable and easy.

Brand strategy is all about finding the path to earning customer loyalty, increasing margins, and keeping customers coming back day after day. The following section explores ways to set strategy.

The Reasons We Ask Questions

WHO SAYS SUPERMODELS ARE DUMB?

Which came first: the answer or the question? Unlike that vexatious chicken and egg, the answer to this riddle is fairly straightforward. Questions—What's the meaning of life? Is there a heaven? Where's the other sock?—can and do exist without clear-cut answers. However, answers—"happiness," "maybe," and "in the dryer"—cannot be uncovered without first asking a question. This applies to planning strategy. The more questions, the more answers. The more answers, the stronger and more relevant the consequent design.

Sometimes designers must set their own business strategy, as is the case for many freelancers. Sometimes they just need to be able to communicate with account people. What exactly do you know about business?

To learn a little more, gather and organize your questions. Then take the list and go to the nearest sphere of business thinking, be it the "business" section of the library, the bookstore, or the Internet. Don't waste time with reheated strategy. Get answers from the leaders of the pack.

If you're a designer creating a business strategy, it's good to read up on modern business thinkers such as David Aaker, Peter Drucker, and Michael Porter. There are plenty of authors to pick from, and it's not difficult material. Like most business strategy, their work is straightforward and fairly easy for beginners to understand. You might find it dry at first, but eventually you can start to connect it back to your world and apply it in your daily client work.

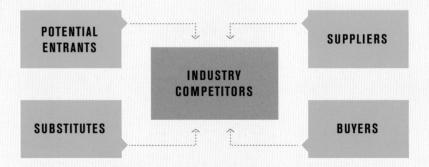

Porter's Five Forces model, a simple tool that frames industry power dynamics, is just one of countless business tools that can help focus design toward the client's business objectives. The Porter's Five Forces model identifies market forces that impact the client's business.

Even designers who have the benefit of account people should maintain a certain level of business strategy in their own right. With it, you can better showcase the power of your design to business audiences. This will strengthen the case to any business manager at any level of any organization.

For PrairieStone Pharmacy, a new entrant into the highly competitive medical category, business strategy was a key driver of the brand strategy. Part of the company's business strategy was to recruit a quality workforce by offering a better work environment for pharmacists, employees who are hard to find in a competitive market. One way PrairieStone improved the work environment was by introducing automated pill-sorting technology that allowed pharmacists to get out from behind the glass wall.

A peripheral benefit of this was that functional space behind the counter could be reduced, lowering the cost of operations and increasing profit per retail square foot. This in turn attracted retail clients who planned to add a pharmacy to their retail operations—they were drawn to PrairieStone's service quality and ability, consistently, to increase overall store traffic. These dynamics helped strengthen a powerful and valuable business strategy that led to a thoughtful brand strategy. These strategies then informed a logo design that exemplified the PrairieStone Pharmacy story. Understanding the business strategy made the design stronger and more relevant.

Early pharmacies in the Midwest region of the United States used prairie stone to create mortars and pestles. PrairieStone Pharmacy's logo functions nationally while alluding to its agrarian roots. CAPSULE

Design as a discipline is a competitive advantage. It's a fundamental part of the business strategy. Therefore, citizens of any design community need to believe in business strategy and understand it before they begin designing.

Purpose of Planning

DON'T TICK OFF THE CLOCK

"I do my best work under pressure." Ever heard that? Ever said that? It's the credo of procrastinators everywhere. We'd all like to think that great work is the product of ingenious, "Eureka!" moments, when lightning strikes and creations miraculously spring forth. This is risky. Even if procrastination has worked in the past, a happy fluke does not a modus operandi make.

One hour of planning usually eliminates two hours of reworking. Plan now and enjoy extra time later.

Beware—or, before you know it, you're holding a snarling deadline at bay with nothing but a mocha-fueled all-nighter and a presentation riddled with more holes than Grandma's latest crochet project. As for that "work under pressure" nonsense? Pure poppycock. Your thrown-together presentation may very well be better than another person's well-planned presentation. Fine. But your thrown-together presentation will never be better than your own well-planned presentation. If you want to progress as a designer, plan in advance and check excuses at the door.

Also, keep in mind that success is not synonymous with perfection. Planning never removes all risk. In many organizations, strategic planning constitutes hours of meetings spent setting strategies and tactics. It can become easy to worry over little details of the planning effort and rigidly follow the rules. But a successful plan is gauged by big-picture success. When you encounter bumps in the road, simply adapt the plan. The more bumps you encounter, the more proof there is that a definitive plan was in place to begin with. Don't get tangled up in execution. Keep your eye on the big prize.

THE OUTSET BRAND: RARE DESIGN, DONE WELL

"Foodies" are a growing force in the marketplace. They are mostly baby boomers who view the creation and enjoyment of cuisine as a refined hobby. "Grill masters" are a particularly passionate subset within this category. Seasoned grill masters are concerned with three things: the quality of the grill, the meat, and the tools.

The Outset brand increases the impact of its mark by making it a primary focus of the product design. In traditional execution, the logo is part of the packaging, which is discarded soon after purchase. Or it is a small mark on a corner of the product, to be seen or ignored at the user's discretion. Outset made the logo a primary focal point of its products, so users are reminded of exactly what brand they are using every time they grill, wash, or put away their grilling utensils.

The logo becomes part of the product as a simplified graphic element. It pleases aesthetically and provides a point of conversation between the grill master and the grill master's friends and family.

Creating the Ideal Logo Design Brief

KEEP YOUR EYES ON THE ROAD

Design briefs: keep them brief. Seems simple enough to remember, no? It may be simple to remember, but lassoing 100 years of a business, three months of current research, and a gaggle of planning meetings into one brief document is a formidable task—and this will often be the case. Keep design briefs brief, to the point, and easy to follow.

Beyond being spare, design briefs must set direction and inspire design. So the more focused the language, the better. And the more inspirational the language, the better. Start preparing the brief by defining brand strategy. From there, pinpoint the brand's core competitors, collaborators, and customers.

Once you identify the basics, set expectations. Write with precise, thoughtful language. Communicate the final objectives and goals with a rich (but concise) explanation that properly sets client expectations. Establish a wide variety of objectives concerning components that are measurable: timing, budget, sales, etc. But also remind the client that, though creative goals aren't necessarily quantifiable, they are observable and just as important. If only measurable objectives are set forth, then those are the only objectives by which the work is judged, irrespective of other accomplishments.

Successful briefs don't just set expectations, they also translate. The brief is the bridge between the thought and the image, so it must be descriptive. Therefore, language is essential—the more illustrative, the better. For example, what does the frequently encountered word "innovative" really mean? What is the visual association? Does it translate visually? Not necessarily. Dynamic words don't always make dynamic visuals. A better way to create visual associations is to reference existing images or abstract iterations. Spend time experimenting and figuring out which visual option works best.

The design brief should also consider and answer the classic *whos* and *whats*. Who is the client (history, people, size, and industry)? What are the budget and timeline (overall and broken down piece by piece)? Who is the audience (age, income, location, habits, and tastes)? What has occurred to date? What is the catalyst for changing the logo, and what has been done so far? What does success look like for the client (specific analytical goals, return on investment, sales, usage rates, internal rate of return, or any other predetermined analytical benchmarks)? And, what is the makeup of the decision-making team (people, personalities, individual goals, and a final decision-maker)?

Finally, how much time should it take to create a brief? After all research and strategy work is complete, no more than two hours. If it takes longer, you're likely starting to rehash existing strategy or language. How much time should it take to review a brief? Two hours is bordering on excessive. If you catch yourself admiring the increasingly elaborate doodles of your design team, it's a not-so-subtle sign that things have taken a turn off the productive highway. Boredom is a bad way to kick off a project. Keep the brief clear, focused, and brief.

DESIGN BRIEF QUESTIONS

••• What three audiences will see this logo design the most often?

••• If there was one thing you could communicate to each audience, what would that be?

••• What are the brand attributes, promises, features, benefits, and positioning statement?

••• What words describe the brand personality? What visuals communicate the brand personality?

••• Where will this logo appear most often? On what media: golf balls; billboards; business cards?

••• Are there any must-haves or nice-to-have items?

••• Who are your competitors? Who are your collaborators?

••• What is the budget in hours? When are presentations scheduled?

••• Why do you need a logo? Or, why are you changing the existing logo design?

••• How will you measure this logo design's success? Smooth implementation? Awards? A change in signals? An energized staff? Other tests or benchmarks?

AT&T: THE INFLUENCE OF A BRIEF ON AN INTERNATIONAL LOGO REDESIGN

When SBC and AT&T merged, AT&T required a logo to signal significant changes to the business strategy. Ed Whitacre Jr., AT&T's president and CEO, voiced the brand's vision as aiming "to be the only communications and entertainment company our customers will ever want."

Interbrand was asked to design a new entity to help actualize this goal in both business and residential sectors. The firm worked off a design brief based around Whitacre's vision, as well as around anticipated changes to the brand resulting from the merger. Extensive brand research confirmed that AT&T was an internationally recognized, iconic brand with a valuable heritage. But many consumers said the company had disappeared from the residential arena and primarily served business-to-business customers.

The goal was to change the perception of the AT&T brand from the monolithic Ma Bell of the past to an evolved company, by balancing AT&T's innovative heritage with SBC's ability to deliver communications and entertainment.

The creative brief defined the brand's positioning strategy by first defining who the key targets were, what the compelling promise was for both residential and business customers, and why consumers should believe this promise. Guided by the creative brief, research uncovered that, over time, the logo had become attached to negative consumer perceptions. For some consumers, the "death star" globe and bold AT&T type appeared bureaucratic and impersonal.

After deciding to change the globe, the team created logo options ranging from evolutionary treatments to revolutionary transformations. Although they had uncovered negative associations with the old globe, the team also found that the drastically retooled identities were too far removed from the original globe and lost the original brand mark's core value and positive consumer equity.

Saul Bass designed the original AT&T logo. For years, it adapted smoothly from one medium to the next. After a lifetime of dutiful service, however, the logo began showing age and became bogged down by consumer brand perceptions and other external factors.

BASS & YAGER

Rather than change the primary color, blue, the designers alluded to modern technology by adding dimension to the globe. The original horizontal wires enveloping the globe symbolized worldwide communications. Updated wires now also impart transparency and luminosity, increasing the brand's approachability and capturing a sense of openness central to the revitalized brand.

Beyond the globe, an even more dramatic change occurred in the logotype. Designers created a custom lowercase font based on the Cingular identity's font, Avenir. Solid monolithic type switched out in favor of softer lowercase type. The resulting tone was more personable, dynamic, and fitting of a business spearheading innovative technology.

Modern improvements to the classic globe don't detract from existing brand history. They expound upon original visual assets to better reflect internal brand development. The ultimate purpose is to show consumers that significant change is occurring—something has improved.
INTERBRAND

ONCE UPON A PANCAKE, PEOPLE INSISTED THE WORLD WAS FLAT. THEN SOMEONE DID A LITTLE RESEARCH. WITH JUST A WHIP OF CURIOSITY AND A DAB OF EXPLORATION, THE WORLD SWELLED INTO A ROTUND, COMPLICATED, SOUFFLÉ OF POSSIBILITIES. RESEARCH, IT SEEMS, LITERALLY MADE THE WORLD GO ROUND.

Conducting Research

A number of things qualify as research. Browsing the Internet. Full, in-depth research, using thousands of individual interviews, months of video analysis, and summary reports stacked on their own dolly. It's all research. Some research methods have a larger price tag, in return for a higher level of confidence in the information they provide. Others offer a much smaller price tag or are completely free. These must be taken for what they are—unregulated and potentially unreliable.

When researching, consider two things. One: know your source. Where does the data come from, and how does the source impact the data received? If you have a research company conducting research, it is part of the source. If you don't trust it, don't use it. Two: conduct enough research to be confident in the results and your opinion of the results. However, also keep in mind that 100 percent confidence doesn't exist.

What to Research and Why

THE PATH TO KNOWLEDGE IS PAVED WITH SHARP STONES

Drooling with excitement. Nodding in unison. Your team is really getting it. Getting a nap in, that is. Research can be pretty boring business. Unfortunately, it's unavoidable if you want to do a proper job. You'll sift a fair amount of sand before you hit pay dirt. Understanding the three stages, three elements, and many methods of research helps hasten the hunt.

Elements are the things being studied. They always remain the same: people, objects, and culture. People are the individuals whose actions and personalities influence—and are influenced by—the experiences of others. Researchers study people by listening to them and observing behaviors. Objects are the things we interact with every day, the physical devices that impact our lives. Researchers study objects by holding, handling, and dissecting them, then questioning how they affect lives and watching how people interact with them. Finally, culture comprises all the history and patterns that make up the human race. To understand cultures and even subcultures, one must study the history, traditions, and values of the community.

Most important, start by memorizing the three elements: people, objects, and culture. Got it? It's not always that simple. But fundamentally it can be simplified to these three.

Thorough research includes three core stages: exploration, data gathering, and testing. Exploration outlines broad issues surrounding the subject matter or elements being studied. Data gathering is about, well, gathering data. At this point you convert the data into information and eventually to knowledge. Testing is the final stage. It's an interaction between individuals and ideas or concepts, meant to identify issues or create a higher level of confidence.

✳ smith&nephew

*The "burst of energy" symbolizes Smith &
Nephew's ongoing passion. The bright,
sunny orange sways contrary to most
medical product brands, setting the brand
apart and conveying warmth and energy. The
casual typeface radiates casual friendliness.*

WOLFF OLINS

SMITH & NEPHEW: TEACH AN OLD BRAND NEW TRICKS

Research was essential to Wolff Olins' redesign of Smith & Nephew. When the
150-year-old firm took on several big acquisitions, it required a logo and brand
image to reflect its new direction.

Wolff Olins started by gathering common language and beliefs from among
Smith & Nephew's various business units around the world. Findings suggested
that they were united in one goal: helping patients by "giving them their lives
back." This became the simple, elegant, and highly emotional core of Smith &
Nephew's brand, from logo design to videos and packing boxes.

*Use launch tools to help introduce the brand
into employees' lives. This is especially
valuable for companies like Smith & Nephew,
whose thousands of employees can be
leveraged to help spread the brand's story.*

*Never overlook a moment to make a
connection. Even on shipping containers
the opportunity exists to communicate a
message. Wolff Olins used several media to
communicate Smith & Nephew's message.*

THE THREE ELEMENTS OF UNDERSTANDING ANY MARKETPLACE

The three research fundamentals are people, objects, and culture. No study can be conducted without influence from these fundamentals. No conclusions can be drawn without understanding how they influence each other. The iPod as a marketplace phenomenon is a good example for illustrating the interdependent relationship among these fundamentals.

PEOPLE

In simplified terms, the iPod phenomenon involves two sets of people. One group is made up of the individuals who listen to music. The other is made up of the people at Apple who created the iPod.

OBJECTS

The iPod is one of several objects within the history of mobile music: before it came the boom box, Walkman, and Discman. Understanding the iPod as an object entails looking at it within a historical context.

CULTURE

Culture includes the belief systems, history, and past patterns of behavior that are the glue holding objects and people together. The iPod blends into behaviors and history surrounding music, commuting, sports, and many other aspects of regional and global culture.

These three elements cannot be separated or substantially defined without one another. Consider all three carefully throughout the research effort. The most common research methods are observation, surveys (print and digital), face-to-face interviews, focus groups, and field studies.

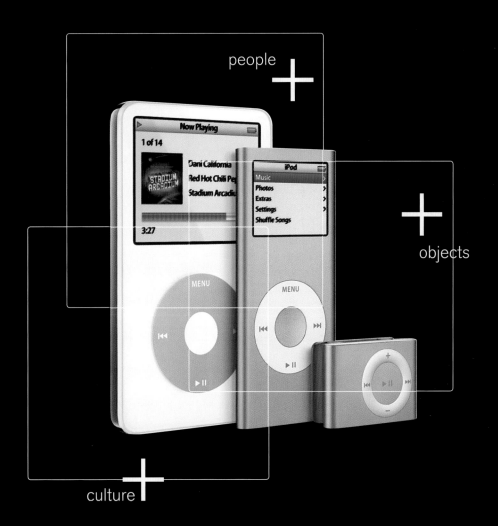

people +

objects +

+ culture

People, objects, and culture are inextricably interwoven. They cannot be separated or substantially defined without one another. Consider all three carefully throughout the research effort.

URBAN LEGEND OR SUBURBAN MYTH?

Pirates no longer sport eye patches. They look like average citizens, looting digital music right from the family computer. Because of this, performers are returning to the road in droves, increasingly relying on live-performance income to supplement shrinking record sales. Leading up to this trend, demand for road venues had been waning for a solid decade, and during that time, not enough locations grew to support current industry needs.

Engage in primary research. To experience club atmosphere firsthand, the design team traveled to Las Vegas and visited, among others, the club Tangerine.

Today, intense competition for audiences and demand for space is pulling artists out of traditional music hubs and into the arms of swelling suburban audiences. Myth Nightclub in Minnesota is one of the first to recognize and cater to this trend. Capsule strove to infuse Myth's logo with this innovative spirit.

Myth's founders dreamed of a concert venue rivaling the dazzling boutique clubs of Las Vegas and chose Capsule to design a logo that would help launch a new suburban concert venue with urban appeal. The challenge was to adapt a Las Vegas atmosphere to attract suburban audiences. To capture the client's vision, Capsule needed to develop a business strategy and conduct qualitative research.

Capsule began by splitting the client team into two parts: one undertaking a brand definition process and the other engaged in a visual ideation process. Visual ideation is an important first step because it helps inform and inspire the design team. The process began with brainstorming. The team gathered relevant resources from the worlds of fashion, technology, music, sports, and travel. It then clipped visually intriguing images from each world and filtered them into three style categories. Each category was created on a separate style board that framed the brand visually in a unique way.

The boards accomplished two essential goals: they brought the client directly into the process by setting style, color, and tone, and, most important, they provoked and guided dialogue to answer objectives for the brand.

Use style boards to articulate a visual language. Style boards, such as these designed for Myth, are especially helpful for soliciting client feedback and creating a common language that both designer and client can understand. CAPSULE

The group that undertook the brand definition process outlined the brand's personality, functional benefits, features, and key messages for the designers. When both groups were finished, Capsule headed to Vegas to bring the visual ideation and brand together. Primary research, which included face-to-face interviews and artifact gathering, outlined expectations and provided tangible inspiration. Capsule spoke with patrons, club owners, artists, and talent agents, who provided insight into club life from several perspectives. Additionally,

Capsule went into clubs seeking artifacts: menus, matchbooks, flyers, coasters, T-shirts, and more. By collecting paraphernalia with a function or look that said something about its respective club, the team was able to bring home physical items to inspire its work.

The preliminary planning and client exercises were an essential part of achieving a logo that reflects the client's vision and also sets the framework for future collateral and designs created after the logo.

Integrate logo design elements into consequent design. Myth's interior design elements were based on the color and design tone first established by the logo.
CAPSULE

MYTH

Strengthen design with observation. To attract multiple audiences, audience, market, and client research guided Myth's logo away from a bias toward any single music genre.
CAPSULE

How to Manage Your Research

AVOID SPLIT ENDS

The research process is like a head of hair. If not maintained, it tangles eventually into a big, snarly mess. If the research process is combed through carefully at the outset, it remains more manageable. There are four steps to achieving this:

1. Temper bias. Bias has a major effect on research outcomes. So give thought to where specific bias originates and then work to offset its influence. Keep in mind that bias exists in any and all research, so completely eliminating it is impossible.

2. Understand a variety of methodologies and what they deliver. Observation is the most authentic methodology, because there is little or no interaction between the observer and subject. This method best identifies specific behaviors.

Surveys are often the most efficient data-gathering method. Historically, these relied heavily on the U.S. Postal Service. Today, the Internet has made this process very convenient. It allows researchers to gather mountains of data from willing participants in the form of either open- or closed-ended questions. Data integrity relies heavily on question wording and the sample used.

Face-to-face interviews are done in one-to-ones, dyads, or triads. There is always one interviewer; the terms refer to the number of interviewees: one, two, or three, respectively. Each combination offers its own unique benefit. However, face-to-face interviews typically offer much of the authenticity of observation, along with the convenience of survey-like feedback.

Focus groups are ideally suited to researchers looking to discover ideas, beliefs, or language around the subject matter. However, focus groups are dangerous when testing ideas or gathering specific data for analysis.

Field studies combine observation and face-to-face interviews done "in the field." They offer authenticity because they probe near consumers' moments of decision. They lend brand research the credibility of authentic context. Field research is often more expensive to conduct, but resulting data is likely more robust and valuable to the creative process. When in doubt, field studies are always a good bet.

3. Use thoughtful sampling. When predicting something specific— say, the outcome of a country's

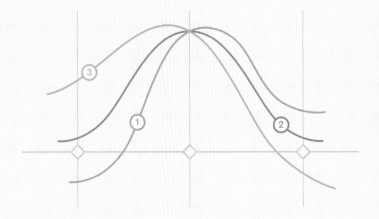

Fringe segments are not static. They are defined relative to the perspective of the researcher. The person on the fringe according to one subject area could be considered mainstream according to the parameters of another study.

① POPULATION OF MUSIC LISTENERS ② POPULATION OF MOVIE WATCHERS ③ POPULATION OF PEDAL BIKE RIDERS election—a larger percentage of the target market size is required. This percentage is a confident gauge of the prediction. In situations in which researchers seek general knowledge rather than hard numbers, a sample size of ten percent or less of each audience segment should suffice. The key is to have a sample large enough to defend findings confidently.

4. Believe in the bell curve. When conducting research with large sample sizes and situations in which you're predicting future behavior, confidence levels and margins of error are important. In most situations, you will only have to understand that large confidence numbers are good and small are bad. And for margin of error, the opposite is true.

The following eight steps should steer research projects in the correct direction. Once these are covered, move on to the details. And do it quickly, because there are a lot of them. Here is a basic checklist:

1. *Recruit participants*
2. *Write a discussion guide or questionnaire*
3. *Conduct interviews or research*
4. *Transcribe findings*
5. *Analyze results*
6. *Draw out recommendations*
7. *Create the report*
8. *Present it to the client*

Sounds daunting, but rest assured: If you manage the details now, you'll have better research later.

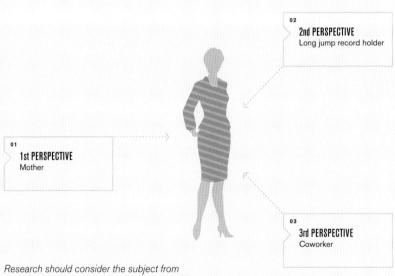

02
2nd PERSPECTIVE
Long jump record holder

01
1st PERSPECTIVE
Mother

03
3rd PERSPECTIVE
Coworker

Research should consider the subject from multiple perspectives. One research method equals one perspective. Three methods equal three perspectives. To her children, this woman is a mother; to judges, she's a strong competitor, etc. No one perspective completely represents the whole woman.

How to Test a Logo

HOUSTON, WE HAVE A HINDENBURG

"Fantastic squirrel!" Encouraging words, if said logo is indeed a squirrel. If it's supposed to be an elephant, you've got a small problem. But not to worry. The planning phase is the time to uncover these issues. It allows you to wrangle them before they charge into the real world and do any major damage.

Testing is a euphemism for disaster management. It uncovers any previously overlooked flubs—because it's surprisingly easy to miss big-picture stuff when working so closely to a project. Before embarking on a project, keep in mind that testing can do great damage when applied at inappropriate stages of the design process. For instance, never, ever, use testing to make a final decision on a logo. You risk nixing a design that is ahead of its time—which would be a pity, since those are often the best designs.

When you've got some work and you're ready to test it, a discussion guide is indispensable. It's a simple document that expedites information gathering by organizing the process. Effective discussion guides include both simple rating questions and plenty of open-ended questions asking how individuals feel about the design. Keep it close—you'll need it.

Then, start scheduling face-to-face interviews. Phone interviews will suffice, in a pinch. Ask questions based on your guide, but also feel free to ad-lib if it feels more appropriate. When you get responses, learn to recognize when and how personal views influence feedback. Sniff out highly emotional language. Once you find it, dig. Participants may say they hate the design. Or overwhelmingly love it. Neither reaction is better or worse than the other. The value is in finding out *why* people feel what they feel. Keep probing until the genesis of

the emotion reveals itself. Consider feedback against that of the entire population. Then determine whether it's specific to the individual or is shared by others.

Research is often counterintuitive, especially at this point. Logically, it follows that the more people who love the logo, the better it is. Right? Isn't it a bad thing when everyone hates it? Not necessarily. Actually, the more emotion involved, the better the chance that someone will remember what he or she is observing. Average gets ignored. Love and hate get people talking, looking, and thinking.

However, it should be noted that, though a logo can work if it is hated, it can't work if it's offensive. Logo testing should filter out any logo components that offend or insult any segments of the audience.

DOMAINS OF TESTING: BOUNDARIES PROVIDE A SAFE TESTING AREA

Anything can be tested and proven to have bad attributes, given a large enough sample. Focus on the following four domains of testing, to avoid the individual who tests well from damaging every other comment on the logo design.

Emotional responses:
The first emotional word an audience associates with the logo. Then, the second.

Competition:
How does the logo fit in with, remind them of, or stand out from the competitive set?

Brand attributes:
Which brand attributes does it communicate? Which ones does it miss?

Cultural connotations:
What cultural messages are being communicated by a logo like this? Of what other images does it remind the audiences?

The obvious might not be so. Testing reveals that this preliminary concept for the Gear6 logo has a negative visual connection. It's too easy to misconstrue it as offensive, so it's removed from the options. CAPSULE

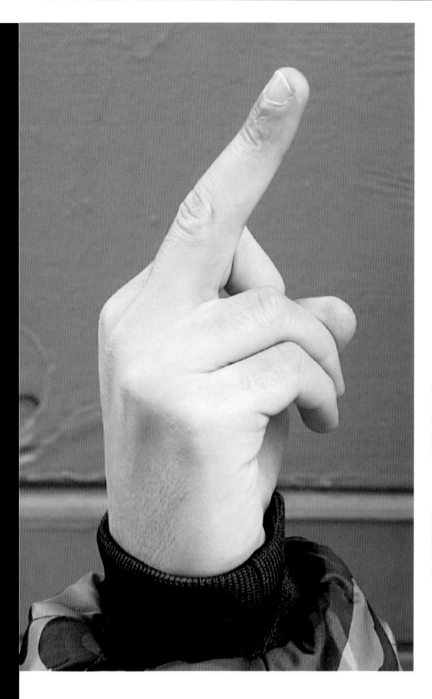

GEARSIX

THERE ARE TWO SPECIES OF DESIGN BUDGET: WHALES AND SHRIMP. DON'T FRET IF YOU'VE GOT A SHRIMP. THE TRUE DETERMINANT OF SUCCESS IS IN THE TECHNIQUE, NOT THE BAIT. GREAT STRATEGISTS KNOW HOW TO CAPTURE GREAT DESIGN WITHOUT THE AID OF SHINY BELLS AND WHISTLES.

EFFORT,
PLAN, AND
SIMPLE

Fundamentals of Planning

The beauty is in the process. Planning before pencil meets paper or palm meets mouse is essential to any logo design, small or large. The old adage is true and easy enough to prove: "Fail to plan and you're planning to fail."

Why doesn't everyone plan? Most do but don't plan enough, because it's considered boring. But planning doesn't have to be tedious and long-winded. It just needs to be thorough, mindful, and well thought out. And remember, work done in planning strengthens the brand story, inspires better design, and engages the client in your process. All of these impact the "P" on your P&L. Provide a healthy habitat for your design by spending time understanding four important groups: company, collaborators, competitors, and customers.

Company

LAYING THE BRAND ARCHITECTURE'S FOUNDATION

Brand architecture is a loaded term. But what does it mean, really? For the purpose of explanation, imagine a brand as an office building. Brand architecture is the congress of vents, boilers, and copper guts supplying power to the building's occupants day after day, keeping everything running. The logo is the lobby of the building, the gleaming, sleek, leather-bound wrapping. Before fussing over the lobby's light fixtures, worry about the state of the building's wiring. Because all light fixtures look the same in the dark.

A brand's architecture has four basic components: features, benefits, emotional rewards, and archetypes. Features, benefits, and emotional rewards explicitly express brand offerings, outlining exactly what the brand does for individuals. The brand archetype is a metaphor that communicates the same offerings on an abstract level. Rather than *say* what the brand stands for, the archetype *shows* what it stands for.

To understand the difference between the four components, let's dissect the messaging on a tube of toothpaste. *Features* describe the product or brand itself, often in single words such as "minty" and "whitening." *Benefits* are tangible advantages individual consumers enjoy, such as "fresh breath" or "whiter smile." They're mainly rational. *Emotional rewards* are the psychological advantages that consumers take away, such as "confidence" and "attractiveness." These often are not stated explicitly on the packaging but, rather, are implied.

The *archetype* is the personality through which offerings are delivered. All four together comprise the basic framework for the brand architecture.

Brand architecture also contains four supporting elements—key messages, position, promise, and one prominent unmet need—and are meant to supplement and reinforce the four basic components. *Key messages* present the brand in digestible amounts: bite-sized sentences or phrases tailored to a variety of audiences. These audiences can range from members of the media to executive teams and customers. *Position* identifies the brand's place in the minds of consumers and in the competitive battlefield. It's relative to the competitive landscape, competing both for dollars and share of audience attention. The *promise* is what a brand pledges to do for the individual. The promise is at the core of the brand and should manifest itself in anything that communicates something about the brand. Successful brands set

realistic, passionate, and valuable promises and then deliver on the promise with each interaction. Language for these three can be inspired by a variety of sources, including in the mission, vision, and values of the organization. With these three, the brand architecture is nearly complete.

The daunting *unmet need* is both a conclusion and a connection. It ties everything else back to the business strategy. So what unmet need does the product, service, experience, or business fulfill? Unmet needs are often hiding out within the pages of business strategies or with the leadership team. To find it, begin by asking, "What does the brand offer that no one else does? What fundamental, currently unmet need does it fulfill?" Enough debate and exploration will clarify the answer. This completes the link between the business strategy and the brand strategy.

PROMISE

BEHAVIORS +
UNMET NEED

ARCHETYPE + POSITION

EMOTIONAL REWARDS

FEATURES + BENEFITS + KEY MESSAGES

A brand's architecture is designed so all the elements support the brand promise. Study the different building blocks before defining a strong brand.

Unmet Need: DrySoda is a sophisticated non-alcoholic drink that seeks to fulfill a perceived gap in the high-end beverage market. TURNSTYLE

Archetype: Fox River Socks' newly launched line of "shucking awesome" socks are woven from sustainable corn fiber. The globe logo, illustrated by a tattoo artist, fuses the brand's outlaw archetype with its responsible practices. CAPSULE

POLYTECH.MONS

Emotional Reward: Polytech.Mons' logo symbolizes the emotional rewards the institution offers students. These include personal and professional achievement, discovery, and higher knowledge. EX NIHILO

Customers

THE CUSTOMER IS A QUIZZICAL CREATURE

Clients like to know that the designer is educated about the customer. When you can speak authoritatively about target markets and key demographics, it reflects well on your design. This doesn't mean the design needs to be explicitly driven by the client's customer. A logo needs simply to reflect the brand attributes and audience. That said, a little business savvy goes a long way with the suits and ties.

Consumer. Target market. Shopper. Business strategists use many words to describe one thing: the customer. Labeling customers seems important, but understanding them is far more important. This is accomplished by understanding the meaning of basic business language, not memorizing labels such as "soccer mom."

Before conducting any customer research, be sure the methods are valid and agreed upon by the client and a research professional. Solid research will build a strong foundation for the rest of the project.

When decoding customers, context reveals quite a bit. Get context by spending a day as you imagine the customer would. Walk his or her path. See what the customer sees. Feel what the customer feels. Then observe the customer to see how he or she behaves in that same context. Watch how he or she interacts with the brand, decides to buy, use, or even dispose of it. Are there differences? Were any assumptions overturned?

Designers work in a world of Pantone rainbows and rich materials. Research interviewing is a world of checked boxes and dry business language. It may prove less than stimulating for most designers, but it is an important complement to raw observation. To begin, formulate questions aimed at understanding beliefs and test previous observations against what the interviewee says. Take down everything, even if it sounds irrelevant at the time. Once everything has been gathered and there is a more complete picture, take time to filter out what truly is not of use. It's imperative to do this because people can be deceptive and often lie to researchers. They'll tell researchers what they think they want to hear and hide embarrassing opinions. Truthfully, raw observation almost always delivers more valid results than interviews. This is because raw observation studies natural behavior and not formulated response. That being said, face-to-face and one-on-one interviews are still very valuable in that they help prove or put to rest theories drawn from raw observation.

The concept behind Buck 'n' Jims line of spice rubs is a quirky blend of redneck soul and gourmet ingredients. Its unconventional approach gains the attention of Internet trend hunters DailyCandy.com. CAPSULE

Engage customers by integrating an interesting cultural reference. Here the Buck 'n' Jims logo invites conversation; it's the visual equivalent of a witty comment.

SPREADING MESSAGES, SOWING GROWTH

Starshine Academy is dedicated to "sowing" the world's best community schools where they've never grown before—in at-risk communities around the world. With its roots in a charter school that transforms the lives of kids in one of Arizona's poorest and most dangerous neighborhoods, Starshine wanted to update its identity before starting the second, third, hundredth, or thousandth Starshine Academy. The challenge for Lucid Brands? Create one compelling logo that would convey Starshine's powerful mission and resonate with many different audiences.

As the ultimate "end users," students needed to relate to the logo. Because the school spans K–12, it had to appeal to kids who are just being kids, as well as to kids *having* kids. For parents, the logo can reinforce their trust in the school.

Starshine's founder, Tricia Adams, and its governing and corporate boards were also key audiences. These supporters comprise a "who's who" in architecture, music, technology, social causes, business, education, and other fields. Because of this, it was imperative that the brand strategy and new logo not only meet their high standards but properly express their ideals, as well.

STARSHINE ACADEMY™

For Starshine Academy to spread internationally, the logo needed to convey the school's identity to prominent influencers. LUCID BRANDS

Kids, parents, and the broader community all interact with the logo design. They are the main end users and part of the many pieces of the complex audience with which the logo must resonate.

In addition to speaking with multiple audiences, the identity and logo needed clearly to position Starshine Academy as a world-class organization—ready and worthy of substantial investment. Seeding schools across the globe takes the support of prominent educators, philanthropic leaders, foundations, pundits, social leaders, NGOs, and governments. These influencers are attuned to the quality and meaning of brand symbols, so to reach this audience, Starshine's new logo needed to be crafted with the same attention as that given Fortune 500 companies.

Starshine's message is, "Imagine if you could grow the world's best schools where they've never grown before. Sow them like seeds through the countryside, into cities, and across the planet. At Starshine Academy, that's not just our dream, it's our mission." Once Lucid Brands understood Starshine's unique ability to change children's lives and bring hope to communities, it envisioned a sower of seeds becoming a sower of stars. This sower symbol, seen in the history and art of almost every culture, captured the "Starshine effect." The idea conveyed that the school and its teachers would bring hope to each of their students. Each student would in turn bring hope to others.

Starshine Academy's logo is integrated throughout its teaching materials, from standard teacher's manuals to instructional CDs. The resulting family of educational resources evokes Starshine Academy's personality and purpose.

The symbol allows children to imagine themselves as sowers. Careful consideration ensures that it appears youthful and gender-neutral. By making stars the seeds, the sower image acts as a bridge between the sowing metaphor and Starshine's name. The thirteen stars are symbolic. They represent Starshine's K–12 grades, generations, and stages of knowledge. The new illustration's color carries over from the previous logo. It's a bright, optimistic, and familiar yellow-orange that kids and adults alike associate with bright school buses. The logotype was created to act as a pathway for the sower. A supporting mechanism, the capitalized Trade Gothic Light type provides the sower with a simple, strong patch of ground, capable of fostering growth.

What's next? The new identity is just one part of the effort to spread Starshine Academy. New schools are being planned, and a training center is under development. The effort is in full swing to rally the support needed to bring Starshine Academy to every child who needs it. Starshine Academy's world-class logo helps gain credibility in the eyes of its target audience of potential supporters: sophisticated international organizations.

"Imagine if you could grow the world's best schools where they've never grown before. Sow them like seeds through the countryside, into cities, and across the planet. At Starshine Academy, that's not just our dream, it's our mission."

While researching the idea of a sower, inspired by Starshine's mission, Lucid Brands found this image of folk hero Johnny Appleseed.

STARSHINE ACADEMY™

Sower
Might be a boy or a girl

K-12 Stars

Positive stride

Logotype acts as a path

Trademark

Lucid Brands collaborated with identity designer Joe Finocchiaro to refine the design and capture the spirit of the sower's stride. The sower figure is gender-neutral and maintains a positive, forward motion. Each of the thirteen stars symbolizes one of Starshine's grade levels, while Starshine Academy's logotype and trademark act as a path for the sower.

Collaborators

DOES YOUR BRAND HAVE STUFF ON ITS FACE?

If you want a brand to be popular, it needs to look presentable. Logo design is the most obvious example of this. The logo is a brand's haircut. Haircuts are surface treatments, but they speak volumes about the person they top off. Where would Elvis be had he opted for a bland, blond crew cut? If a brand bucks trends, the logo should allude to that. If it's buttoned-down and hard-nosed, the logo should look buttoned-down and hard-nosed. Look the part. Pretty straightforward, no?

Mother was right. It's what's on the inside that counts. Of course, she's the one who was always fussing over your shirts and smoothing your cowlicks. Appearances aren't everything, but they aren't nothing, either. How you look is an external reflection of internal values. When a disheveled logo squats in the corner of an advertisement or sprawls out lazily on a piece of signage, it's sure to turn off a lot of people from the get-go.

Brands are a lot like people. They have personalities, names, and values. They even have friends. Except that, in the land of brands, a "friend" is called a "collaborator." And these collaborators come in many forms: competitors, customers, media, and industry organizations, among others. Basically, they're anyone or anything that can promote your brand and advance its reputation without getting compensated with cash. They talk to friends, who talk to friends. And they talk to friends. Word-of-mouth connection is one of the oldest methods of building a strong brand. It's also the best heeded, because it's an authentic form of communication.

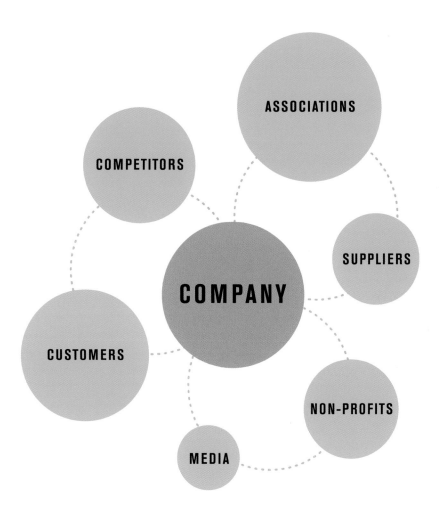

ASSOCIATIONS

COMPETITORS

SUPPLIERS

COMPANY

CUSTOMERS

NON-PROFITS

MEDIA

Collaborators often pop up in unexpected places. Brainstorm a bit about where you lack knowledge and look for people in those areas who can help fill in the gaps.

Competitors

BEATING THE BRAND

See it out of the corner of your eye? Feel the hairs on your neck stand up? That's them. The competition. Why, at this very moment, they're undoubtedly hatching a plan to sneak away a piece of your client's market pie. If you want to beat them, heed that old saying: "Keep friends close; keep your enemies closer." Good advice. But before you invite them over, you should know their names: primary, secondary, and tertiary.

Primary competitors have brand values that overlap yours in a significant way. This is the result of one of two things: either your brand messaging is generic, or it's so good, competitors copy it. Whatever the case, it's important to stay unique. Often, products in a category have similar features and benefits. A distinct brand gives you the upper hand by highlighting a feature or benefit that's unique to your service or product. If it's done well, the brand will go a long way in selling your offering over that of a direct competitor.

Primary competitors butt heads on an hourly, daily, and weekly basis. Understanding primary competitors helps define day-to-day tactics. However, successful long-term strategies look beyond current primary competitors. Long-term design strategy should focus on voyaging to places where there are no primary competitors. The final goal is for the client to compete only with secondary and tertiary competitors.

Secondary competitors include all those above, below, or just outside your client's competitive circle. The brands offer a realistic alternative to your client but aren't competing directly. Secondary competitors appear periodically on the competitive landscape but never offer a consistent threat. But, they do require consideration. If they are successful, they may quickly grow into primary competitors. Additionally, because they offer an alternative, changes in marketplace dynamics, economic conditions, or other uncontrollable factors could change how secondary competitors compete with your client's brand.

Tertiary competitors are like newborn siblings. Technically, they don't compete directly for quantifiable things, such as food and shelter. But they do take away attention that would otherwise go to your client. Tertiary competitors compete for an audience's attention by offering similar distribution or communication channels. They can't always take market share, but they can take mindshare. So they require some attention. For instance, your client may not compete directly with everyone advertising in a particular magazine, but when an advertisement appears in that context, the client does compete for attention.

Other tertiary competitors include the pocket of potentials, those who are not competing directly but have the potential or desire to do so in the future. This group can offer both threats and interesting opportunities. Understand them and know their ability to innovate or acquire. Also, learn a bit about the future of your category. Then make a judgment as to whether these competitors are friends or foes.

COMPETITIVE LANDSCAPING EXERCISE

••• Start gathering artifacts. All communication elements are eligible, from business cards and invoices to signage, advertisements, and vehicles. The more you dig up, the clearer the picture will become.

••• Place everything on a wall, organized first by communication device and then by competitor. Initially, this might feel like a visual audit. But it will soon turn into much more.

••• Invite designers, writers, and objective businesspeople to spend time with the wall. Give the writers a particular flag color. Give the designers another, and so on. Post-it notes are handy for this.

••• Ask each person to identify and mark similarities and differences in both the language and visual presentations of each brand. Have participants look at everything, from size of the business card to type, images, and common colors. The color-coded flags will form patterns where the commonalities exist from the perspective of each group. Have each group articulate the similarities found.

••• Photograph the results. Then articulate the findings by similarity and by communication device.

••• Now flip the exercise. Have the participants identify significant differences. This part of the exercise will likely reveal the leaders in the category—or, at the very least, those most capable of thinking and acting differently, the way leaders often do.

THE GEAR6 BRAND: HOW DO YOU MAKE INNOVATION STAND OUT?

The word "innovation" suffers from the same problem as do the words "strategy" and "creative." Like so many linguistic laser pointers, the business community has overused them to the point where they've lost their original brilliance.

In a world where the word innovative is anything but, how do you communicate the genuine article without sounding insincere? Well, it seems the best way to appear innovative is to act innovative. The logo is the perfect tool for this end. Gear6's logo matches its technology products in terms of innovation and design excellence. And it communicates this in the most convincing manner—through silent, visible reality.

The Gear6 name and identity support one another. Its logo offers a hidden message found on a keyboard. Just hit the shift key + the number six. Green sets Gear6 apart from a sea of blue technology logos. CAPSULE

Silicon Valley is a tough place in which to stand out as innovative. Gear6 knows. It keeps offices in Menlo Park, California—possibly the most competitive stretch of land in the world for technology brands. The technology hardware systems category has plenty of large competitors, including EMC, IBM, Intel, NEC, HP, and Sun Microsystems. However, Gear6 found an area in Silicon Valley in which it could lead in innovation—its logo design.

Industries start to form patterns and behaviors based on historical leaders in the industry. Fit in or stand out—but before doing either one, know how your logo's look and feel gels with the business strategy.

PAUL RAND

Blue happens to be the most inoffensive color globally, but it is also the most common technology brand color. It doesn't work hard to set one brand apart from the competitive set.

START BROAD, GO NARROW, AND THEN FAN OUT AGAIN. PUSH A LARGE RIVER THROUGH A NARROW CANYON AND YOU MOVE BOULDERS. LIKE A RIVER, THE PACKAGING DESIGN PROCESS NEEDS TO FLOW FROM WIDE OPEN TO NARROW AND THEN BACK TO WIDE AGAIN.

The Flow of a Process

Starting broad means seeking to understand all aspects of the category where the package will reside. Moving on with secondary research, then to the primary research, and finally to anything you can get your clammy mitts on will help you gain the global perspective of your packaging endeavor.

Now, start to narrow the river of knowledge. Get to the essential items that will help define what this product and package will mean to consumers. Seek specific answers to specific questions and the river of knowledge will start to narrow itself. Pieces will fall away and others will become much more important. The creative energy around certain aspects will start to move aside the mental boulders, and ideas will start to surface. The idea is continually refined until it becomes a gem floating atop the river. This gem of an idea inspires many other ideas that flow directly out of this intense ideation process. Ideas are engineered, tested, and further refined until they reach a point of execution and delivery, all of which are dependent upon the talented people involved.

The cadre of individuals who explore new territory is always better when equipped with diverse skills and perspectives. Following the river metaphor, no one would rationally choose to be accompanied by rocket scientists on a white-water rafting trip, right? Nothing against rocket scientists, but can they swim, handle a paddle, or fight back the wildlife? Having them around might be fun, but what you really want is a bona fide guide. You need someone with muscle, a map reader, and even a happy observer who can simply watch for rocks to avoid—multidisciplined, multiskilled, and multitalented.

With a budget in hand, as well as clear objectives and the right catalyst, your process has begun. We'll work out the details as we go.

Research

METHODS FOR MADNESS OR BRILLIANCE

In the last decade, research methods for packaging have seen a number of technological and creative advances. These advances allow a marketing manager to set up tracking studies to see how a shopper eyes a package or an entire category. Other creative methods get at the underlying psychology behind the decision a shopper makes by inviting them to create collages depicting your brand as it relates to their life and talking at length about relevant metaphors and emotional factors. Going even farther, current research techniques by Dan Hill read emotional reactions to visual language, translating the ever-elusive emotional landscape of consumers. With so many methods for and perspectives on how to understand the shopper, it's easy to get wide-eyed and walk right past the fundamentals of research. Seeking to understand people, culture, and objects is the baseline—from here you should build a plan to gain that understanding while keeping any biases in check.

Context is essential. When observing behaviors, asking questions, or just getting a feel for the situation, having the right context matters. What does this mean when it comes to packaging? It translates to: "Where will your package live its life?" Research in consumers' homes will likely reveal certain behaviors and influences when it comes to the packaging they prefer. Research in retail will get at other aspects. These are the big areas, but by no means the only ones. How does the package translate at work, in the car, on the bus, or waiting for the train? Some contexts matter more than others, obviously, but they may surprise you with findings that impact the packaging design.

Objectives are next. The method of research varies from simple individual observation to multivariable analysis with an intentionally predictive outcome. This requires starting with a set of objectives that will drive your choice of methods and set context. Objectives should be measurable, but sometimes it's just good to write them down, measurable or not. Measurable objectives can cover you and your boss's rearview mirror, but sometimes they get in the way of seeking knowledge. It's hard to see the road ahead if you're always looking at what you left behind.

Exploratory research is the place to begin when looking at a package design process. This Texas-sized broad category of research contains everything from gathering secondary research from online sources to visiting the place where the package will eventually be displayed for sale.

Testing concepts in context can provide insights not readily grasped by just creating a design. Adapting the design based on research can improve the chances of success without diluting the original concept.
CAPSULE

Shoppers use fat percentages as an essential part of their milk buying decision. The Schroeder Milk package design uses this research knowledge to create a clean, simple package design. The result? An increase in sales, distribution, and shoppers who actually prefer Schroeder Milk products.

CAPSULE

Field interviews can take place after intercepting shoppers or recruiting them to a specific context (mall, store, home, etc). Using an experienced interviewer to ask open-ended questions can yield amazing insights into your package and how it performs in the chosen context. This method can be qualitative with a large enough sample size, but the real focus should be on the questions and the interviewer conducting the research. Fieldwork is essential for any brand with a package.

Testing is set up with assumptions and seeks to understand truths about how the larger population will respond to

aspects of the package. Although highly valuable to understand consumer reactions in context, testing can also be one of the most overused methods next to focus groups for exploratory research. For instance, over-testing something to ensure that it doesn't offend anyone leads to a rather boring package design.

Facial recognition techniques explored by Dan Hill in his book, *Emotionomics,* offer a field full of amazing discoveries. Interpreting facial reactions allows you to see true emotions coming from consumers. The innovative techniques interpret visible reactions to better understand an emotional decision-making process. For example, try opening

a bottle of curdled milk in front of a friend, smelling it, and then asking him to try it. Unless your friend has an odd fascination with spoiled food, he'll likely refuse with only a few words exchanged. Such techniques offer much more reliable, emotional information to inform packaging decisions.

Research is only as good as how it is implemented in setting strategy, informing creative, or redirecting an effort. Leveraging research sometimes means not doing anything at all and having enough confidence in the current plan to take no action. On the side of change, the right research can lead to significant advantages at the shelf. Having a better understanding of the consumer in certain contexts can be the tool to unseat a complacent competitor or stay ahead of the horde of new entrants.

By understanding the visual patterns in the category, the Sommerfield private label line of products can flex to candy, foods, and even baby products. Letting the food category lead creates opportunities to add category-specific personality within each product line.

TURNER DUCKWORTH

RESEARCH PLANNING

RESEARCH PLANNING: CHECKED TWICE, TRIANGULATED ONCE

Conducting research has many facets, opportunities, and painful realities. Using research to gain understanding is smart; using research simply to prove your point is dangerous. Start with a checklist and confirm your findings with triangulation.

1) What are you looking to understand?

2) Specifically, what is/are your objective(s) for the research?

3) What methods will be the most efficient?

4) What methods will have the least amount of bias, or where can bias be managed?

5) What level of confidence can you expect from the research?

6) What do you expect as an outcome?

7) What do you not want to see as the outcome? What are the implications of this?

8) Who will be researched? Who will be profiled? What individual or group of individuals?

9) How will you connect to them? How difficult or expensive will it be to research them?

10) How long will the research take? How does the time factor influence your market plan?

11) What will it cost? Will the knowledge gained be more valuable than the cost?

12) What else can the research be used for? Selling tool? Secondary report for sale?

Strategy

RATIONALIZE STRATEGY, EMOTIONALIZE DESIGN

Business strategy, brand strategy, experience strategy, channel strategy, creative strategy, retail strategy—insert a word in front of "strategy" and you've gained fifteen IQ points and a master's in business. Translating what you just said when a weathered and experienced entrepreneur says, "Son, what did you just say?" is when street IQ shows up. Strategy is just another word for applied knowledge: in other words, IQ points that have been earned, not purchased from business school. If we learn from experience, we should be able to set a better strategic course for the future.

Packaging is one of the essential places where a strategy comes to life and forms meaning with consumers. Packaging is often the result of many strategic paths to achieve set objectives. In other words, the longer a package has been on the shelf, the more likely it has traversed many strategic paths. Managed well, this can translate into a package connected to consumer culture and reflective of the brand strategy set forth by a capable management team. Managed poorly, the results are either obvious or become obvious when the nearest competitor takes advantage and translates the results into increased distribution, sales, and/or brand loyalty.

In the same way the operations team makes a large equipment purchase to create a new product, enter a new market, or increase efficiencies of an existing operation, the package design process should result in the creation of a custom built asset. This asset, if designed right, can be a strategic tool. The difference is contained in a rather large, scary, and gooey word—emotion. Although a double-duty, 65 percent more efficient, and 25 percent less expensive piece of equipment can be rationalized, a package design change is emotional. Even if we rationalize it with competitive case studies, it is still emotional. And it should be. Consumers buy emotionally in a way that seldom can be rationalized. The package design needs to be emotional, while also being rational. Thus is the intersection of business strategy and design methodology.

Design as a methodology for visualizing business strategy is not a new concept, as Walt Disney had an entrepreneurial grasp of the idea over half a century ago. It has been taken to new heights of awareness more recently by Procter & Gamble, Target, and Apple.

How does this translate to a packaging design process? Simple. Take equal parts strategy and design, blend them by a team of open-minded, educated individuals, and a strategy comes to life in the form of a package. Over-emphasize the business strategy and you'll end up with a litany of brand extensions with no design authenticity or rationale for that matter. Over-emphasize the design and you'll end up with a beautiful package without a single customer interested in buying it.

Balancing design and strategy creates an opportunity to appeal to unique, separate audiences—men and women—both of which are targets for this brand of sunglasses. The design creates an appealing solution to a smart strategy.
SUBPLOT DESIGN

No rational person would put wine in a solvent container, would they? Rational and emotional working in balance offers opportunities to see a new market of wine consumers, willing and proud to pour their wine from what could also be used for mineral spirits at your local hardware store.

KOREFE

PRIVATE LABEL BRANDS

With advancements in packaging technology and the cost of creating a package falling, the old black-and-white version of private labels is long gone. Today, many private label brands are not using the store brand name and have come close to equaling or surpassing the manufacturer's brand. ACNielsen recently studied private label brands globally and found that 69 percent of consumers believe private label goods are an extremely good value, and 62 percent think private labels offer quality that is equal to or greater than the big brands. This finding, along with the fact that 30 percent of Ahold's (a European-based grocery conglomerate) overall sales come from private label and Sweden's ICA captures somewhere between 30 and 40 percent, means private label brands are an increasing competitive threat to stagnation.

How does private label packaging impact you? If you're representing a private label brand and find the product categories innovation challenged, you'll find an opportunity to capture more margin through private label programs. If you're representing a manufacturer's brand, innovation is one of the best battle-axes to keep out private label competitors.

Some retailers have taken the tactic of being a close follower of the national brand as an appropriate competitive behavior. Others have gone as far as designing a package that some might say fools the consumer when trying to decide at the shelf. This second tactic may offer short-term gains, but it fails to build trust with the consumer or the general population, and fails to establish a national brand, so in the long term, everyone loses.

RETAILER CONCENTRATION OF THE MOST DEVELOPED PRIVATE LABEL MARKETS

Country	Region	Private Label Share	Retailer Concentration
1. Switzerland	Europe	45%	86%
2. Germany	Europe	30%	65%
3. Great Britain	Europe	28%	65%
4. Spain	Europe	26%	60%
5. Belgium	Europe	25%	80%
6. France	Europe	24%	81%
7. The Netherlands	Europe	22%	64%
8. Canada	North America	19%	62%
9. Denmark	Europe	17%	89%
10. United States	North America	16%	36%

SOURCE: ACNIELSEN'S THE POWER OF PRIVATE LABEL REPORT

Private label growth correlates to retailer concentration and generally has the greatest penetration in European countries. The opportunities for private label packaging are growing at a substantial rate.

Waitrose private label packaging is designed in the most honestly beautiful manner. Simply showing the beauty of the individual products using a consistent design approach is a great example of the power of private label brands.

TURNER DUCKWORTH

Constraints

WHISPER SWEET DESIGNS TO ME, BABY

If necessity is the mother of invention, then constraint is your scholarly aunt. Set your boundaries and it becomes a matter of what can be done within the limitations. Set more boundaries and you'll be amazed by the results you achieve, whether you stick to the constraints or stretch the rules. Authentic creative behaviors thrive on constraints and become paralyzed by the blank page. Limitless opportunities are good; setting boundaries on creativity is better. What may seem like a paradox offers a perspective on fueling the creative process.

What makes constraints so helpful? It might be the comfort in having the requirements on the table and allowing the creative ideas to flow down a focused path. It might also be that we yearn for limitless opportunities but can't cognitively deal with infinite possibilities. The Web is an elegant example of what seems limitless, yet we navigate it with simplified search engines such as Google. Or consider how the complexities of computing and all the technology in our lives have been simplified by Apple's design. Constraints are all around us; acknowledging and understanding them is design's challenge and the place where it can shine.

Once you know that limits exist, the next step is identifying and articulating them. As a brand owner pontificates the vision for the brand and how the package must be the opening page of the brand story, design thinkers must interpret this message. Global, visionary speeches often sound like they don't have constraints, but listen harder and you'll hear key words that bring ideas into focus. What is the brand story? Does it have all the elements of a good novel or does it read like CliffsNotes? Who are the characters (sub-brands, partnerships, parent brand, etc)? Asking paired comparison questions can further define the constraints. Questions like, "Do you expect to see this package on the shelves in Seoul, South Korea, or Detroit, Michigan?" This type of question helps to form conceptual boxes for the design process. Generally, the more questions, the smaller the box becomes. And as my stepmother always said, "The smaller the box, the more valuable the contents."

Please, not another box on the shelf, anything but a box. Constrained to the efficiencies that come with said box, the Full Tank packaging design takes the box in an entirely new direction. Every detail is considered and given a role in communicating the brand personality.

TURNSTYLE

CREATIVE BRIEF

Putting words and visuals on paper—one to two pages at most —is what writing a creative brief is all about. The brevity of a brief—and identifying specific goals—is important. Done right, the brief gets better—and usually shorter.

Here are some of the fundamentals that should be included:

••• Background on the brand and the company behind the brand

••• Brand attributes (promise, personality, archetype, features, benefits, emotional rewards)

••• Distribution of the brand (types of retailers, international, countries, regions, etc)

••• Market research recently conducted and top findings from research

••• Trends or other external factors influencing the brand and package

••• Target audiences (purchaser, influencer in the decision, and end user of the product/package)

••• Timeline with critical dates and budget with hours broken out by critical dates

••• Production issues, structural parameters, and other constraints

••• Regulatory issues and environmental opportunities

WANT TO ILLUSTRATE THAT YOUR CREATIVE
TENDENCIES ARE FAR-REACHING AND ENCOMPASS
A MYRIAD OF DESIGN RATIONALES? PROVE IT.
ARE YOUR LOGO DESIGNS DEFINED BY UNIQUE
TYPOGRAPHY AND COLOR CHOICE? SHOW IT.
CREATE PROMOTIONAL ITEMS THAT ARE JUST
THAT, PROMOTIONAL. SHOW YOUR TRUE
COLORS. BRAG. FLAUNT YOUR STUFF LIKE
A BIG, BLOOMING PEACOCK.

The Big Picture

We've all seen them: portfolios and self-promotions that seem to have a life of their own. Teeming with well-designed, innovative graphics, these portfolios are not the cookie-cutter renditions of yesteryear. Rather, they are streamlined masterpieces that stand out in the minds of a targeted audience.

Remember when you were a kid and your mother used to say, "If you can't say anything nice, don't say anything at all"? These days, many people espouse an updated version of that philosophy: "If you can't build a portfolio right, don't build it at all." Portfolios are core marketing tools, and the statement they make by their appearance and functionality is critical to the business they represent.

Planning your portfolio, namely what form it will take, the contents within, and to whom it will be distributed, is the first step in portfolio development. This stage of the process will allow you to step back and see the big picture in terms of how you want your portfolio to impact you and your company. Do you want your portfolio to be a permanent symbol of who you are and what your company does, or do you want it to be customizable to each recipient? Should your portfolio content include visual as well as verbal components, such as case studies, that will clearly define your creative vision? Or perhaps the visual components of your portfolio should simple speak for themselves. As with all things design, take your time to get it right and remember the adage, "Planning makes perfect."

Sleek and Chic

A LITTLE BLING GOES A LONG WAY

▼► *Choosing a sleek portfolio with simple, well-defined imagery and minimal copy draws the viewer in. A silver cover with coordinating bright orange vellum inserts is a defining characteristic that is carried throughout b-on creative's engaging portfolio.*

B-ON CREATIVE (SOUTH KOREA)

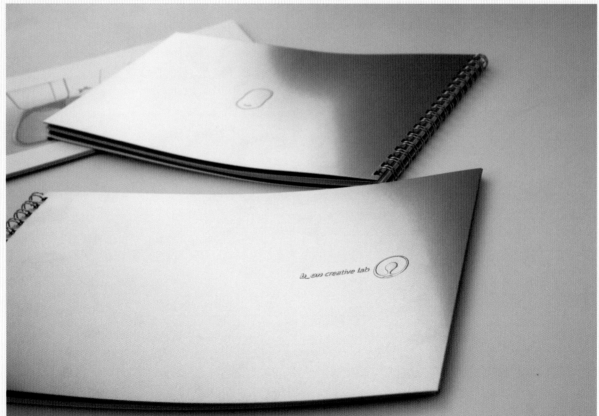

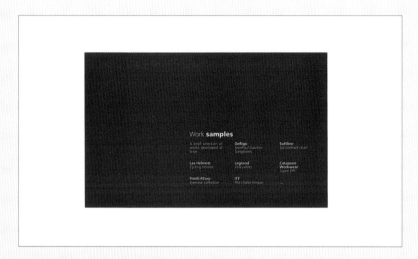

Taking the Bull by the Horns

MAKING YOUR PORTFOLIO WORK FOR YOU

In the past, designers and creative firms commonly approached marketing and self-promotion in an uncoordinated fashion, with portfolio development relegated to the lowly status of being addressed only after the garbage was taken out—if then.

While creatives play a huge role in the global economy, these individuals and firms find themselves reinventing their marketing techniques to compete in a saturated market.

So how do the best creative firms create portfolios and self-promotion campaigns that make targeted clients comfortable enough to loosen their purse strings? Portfolio design and self-promotion can be a relatively simple matter: Take examples of your existing product or service and let a particular group know you're there to serve it—albeit in a fun and unique way.

Conversations with experts produced a list of old-standby practices that, with a couple of unique twists, make for a lucrative portfolio campaign. Among those practices are evaluating how your portfolio fits in the market and crafting an appropriate message ensuring that you leave a lasting impression.

In fact, one of the most difficult problems facing many businesses is establishing a promotional strategy that is profitable, logical, and competitive.

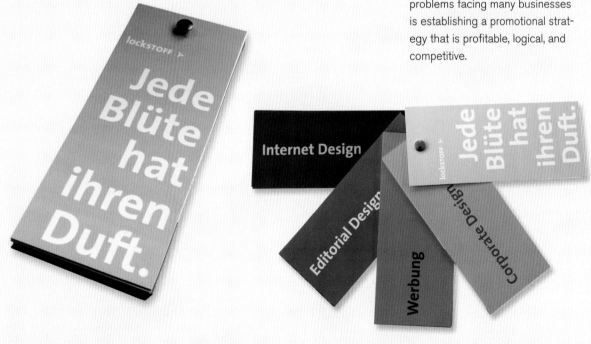

Determine your marketing objectives, which will result in different promotional strategies. For example, your promotional objective might be one (or all) of the following:

- Increase sales

- Increase your customer base

- Maximize long-term profits

- Stay competitive

- Establish a stronger market position

You need to understand your competition by keeping abreast of what the guys down the street are doing in terms of portfolios and self-promotions. Find out what is working for them and what is not. Then create your own strategy.

But remember: Simply deploying a series of promotions or designing a stand-alone portfolio isn't enough. Although strategic use of promotions has proven to be a good system for some designers, it is important that it is not the quick fix. Instead, it should be a coordinated effort between your marketing and sales functions.

◄▲ *The portfolio of Lockstoff Design is cleverly bound together with a single metal rivet, which makes it attractive and functional. When fanned open, recipients can see a snapshot of several projects the firm has worked on. The opposite side of each fan leaf offers detailed information about the project on the front. The single fan leaves are interchangeable, offering a flexible way to update the portfolio when necessary.*

LOCKSTOFF DESIGN

EIGHT TACTICS FOR PORTFOLIO DESIGN

··· **A PICTURE IS WORTH A THOUSAND WORDS.** Include more visuals and less verbiage on your promotions. The visuals should tell the story.

··· **MAKE IT MEMORABLE.** "A memorable portfolio is the key to a successful designer. A good designer must know his audience, and one step further, must know the target market," says Marshall Haber, president of Marshall Haber Creative Group. "We get dozens of portfolios every week from designers looking for work. The ones that stand out demonstrate quality and cohesive-ness. The last thing I want is a designer that is all over the place. If showing quality means showing less, I'm fine with that.

"I look for design that communicates and motivates rather than just design for design's sake. Bells and whistles in design are great, even necessary, but they need to enhance a project, not overtake it. Our business essentially services clients in sales, so the reality is that our work has to inspire action. I never forget that my job is to com-municate a message for our clients clearly and effectively. When I see a portfolio that demonstrates that understanding, it stands out as a winner."

··· **TIMING IS EVERYTHING.** Timing a promotional campaign is an art. Marketing is 99 percent good timing. Synchronize your portfolio design to back up a direct-mail or email campaign. Promotions that appear out of nowhere, with nothing else to support them, usually do not generate the desired results.

"Digital technology makes customization easier. It also means that work can be sent across the globe in seconds," Haber says. "I've hired a freelancer within minutes of getting a portfolio via email. If you got the goods, you'll make an easy sell."

··· **IT'S A BALANCING ACT.** Whatever the method, a good promotional strategy is determining frequency, reach, and timing. The decisions you make about these three factors will determine how your portfolio campaign is weighed.

"The main purpose of creating a portfolio is to show the quality of your work. Exquisite work is a designer's best asset," Haber says. "An equally important part of any new business presentation is providing a prospective client with case studies and sales figures of previous jobs. That's what helps to land the account. Portfolios aren't just important to a designer or a design firm, they're essential. If you want to claim your territory as a great designer and distinguish yourself in one of the most competitive creative industries out there, take your PDF and stick it in the ground."

··· A COMPLEX FORMULA. One thing we know from tapping the heads of consumers of creative services is that portfolios and self-promotions alone are rarely the primary motivator in selecting a creative professional. That's true whether you're in a high-, medium-, or low-price niche, a large firm or a one-person shop. The selection process is part of a complex formula rooted in how customers know and understand your experience, your credentials, and the products and services you offer—both in terms of quality and confidence.

"Portfolios that speak to the target are very powerful," Haber says. "Digital technologies make it easier to customize a presentation or portfolio for each target. That's not a unique trend so much as it is a smart trend, and technology has made customizing easier. Something that doesn't work is complexity. I've seen portfolios and presentations that seem to go everywhere. The key word in good design is focus. A designer must also have a sharp business sense and a planned strategy."

··· MARKETPLACE KNOW-HOW. Your promotional strategy should be continually evolving. Strive to take the continuing pulse of your marketplace, creating your own

scenario of how your portfolio can capture the attention of your audience, and revising your promotional strategy accordingly to help maximize your profits.

"Technology has dramatically transformed the nature of portfolio presentations. Today, portfolios are either sent as PDFs or as website links," Haber says. "Virtual portfolios allow the client to interact with the work, and more importantly, with the designer. Obviously, this shift demands a different and wider skill set. Classic black cases and spiral flipbooks are not totally obsolete, as I'll often present a new client with a hard copy of the portfolio at our initial meeting as a tangible reference of our scope and capabilities. It is therefore critical for a good designer to have both digital and print skills."

··· DEMOGRAPHICS, HERE WE COME. Getting to know the demographics of your potential customer base, including their purchasing power, can greatly enhance how well your portfolio is received.

··· PARTNERS IN PROGRESS. Tap into your existing client base—many of whom may be more valuable than you realize. The beautiful thing about having an accurate database of existing and former clients is that these people know other people. And assuming you offered a gratifying client experience, there is no reason that your old clients wouldn't refer your offering to potential new clients—especially upon seeing an updated portfolio.

Defined Design

▼► *Carefully selected images and a clear vision that walks viewers through each page is at the heart of this portfolio book. "The book is intended to work as a personal portfolio for potential clients," says Nikolaus Schmidt. "The overall intention is to show clients the diverse production techniques that can be achieved." Featuring commercial as well as personal projects, the images shown on the French-folded pages are clearly defined with clean visuals. The blue inserts feature a thicker stock with the key facts of each project including client name, date, and kind of work.*

NIKOLAUS SCHMIDT GRAPHIC DESIGN

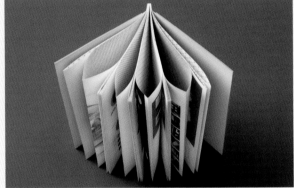

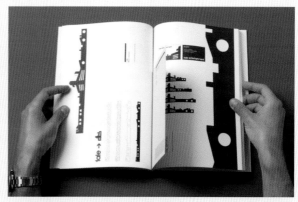

The Medium Is the Message

NO ONE SAID YOU HAVE TO FOLLOW ONE PATH ON THE ROAD TO SUCCESS

Good portfolio design is a critical element in attracting potential prospects. Your content is your greatest lure— no tricks or gimmicks, just the goods. You've got a story to tell, so tell it. But *how* you tell it is as important as *what* you tell. Marshall McLuhan has long been known as the man behind the message—the coined phrase, "the medium is the message." In his book *Understanding Media*, McLuhan asserts that "the form of a medium embeds itself in the message, creating a symbiotic relationship by which the medium influences how the message is perceived."

If you determine that the best medium for your portfolio is a whiz-bang CD filled with interactive elements, perfect. Or perhaps a traditional printed portfolio that showcases your firm's work is more suited to your designated audience.

Better yet, maybe simple, straightforward e-blasts will get your message across. The medium that you choose to display your work needs to reflect who you are as a creative professional. In declaring "the medium is the message," McLuhan goes one step further to propose that the media itself, not the content it carries, should receive the most attention. However, in the creative world of design, the content of your portfolio is a vital component of showcasing who you are and what you do. The medium should grab their attention and usher them inside—eager to find out more.

The medium in which your portfolio or self-promotion piece is housed can be the most memorable component. Whimsical, fun, knock-your-socks-off-creative—that's what will get you noticed.

► *These portfolio cards were designed like mini case studies, showcasing various facets of Brand Engine's most notable work. Each card gives a glimpse into the stages of brand development, the breadth of the projects, the assorted applications of the brands, as well as some contextual placements. The goal was to create a system that would be convenient to customize and print in-house and easily mailed or carried for quick hand-offs at meetings. The result? A color packet of cards strategically designed to create a memorable impression of what Brand Engine is all about.*
BRAND ENGINE

At Brand Engine, we specialize in designing successful, sustainable consumer brands through strategic rigor and insightful creative expression.

It's what we do best.

Finding the Right Mix

PERFECT INGREDIENTS, PERFECT PORTFOLIO

Remember back to the good old days of kindergarten when you couldn't wait to grab the attention of your fellow comrades with the beloved show-and-tell? At the ripe old age of five, you knew that it is far more powerful to "show and tell" than to just "tell."

The same holds true for portfolios and self-promotion.

Indeed, a lot of designers may say, "I tried it and it didn't work." And to that, the little person in your head should respond, "You tried it and it didn't work as well as you wanted *that* time." Who's to say a similar self-promotion piece won't woo a potential prospect the next time around? You just need to make sure there's going to be a "next time."

"Never underestimate the obvious," says Andrea Cutler, professor of design at Parsons School of Design and owner of Andrea Cutler Design. "Your portfolio, along with a well-designed and organized résumé, and good cover letter are *you*. They're the first impression. And a great business card for networking is critical. If you are a designer, especially a freelancer, then that single item alone speaks volumes about your capability. I never go anywhere without my cards. I also have a mini business-card-size 'port-a-folio' on a key chain, that I make on a need-be basis to give people. They are an effective marketing tool for me."

◄► *A key chain–size mini portfolio offers a great leave-behind piece for potential clients to take with them and share with others.*
ANDREA CUTLER DESIGN

With well-designed portfolios, you feed the passion. You create aficionados. The way you do that is to get them in the proverbial "door" with other aficionados—your "followers"—the ones who keep coming back for more.

Create your own fan club. Educate them about who you are and what you can do. You want to fuel the passion, fuel the flame. And portfolios and self-promotions are absolutely the most cost-effective way to do it.

Of course, zeroing in on the potential audience most likely to respond to your portfolio is essential. This is achieved through choice of media, position, or placement, along with the messages your self-promotion delivers. The more you are "front and center," the more they will remember you and your capabilities.

Ideas at Work

DON'T FORGET TO LEAVE THE LIGHT ON

So what are some portfolio techniques that really work? Some people say tangible portfolios (versus the virtual ones) and self-promotions are a waste of money—it's word of mouth that sells *you*. Others feel that it is the total communications mix—and the appeal of your creative know-how—that really sells. One thing is for sure: By putting your portfolios in front of your target audience, across a variety of communication channels, the message begins to strike home.

A good portfolio strategy also is a balancing act between targeting frequency, reach, and timing. The decisions you make about these three factors will determine how your promotional campaign is weighed. But the form your portfolio design takes is also paramount. Whether you choose to create traditional portfolios housed in the standard sleek black case or nontraditional portfolios, such as magazines or PDFs, you need to make sure form and function meet.

► *Based in Bologna, Italy, LLDesign creates their self-promotional portfolio by including selected works from the last four years. Measuring 17 × 24 cm (6.7 × 9.4 inches), this portfolio is digitally printed on different kinds of paper and hand bound. It's a great example of how the form the portfolio takes complements the function of the design elements within.*

LLDESIGN

OUT OF THE MOUTHS OF THOSE ON THE FRONT LINES OF DESIGN

For many creative professionals, how you format your portfolio is dependent on how long you've been in the creative business and what you see as the best way to showcase who you are and what you do. Andrea Cutler, professor of design at Parsons School of Design, asked a variety of colleagues and students, some of whom have been in the design industry for decades and others who are "wet behind the ears," how they format their portfolios. Here's what they had to say:

"I am just taking my first baby steps in graphic design, and since I already want to apply for different jobs, I decided to use a blog temporarily to show my humble portfolio pieces."

"As with any portfolio, if you're going to show your work, your blog needs to look first class. Just like a website, don't present it until the medium itself is a portfolio piece."

"I have an online portfolio. If requested, I send a PDF, which I also have on my website. I have a book that I show when I get invited for an interview so that I am able to speak about my body of work in person."

"I've been a designer for five years, and I still have an 11 × 17-inch [28 × 43 cm] book, but I also have my website, and other online profiles that allow for a portfolio gallery."

"My initial contact is always my website. Sometimes it's email, sometimes phone, and sometimes a self-promo, but always the website."

"I am still using the same formula I have used since I graduated from art school ten years ago: a traditional book on the smallish side [11 × 17 inches; 28 × 43 cm] and a PDF for emailing and online samples. I send the PDF most often. I have never been asked for a leave-behind book nor have I mailed one to a client, agency, or studio. I have gotten most jobs networking."

"I have been in business for twelve years now (in-house and freelance), and the way I refer to my work is via PDF, on my website, and with a custom book. When I first started out, I had the standard black leather book with samples attached."

"I have been a graphic designer for over twenty-three years. I originally used a traditional book with vinyl pages, but now use a hard case with individual boards and mounted images and a few hard copies of brochures, etc."

"I've been practicing for over twenty-eight years. I used to drop off a physical portfolio. Now I use only my website with downloads and direct mail support."

▲◄ *"As a graphic designer whose expertise is in print, it is important for me that my portfolio reflects my abilities in this discipline. Therefore, I chose to display my design pieces in a book. I selected the most outstanding case studies that I had created in the past few years. The layout is simple, clean, yet keeps the viewer engaged, as there's still a lot of movement inside the spreads. The focus is always on the images, whereas the text is used as a complementary—and balancing—element."*
Carmit Haller

CARMIT DESIGN (BELMONT, CALIFORNIA)

◄ This self-promotional package of business cards uses the small dimension to showcase an intriguing miniature portfolio on the back of each card. The extraordinarily colorful packaging in the form of a little bag provides the bling-bling needed to grab the viewer's attention.

804 GRAPHIC DESIGN

Portfolios and Brand

A SYMBIOTIC RELATIONSHIP

Many a provider of goods and services would like to do for their business what Starbucks has done for the coffee shop—get the consumer or client to spend about three times what they used to spend. It is not that their coffee is so superior, although it is very good. Rather, it's their innovative marketing. Starbucks has transformed the ordinary task of getting something to drink into a delightful experience. And it resonates throughout their brand.

Experts define brand as every prospect or customer interaction with your company that creates an impression. But a corporate or product brand is clearly more than just a logo or an advertisement—it's the personality and soul of a company. When it comes to branding your portfolio, there are some common mistakes to avoid:

- **Inconsistent messages.** A good self-promotional campaign is dependent upon consistency to build trust and strength in a message. For example, let's say your portfolio features an award-winning website followed by an outdated logo design for a company that's no longer in business. Having such inconsistent design elements featured in your portfolio can send a wrong message about who you are and where you're taking your company.

- **Failure to differentiate.** Creativity is the key to differentiation. And creating a unique position for yourself and your company provides a solid foundation for your brand.

"Your brand is defined by other people's perceptions," says Karl Speak, president of Brand Toolbox, an organization that helps companies and individuals define their brand. Speak is also the former chair of the board of directors of the Design Management Institute, a nonprofit, global organization dedicated to demonstrating the strategic role of design in business and to improving the management and utilization of design. "Strong brands are perceived to be distinctive, relevant, and consistent. The most distinctive brands are perceived to make the biggest difference."

For example, if you fail to distinguish yourself at a trade show, by offering a standard candy-dish-topped booth display, you fail to give potential customers a reason to select you rather than the gal next door. Simply put—make every meeting and event memorable in the minds of your audience. Have creative stand-alone portfolio items that you can hand out at a moment's notice. Create surprise and delight at every turn. That's what differentiation is all about.

- **Inconsistent, ineffective identity.** A brand is everything from how your phone is answered to the quality of your customer service to the content of your blog, not to mention your company logo, office interior, and marketing materials—it's critical that each of these elements appropriately represent your company's identity. If one or more of these elements is inconsistent with the total message, you are confusing your audience. Make sure your identity is consistent. A strong brand is the result of good experiences, consistent messages, and positive, reinforcing images. "The process of building a strong brand is to define your brand platform and deliver on your brand promise," Speak says.

inspiring

You'll see

gerard design

classic style

You'll see

gerard design

▲▶ *A strong level of brand consistency is evident throughout Gerard Design's portfolio and self-promotional pieces. The "You'll See" piece was developed to support the agency's rebranding. Treating itself as a client, Gerard Design took a research-based approach that ultimately highlighted the need for sweeping changes to the core facets of its brand, including repositioning itself as a strategic branding firm (not just design), refining its messaging to clearly communicate the agency's capabilities, and creating a visual identity that consistently supports Gerard Design's image and culture.*

The "You'll See" piece is a mini portfolio targeted toward new and potential clients to demonstrate the company's branding abilities. Using a coated paper highlights the photography and images, which together emphasize the company's high-end work. In other words, the firm lets the images do most of the talking.

GERARD DESIGN

CREATI

- BROCHURES
- LOGOS
- PACKAGING
- PORTFOLIOS

NG

"SUCCESS CAN MAKE YOU GO ONE OF TWO WAYS. IT CAN MAKE YOU A PRIMA DONNA, OR IT CAN SMOOTH THE EDGES, TAKE AWAY THE INSECURITIES, LET THE NICE THINGS COME OUT."

—BARBARA WALTERS

A GREAT BROCHURE NEEDS BEAUTY AND BRAINS. SURE, IT NEEDS TO LOOK GOOD, BUT IT ALSO NEEDS TO EFFECTIVELY DELIVER A MESSAGE–TYPICALLY MORE THAN ONE. WHETHER IT'S MEANT TO SELL CONDOS OR RAISE MONEY FOR A NONPROFIT, A SUCCESSFUL BROCHURE SHOULD DRAW READERS IN WITH A SMART LAYOUT TO ACHIEVE A LARGER GOAL.

Layout: Spinning a Yarn

"It's really a storytelling challenge," says Tamara Dowd, a creative director at Hirshorn Zuckerman Design Group (HZDG) in Rockville, Maryland. "How does it unfold?" The best designers lay out a brochure with the same care a fiction writer takes when plotting a short story.

Unlike a postcard or print ad, these multipage pieces require a narrative to pull people along. Great brochures deliver compelling messages in just the right order. Like an engrossing novel, they keep readers turning the pages. A brochure might pose a question on the first spread or two then provide the answer later in the piece. Another approach? Lead with the sexiest message and then present more in-depth information once the target audience is hooked. "I think, in general, a lot of people don't think about flow," says Andrew Wicklund, a design director at Hornall Anderson Design Works in Seattle. "They don't see the big picture."

A multipage print piece should build suspense or interest, and there needs to be a natural progression from spread to spread. If there's too much redundancy, readers are likely to lose interest, but a layout that changes radically with every page flip doesn't work, either. A winning project must master this and countless other balancing acts. "With a brochure, there's a lot of interplay between words and images," says Travis Cain, a senior designer at Planet Propaganda in Madison, Wisconsin "They're constantly being put together." A successful layout needs to integrate these two elements in service of the larger message.

▲ *"If it's long-form like this, you have to think in terms of the story as opposed to the design at first," says Andrew Wicklund, a design director at Hornall Anderson Design Works in Seattle. "Put the bones in. Develop the structure and hierarchy and then start to develop aesthetic." This promotional piece for an upcoming commercial building, for instance, revolves around three key selling points: professionalism, productivity, and proximity.*

The Director's Chair

Dowd believes that planning out how a brochure's story will unfold is a bit like directing a movie. After all, you're in control of the images, order and pacing—and you probably hold some sway over the copy, too. She's a big advocate of taking the time to rough out a storyboard before moving to the computer. This process gives you the chance to think about pacing and creates a structured outline of all the elements that a particular brochure requires. You won't find yourself missing a crucial image or message halfway through the final layout.

So grab a stack of 3 x 5–inch (7.6 x 12.7–cm) cards—they make it easy to play with order—or draw squares on a sheet of paper to represent each spread. Then start making simple notes about what goes where. At HZDG, for example, Dowd and the design team often tackle real estate brochures, which present a special set of challenges. How do you make people fall in love with a building that isn't built yet? You create a piece with personality, emotion, and a strong concept. The design team at HZDG, for instance, might debate whether to tell the story of the community or building first. Which one is the better hook? Or they might flag a particularly striking image to run across the center spread. Once there's a rough map, they ask another critical question. "This all makes sense, but what part of the story aren't we telling?" Dowd says.

There's also something to be said for making your first layout on the computer a rough one. Cain likes to place the images and copy all the way through—even if he's using placeholders for some elements. This gives him a good idea of the ratio of text to artwork and allows him to figure out where everything needs to go. "A rough layout allows you to start thinking spread to spread how these images and copy are going to come together," he says. From there, he works to refine the design and fill in sections with the actual art and copy, as they're available. Sometimes he needs to make adjustments once those final elements are in place. "It's a fluid process," he says. "You need to be flexible."

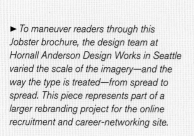

▶ *To maneuver readers through this Jobster brochure, the design team at Hornall Anderson Design Works in Seattle varied the scale of the imagery—and the way the type is treated—from spread to spread. This piece represents part of a larger rebranding project for the online recruitment and career-networking site.*

Too Busy to Read

In an ideal world, your target audience would spend half an hour pouring over every detail of your brochure. In reality, however, they're more likely to spend a few seconds making a snap decision as they sort mail over the trash can. Or if you're really lucky, you'll garner a minute or two as they wait for a delayed flight at the airport. "What's the chance of getting them to sit down and focus on it with a glass of wine?" says Kenn Fine, founder and creative director at FINE Design Group in San Francisco. "You need to appeal to people who only have 15 seconds to determine if they have more time to spend with the piece."

What is his antidote to this time crunch? Figure out the most important thing a brochure needs to say and make sure that message comes across in five seconds. Then identify the second and third most crucial points and think about them as the 30-second experience. Since what a piece says is just as important as how it looks, you'll want to consider the experience of reading a brochure as you're designing it. What comes

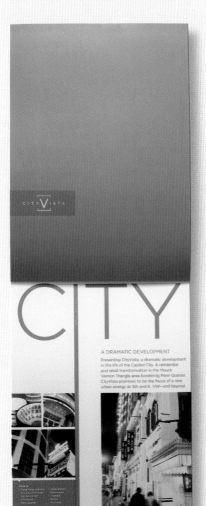

◄ This brochure's pages—printed on heavy stock—are held together with a rubber band at the top of the piece. "We're always trying to find a way to differentiate," says Jennifer Higgins, a senior art director at HZDG. "The condominium market is oversaturated."

across after glancing at the cover? Or after flipping through the first few spreads? Is the message easy to digest in the middle of a hectic day? Do the key points stand out first?

It might also help to adopt Dowd's approach and think about three different levels of reading: main headlines and pictures; main headlines, pictures, and sidebars; or the full piece. Take a few minutes to consider what readers would take away from each of these experiences. Does the core message come across in the display copy and images? Or is it buried in the body copy? "You need to communicate the basic sell without the full read," Dowd says. "You can't guarantee that someone's going to give you that much time in their life to read an entire brochure."

▼ Seattle-based design firm Hornall Anderson Design Works created this brochure as the first piece of collateral for Eos Airlines. "We were pretty generous with the amount of space we allowed for each idea or topic," says design director Mark Popich. "The type is fairly quiet. We wanted to create a calming, refined aesthetic." This type of approach matches the upscale feel the design team created for the whole piece, with such thoughtful details as iridescent paper.

Vying for Attention

With to-do lists growing like weeds, sometimes it takes a slightly different approach to get someone to pick up a brochure at all. "We really push hard on formats," says Dowd, about her work at HZDG. The firm does a lot of pieces to promote upcoming condos—a competitive market in the D.C. area. One way they help clients stand out is with format ideas that are original but still appropriate.

A brochure for a mixed-use development called Rockville Town Square, for example, comes in an interesting package. "Early on we thought, 'This needs to be in a shopping bag,'" she says. "It's a live, work, shop, play concept. We really wanted to call attention to the fact that you're going to be living above everything you'll ever need." The piece comes inside an elegant brown shopping bag with ribbon handles—one that fits right in with the bags used by high-end retailers. For another development, the firm created a cover for a brochure that slides off to reveal a friendly neighborhood map. "I had a professor in college who would call it 'the kiss,'" Dowd says. "It's one little thing beyond what's expected, and it's always in service of the product."

When considering alternate formats, however, it's key to think about what the audience is used to getting and how they're going to use the piece. For example, Wicklund worked on a brochure for an upcoming commercial development in Seattle, and he originally wanted to significantly break from the 8½ x 11–inch (20.3 x 27.9–cm) format used by most of the building's competitors. After talking with the client, however, he discovered that this conservative audience was comfortable with this standard size—in part because it fits easily in file folders and binders—so he went with a 7½ x 11–inch (17.8 x 27.9–cm) piece. This information also led to another functional design detail: Wicklund chose looped staples so the piece would easily slip onto a three-ring binder.

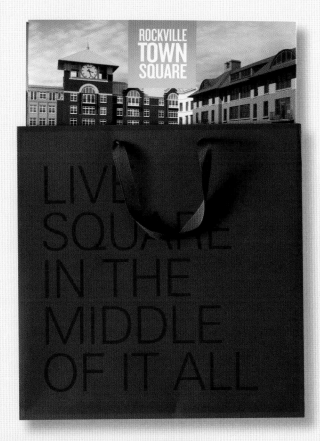

◄▼ *Instead of a ho-hum product folder, designers at HZDG put this brochure in a shopping bag to grab attention. This choice also reinforces the development's "Live, Work, Shop, Play" concept. Along with a migrating varnish, the bag gives the piece an upscale feel.*

LIVE. WORK. SHOP. PLAY.

The four sides of your life that make a perfect Square: **Rockville Town Square**, the new downtown Rockville. Five buildings of luxury condominiums directly above street-level retail. It's a whole new way of life. A place where everything you need is moments away, not miles. Where commuting means you're just **two blocks from Metro**. Where your favorite shops and restaurants are your neighbors. And the centerpiece is a **vibrant town square**—a gathering place bigger than a football field for farmers' markets, concerts, community celebrations, and **simply enjoying life**, every day.

ONCE YOU'VE GOT THE BIG-PICTURE DECISIONS DOWN, THERE ARE STILL THE SMALL-SCALE ONES TO IRON OUT. IT'S A BIT LIKE CHOOSING EXACTLY THE RIGHT PROPS ON A MOVIE SET. IS THAT LAMP WORKING? OR SHOULD IT BE A LITTLE SMALLER? "IT'S VERY IMPORTANT THAT DESIGNERS REALIZE THAT, TO TAKE A PIECE TO ANOTHER LEVEL, THEY HAVE TO BE WILLING TO DO THE NITTY GRITTY," SAYS JEFFERSON LIU, A SENIOR ART DIRECTOR AT HZDG.

Finishing Touches

When he worked on a promotional piece for a condo development called View14, he rolled up his sleeves and made sure the smallest details were just right. The brochure features a series of interior renderings, but to make them more engaging, Liu and the interior designer teamed up to decorate these virtual rooms. They searched for real pieces of furniture that sent the message they were trying to convey and worked together to arrange them in the spaces. All these details were sent to the rendering company, so they could make each virtual room come to life. As a result, the condos in this yet-to-be-built development seem tangible. You can imagine living there, because the design shows you how the condos might look once you add your own style.

As details evolve, it's also essential to approach the design process organically. On View14, for example, everyone from the architects to the developers was just as detail-oriented as the graphic-design team. These collaborators might request that a sink or cabinet be moved an inch or two within a particular rendering—small adjustments that more accurately reflect the final product. "I think it's important in design not to be married to anything," Liu says. "Beginning designers, once they get things perfect, are afraid to change it." Fine suggests another important strategy: if time permits, step away from the design for a day or two and come back to it with fresh eyes. It's an easy way to check your own work.

◄▼ These renderings show what it might be like to live in these future condos. Liu worked with the interior designer to pick out furniture and arrange the pieces within the spaces. These details were forwarded to the rendering company.

► "Our mission here was to create an almost anti–real estate brochure," says Jefferson Liu, a senior art director at HZDG. "No shiny happy people." Instead of showing a generic couple or someone jogging in the park, this piece focuses on the condo development's style. Small details—like the fish swimming down this spread—help set the piece apart. A koi pond planned for the building's lobby inspired this addition.

COMMITTING TO THE DETAILS

If this elegant fundraising brochure somehow morphed into a mystery novel, its title just might be *The Hunt for Blue Matches*. Hornall Anderson Design Works designed this piece—largely as a pro bono effort—to help aishSeattle solicit funds from prominent donors. The Jewish educational and outreach organization needed something to leave behind when calling on potential supporters.

The Z-fold brochure features two covers and, in essence, two different stories. One side reveals the organization's emotional and spiritual side, following a little girl as she celebrates with her family. "It needed to touch the heart," says Yuri Shvets, a graphic designer at the Seattle firm. "It could not look like a capabilities book." The piece's flip side focuses more on the businesslike details, explaining aishSeattle's programs, goals, and budget.

But for designers, there's a bigger message: don't give up on the details. Shvets wanted to include an actual

match on one of the covers, but its tip needed to be the same shade as the blue candle on the other cover. "I was researching all the matches in the world," Shvets says. "The vendors had every color in the rainbow but that exact hue." Finally, he found a company that could reproduce the color, but the custom mix was simply too expensive for this low-budget project.

The vendor, however, sent 50 matches as a sample, which meant Shvets only needed to locate 200 more for this tiny print run. As luck would have it, one weekend, he stumbled upon the solution. He was eating at a restaurant whose matchbooks contained the perfect shade of blue. Shvets pocketed a sufficient quantity for his project—hardly more than any other patron might pick up. "We got lucky," he adds.

So why not take the faster route and create a 3D effect in Photoshop? Shvets wanted the additional value offered by a tactile object—a choice that makes the brochure seem less manufactured and more tailored. "We strive for the highest standards," he says. "Even for pro bono pieces." Additionally, aishSeattle made the commitment to place all those matches in the tiny envelopes and glue them on each cover by hand. Shvets even took the time to write up instructions for the process. After all, it's the details that light the fire.

▼ *The design team at Hornall Anderson Design Works in Seattle felt strongly about including an actual 3D match on the cover of this fundraising brochure, but finding matches in the right shade of blue—and at the right price—was harder than they imagined.*

EIGHT TACTICS FOR SMARTER TYPOGRAPHY

··· **READ THE COPY.** When you're on deadline, it's tempting to skim the text rather than take the time to give it a thorough read. But really understanding what's being communicated in all that gray gives you the knowledge to present the copy in the best way for readers. You might come up with ideas for making the copy more accessible—with headlines, subheads, and sidebars—and you'll definitely have a better handle on the overall message.

··· **LESS IS MORE.** There are countless typefaces to choose from for any given project, but your best bet is often restraint. Thinking about using more than two fonts? Take a few minutes to consider whether those extra typefaces are really enhancing the project. Put yourself in the reader's shoes and reflect on the piece's overall readability.

··· **LEARN THE HISTORY.** The right typeface should enhance your project's concept rather than fight against it. But in order to know what message you're sending, you need to familiarize yourself with a font's history. Is it 10 years old? 20? Or older? What was the intention when it was created? These answers should tell you whether a typeface works for that brochure or whether it's time to look at other options.

··· **SWEAT THE SMALL STUFF.** Much of good typography lies in the details. Pay attention to letter spacing—especially between upper and lowercase letters—and be on the lookout for widows and orphans. Also take a close look at the rag to make sure it isn't inadvertently attracting a viewer's attention by forming odd shapes.

··· **EMBRACE HIERARCHY.** Sure, there's a movement toward less hierarchy at many businesses. But when it comes to type, these differing levels of importance make copy easier to read and understand—not to mention less intimidating. Everything from headlines to pull quotes gives people a hand organizing and remembering information. A good rule of thumb: there shouldn't be more than three levels of importance within a single layout.

··· **CONQUER TEXT OVERPOPULATION.** Too much text—coupled with too little art and space—creates another problem entirely. If you're dealing with reams of text, try going back to the client and working with them to hone the message. Also look for ways to use some of the text as artwork, either with pull quotes or attractive sidebars. It can also help to experiment with the color of the type and the space between paragraphs. Focus on ways to break up those heavy text blocks so you're not creating the same shape on every page.

··· **EXPLORE YOUR OPTIONS.** Rather than rely on a handful of tried and true typefaces, make an effort to keep up on the latest offerings in the type world. Not every project calls for a trendy new font, but it's good to know what's available. Other ideas: Try using an ampersand instead of the word "and" in display copy. Or experiment with old-style numbers; since they don't sit on the baseline like more typical numbers, they blend in better with body copy.

··· **COLLECT TYPE.** Feel like your approach to type is getting stale? Restock those creative stores by starting a type collection. Whether it's the placemat at the Chinese restaurant or a quick snapshot of a poster on the street, make a point to collect things that catch your eye and store them away for those rainy days when your inspiration is flagging.

MILK COMES WITH A DEFINITE EXPIRATION DATE. LOGOS DO NOT. WHEN YOU SELL A BRAND OWNER A FRESH LOGO, MAKE SURE THAT PERSON KNOWS HOW TO STORE IT PROPERLY. OR IT MAY SOUR PREMATURELY.

STANDARD
BY YOUR
LOGO

Essential Criteria

Set standards for your logo design work. Beyond that, know your client's and your creative community's standards. Your work will be more grounded, and you'll project confidence in the design philosophy to the client. Standards are necessary, reaffirming, and reassuring. It's not so much what the specific standards are but simply their existence and consistent presence that is important.

There are three main design criteria by which to build standards: simplicity, uniqueness, and metaphoric symbolism. *Simplicity* equals strength. The less convoluted and the more direct a concept, the more memorable and effective it is. *Uniqueness* establishes visual separation—helpful when your brand is vying for attention in a crowded marketplace. Use of *metaphor* is a core element of brand storytelling. The stronger the metaphor, the stronger the story. And the stronger the story, the more memorable the logo.

In the end, all the standards you set will take aim at memorability. Simple is memorable, metaphors are essentially memory aids, and uniqueness is noticeable and then memorable. The higher and more resolute your standards for these three, the more the audience should remember your client's brand.

Criteria 1: Simplicity

EINSTEIN WAS A MAJOR SIMPLETON

"Everything should be made as simple as possible but not simpler," Albert Einstein said. And he should know. His theory of relativity manages to summarize all existing matter into five simple characters.

Simplification is pivotal to logo design. Consider Google. It is building an empire on a simplified search process, and its logo reflects this strategy. Because the logo is so simple, it can be accessorized with everything from holiday ornaments to specific business sectors. The more simple, the more intuitive, the more approachable. Simply stated, simplicity is a force multiplier.

Simplicity is essential for many reasons, the most important being society's current volume of messages. Consumers are bombarded with more and more information every day. Because of this, designers of all disciplines must simplify their messages so they can be absorbed before another one shoves them aside. Logos marking almost every piece of any given organization's communications or products constitute a large percentage of this visual chaos. It is essential that designers reduce a logo design's elements down to only its most essential components.

Refinement is the act of simplifying or paring down. After a client accepts a design, some may consider the work completed. But, this is the moment when another round of refinement is often required. It is best to leave it and return later with fresh eyes, because the chances of discovering unseen redundancies increase. Diligence is rewarded with uncluttered communication and clear end products.

Simplify creatively. This memorable example for a U.K.-based software systems builder cleverly simplifies by utilizing negative space.
ELLIOTTYOUNG

Convey dimension with simple structure. This logo represents a prepaid card system and elegantly achieves visual dimension.
SEGURA, INC.

Simplify without losing personality. This logo for a U.K.–based paint-your-own pottery retailer conveys a personal, craft-inspired feel through simple, unique, visual gestures.
WOLFF OLINS

RED WINGS

Criteria 2: Uniqueness

REBEL WITH A CAUSE

For some, school was a party in a box, neatly prepackaged with autumn football games and wrist corsages. For others, high school was as uninspiring as cafeteria food. Many of these "others" eventually grew up to be creative professionals, a role in which uniqueness is in the job description and clients applaud creativity.

Uniqueness serves clients in two major ways. Legally, it ensures that clients remain safe from litigation. Creatively, it enriches the client's brand and makes it more memorable. But there's a difference between being truly unique and just being different. Genuine uniqueness stands out from the crowd and provokes further thought. It is different for the sake of something better and permeates its host at all levels.

Being different, though, doesn't inherently denote substance. Many things and people are different just for the sake of being different. It's an aesthetic surface treatment that doesn't push forward so much as shuffle in another direction, for better or worse. Don't confuse the two. If there's no substance, the audience won't have anything to attach to, and the brand message will glop off sadly, like a mashed mound from an upturned lunch tray.

If you seek unique design answers in client meetings, you may find yourself right back in school again. Your new ideas may be treated like new kids, attracting snickers, jeers, and rolling eyes. Don't fold. You are now paid to think differently and to help your client see the brand's creative potential. Fight the little voices of doubt in your head. Fight the loud voices of clients on the conference phone. Fight kindly, gently, and rationally, but fight nonetheless. It's your job to push boundaries. If you make your case and the client still isn't buying, then you've done what you can. Only then should you begin open negotiations.

A fish by any other stroke would not be as unique. The raw brush stroke creates a simple and unique Kanji-inspired logo for the Osaka Sushi Bar. Just any old fish would not pass the test. CDI STUDIOS

Photographer Frank Nesslage uses his nickname, Nessi, to inspire his logo. Professionally attaching to Loch Ness is definitely a unique approach. It's also clever, interesting, and hard to forget. DZIALIFORNIA

Manufactured stories are for kids. The Children's Museum of Utah, USA, has a programming activity and exhibition group called Story Factory. The logo for Story Factory is a unique, playful visual.
CC GRAPHIC DESIGN

A distinct look in the financial services category requires exploration beyond traditional comfort zones. The Einfach Investieren by Fidelity Germany is a great example of uniqueness in a category. LIGALUX

Criteria 3: Metaphor

ALL THE WORLD'S A LOGO

Metaphors make great stories. Ask any writer. Better yet, read a book. Metaphors encode experiences and artifacts into base denominators, so that everyone who shares stock with the common denominator can feel them.

Metaphors target the core of the human psyche by tapping into cultural heritage. Using symbolism and archetypes, they sear memories into the mind. Strong metaphors are essential to the brand story. Worthwhile metaphors extend to logo design. Ideation logically starts with metaphor exploration, and the first step is the briefing.

The challenge of any organization or business is to communicate who it is and what it stands for and to accomplish this for an audience that is often more interested in a nagging hangnail or when it has to pick up the kids.

Any brand's surest bet is to identify itself simply, engagingly, and directly. When this is the case, don't worry about relaying all the intricate details. Rather, ensure that your story is consistent.

We all know of Enron, Goldman Sachs, and Microsoft. Do we know all the finer points of their business? No. Who would want to? The point is not to make consumers completely understand the brand; it's more important to make them trust the brand.

One example of this is the logo for Cerenity senior care facilities based in Minnesota, USA. The logo communicates brand values in a direct way that creates a connection for its audience. The butterfly represents growth, beauty, and flight, among many other things. The interior cross is a highly evocative symbol that makes an explicit connection back to the brand's

Christian roots. Together, the butterfly and cross represent the most important values of the senior care facilities.

The story starts with a simile: "The organization is like a butterfly floating over a field of prairie grass—peaceful and tranquil." Then, it should move to a more subtle approach, which is where the metaphor comes into play. "The tranquility of a floating butterfly" is the phrase that inspires the senior care facility's logo design.

A worthwhile story does not change with time, new management, or external rotation. Great metaphors communicate complex stories to a large, diverse audience. Find the right metaphor and you've struck brand gold. It will be the foundation for everything that follows.

ISLAND QUEEN CRUISE

Canada's largest sightseeing cruise ship's logo helps tell its story. The metaphor is a queen's crown floating over the flowing Canadian waters, symbolizing luxury, national pride, and elegance. RIORDAN DESIGN

Cerenity SENIOR CARE

Cerenity's logo design alludes subtly to the organization's Christian faith through metaphor, whereas the name does not. CAPSULE

Negative metaphors can be spun positively. Playful naughtiness comes across simply and directly in the Gluttony logo design. OCTAVO

During the briefing, establish the brand values. This is made up of the brand promise, archetypes, attributes, personality, and other brand fundamentals. Brand values serve as the foundation for consequent metaphor development and should be used as a barometer throughout the process.

natagora

Inspiration Sources

DON'T BE LIKE A FISH OUT OF IDEAS

Give a man a fish and you've fed him, for today. Teach a man to fish and you've fed him for a lifetime. Or at least until he gets sick of seafood. Fishing for ideas is an art form. Seasoned art directors know which bait nabs which prey. They know ideal times and the special, secret "spots" that greenhorns blindly trample past. And when they sense a real tug, they reel in their tethers with nimble, deft pacing. Catching ideas takes time, dedication, and patience.

If you're looking for a place to catch some largemouth ideas, cast your line in a good book. Words of all sizes and shapes zip and nibble at your mind, tugging it into the author's fluid world. Wade through connotations, splash around in symbolism, and ideas will float to the surface faster.

Awards annuals are fine if you're looking to do what has already been done. For something fresh and new that could end up in *next* year's award annual, find quirky, off-the-beaten-path publications. Or publications that are not traditionally associated with the category for which you are designing. For example, your design for a technology firm could be found while flipping through an old French cookbook—or a world atlas. A word, illustration, or recipe could trigger a metaphor or visual language that can be applied to anything, so long as you connect it well.

Beyond books, immerse yourself in the world around you. The most obvious place to go is where the logo design will eventually live: trade shows, retail stores, or along park trails. To find further inspiration, roam to vibrant locales in which culture coagulates, such as community celebrations, plays, and festivals. Also visit destinations where people seek solace and reconnect with themselves.

Creative inspiration also congregates heavily around your contemporaries. Find peers with whom you can bounce ideas, flesh out concepts, and find encouragement. Hardworking freelancers often need to spend time in a design office with other people doing similar work.

The places and activities in which you likely will *not* find creative inspiration are just as common. Watching television is one of these activities.

Children's brain activity has been shown to list off to nil in front of the boob tube. Avoid places in which you are not only alone but also have no external stimulation. On the flip side, avoid overstimulation; the human brain can handle only a certain amount before it emits a tired shudder and its eyes flicker shut.

Don't give up on finding that perfect creative fishing hole. Once you're there, you'll know. When it happens, look around and sketch a map so you can find your way back.

Before you pick up a sketch pad, review the previous work done during the planning stage. Initial work is often a fertile source of inspiration and ideas.

Seek objects with literal and aesthetic value. The inspiration for the logo of this design house, Root Idea, comes from nature. Branches represent design's two spheres of necessity: logic and aesthetics. The hand symbolizes growing ideas. ROOT IDEA

Immerse yourself in another world. While designing the logo for the children's clothing retailer Goodnight Moon, the designer spent time reading children's books and hanging around kids and in the retailer's environment. CAPSULE

Pick simple ideas. The shape and color of grapes growing in rows play into a visually memorable logo design for Mornington Estates Winery. OCTAVO

IDEATION EXERCISES

One popular metaphor exploration process is called visual ideation, which includes searching magazines, newspapers, websites, video podcasts, and blogs for inspiration. While searching, pick and pull inspirational, relevant images. Once a solid collection has been gathered, hold a team ideation session. Present all the information together and share thoughts. Consider why certain images were intriguing and how this visual charisma can be translated into the project.

A single exercise can run ten minutes; several over a week can add up to multiple hours. There is no need to be overly controlling at this point, but it is important to prepare for a certain level of chaos, because random, unstructured, non-linear thinking is a fundamental component of creative thinking. The only way to find something new is to upset convention. By applying the right amount of focused pressure and conflict, ideas start flowing at an amazing pace. If the initial session does not seem to yield the results you are looking for, remember that patterns can be found later upon closer observation, and when a session is sluggish, move the team on to something completely unrelated.

Don't fall in love with a direction at this stage. Step back and develop several ideas. You may have something genuinely insightful. If you get too attached to one idea, you're shutting out other possibilities and turning off the creative faucet.

Another simple exercise requires one marker, five pages of large paper, and at least three to five functioning brains (or six to ten halfwits, if that's all you can find). More than fifteen will invite chaos and muffle less outspoken members. Ideation sessions should always be somewhat intimate affairs conducted with an abbreviated set of core, creative minds in the room. During these exercises, challenge the group to come up with twenty ideas in twenty minutes. These do not have to be solid, well-formed ideas; members should open their minds and not feel uncomfortable about suggesting seemingly silly things, because these often ignite more legitimate concepts.

METAPHORS: CREATING IDEAS IN A BOX

Identifying metaphors needn't be a random process. Just remember, the structure should focus on ideas, not the process. Try not to overly refine one idea. As an idea develops, have the discipline to put it aside once it has enough structure for someone to get it. Moving on quickly is essential to success.

THE VISUAL METAPHOR MATRIX EXERCISE

1. Gather all relevant materials. Use them to reconnect to the client's brand, promise, and personality.

2. Identify the top five attributes of the client's brand. Examples: speed, simplicity, performance, care, community, love.

3. Identify five basic words that are simple enough for a child to understand. Examples: person, tree, house, nature, animal, word, flight. Start broad. These words can be narrowed and refined into more descriptive terms later.

4. Create a matrix by placing the brand attributes on one axis and the visually descriptive, broad words on the other.

5. Fill in the boxes with ideas, sketches, or whatever comes to mind. These "images" are the interface between a particular brand attribute and a basic word. Images will suggest further words, and words will suggest further images.

6. Keep the machine on spin cycle. From this process, many combinations will pour out. Unrelated elements will reveal unexpected and creative metaphors.

VISUAL DESCRIPTIVE WORDS >>						
BRAND ATTRIBUTES >>	People	Nature	Houses	Tools	Animals	Science
Speed	⚡	🌀				
Simplicity	🧍	🍃				
Performance	🎭	🌱				
Care	🕺	▨				
Community	🤸	🌴				
Love	🧎	♡				

Create boxes and boxes of metaphors. Having places to put ideas helps push the design concepts onto the page.

Surrounding Layout

ARE YOU BUILDING AN ANCHOR OR A SAIL?

Not long ago, plump ships glided into the ports of majestic empires, straining under vast cargoes of spices, textiles, and adventures plucked from faraway colonies. Today, logos act like mighty vessels, transporting brand messages wherever the brand roams, from shopping carts and refrigerators to the opposite ends of the Earth.

Effective logos are like ships, but bad logos act more like anchors, fixing brands tightly to one moment in time and leaving little room for the brand to move. They are often missing one of three principal elements: simplicity, metaphor, and uniqueness. Consider how your designs embody each of these, in what capacity and in what applications. Also consider and visualize how the design fits into both the three-dimensional and the two-dimensional world. Today's technology makes this a fairly easy process. Show

clients logos in their surrounding layouts. For presentations, paste the logo onto signage, stationery systems, and packaging. It's easy to get excited about a logo when it's on your computer screen. Shortcomings spring up in real-world applications.

The logo design's surrounding layout takes many forms. It's not the logo designer's responsibility to make sure all future communications are up to snuff. But if standards are high, you can inspire your client to achieve them.

A logo on its own won't transform a good company into a bad one. But it can make a good company *look* bad. The logo should be an asset, not a liability. A good logo is one that contributes to brand success. The best you can strive for is to design a logo that exemplifies the brand and tells a story in the simplest form

possible. Also, design the logo to reflect where the brand is going, not just where it's been.

You'll know when you've designed an anchor of a logo, one that's stale and heavy. You'll know because you'll encounter it in a trade publication, shrunken and tucked into an inconspicuous corner of a much better-designed advertisement. The small logo will sink under the rest of the brand, hidden from view. That is, until the client finally completely cuts ties with it and hoists a new logo high into the light of day. The surrounding layout impacts a logo design if the logo designer considers it. Consider it and your design will have a better chance of survival.

Become part of the environment. The Union logo design is an integral part of the surrounding layout. It contributes to the rest of the design, making it more memorable. CRUSH

Envision logos in three-dimensional surroundings. The Fashion Center's logo design goes beyond a two-dimensional symbol, solidifying into a three-dimensional brand object. PENTAGRAM

THE
FASHION
CENTER
INFORMATION
KIOSK

Color and Clients

PUT YOUR PANTONES ON ONE LEG AT A TIME

One of the most important things to know about color is how to make a client think about it rationally. A lot of clients burden colors with emotional associations. For no reason in particular, one man's burnt sienna is another man's nightmare. When discussing color with clients, let your swatches do the talking.

Once your swatches have spoken their piece, then you can exercise your lips. Ask what the client likes, what the client's audience would like, what will make the logo design distinct in the existing market. Make sure clients factor in how the logo's color will extend into every area of business, from overall system color to office carpeting.

Let your client pick a few favorites. Then review how each will work with the brand objectives, based on competitors, industry, and brand personality. Tell the client in what ways the color gets people talking and buying into the brand. Remember, the rainbow is infinite. Focus the client, or you may never find the end of it.

If your client wants to build an innovative brand, guide the color accordingly. Drop names of important brands that have dared to color where no one has colored before. Cemstone is a great example. The Midwest construction cement company owns robin's egg blue. However, that specific shade is also internationally associated with Tiffany's jewelry house, a brand perched a million debutantes away from construction's rugged terrain. That's precisely why Cemstone's adoption of blue is so brilliant. The vibrant hue busts the brand free from the comfortable gray fog in which industry competitors quietly drift off.

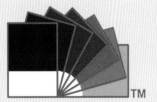 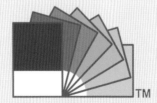 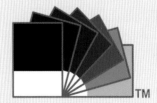

Sometimes color is the brand. One of the world's top brands, Pantone, defines the meaning and standard of color. Its logo is flexible and clear. PENTAGRAM

Think also about what colors have the potential to communicate a negative attribute. Understand the impact and stigmas of specific color, so when your client brings in a swatch of electric grape juice purple, you can deftly quell the situation.

Probably the most common mistake in logo design is creating a logo that requires more than one color to retain the original concept. A successful logo needs the ability to present the same concept in one color as it does in three. If the logo requires three colors, your client will find it necessary always to use more than two colors; in some media, that can be costly relative to the value they will see.

Once a primary color has been chosen, the next big step is finding a secondary color and the rest of the palette. The second color should obviously complement the primary and should also work with any other color in the palette. The color is not what should distinguish the logo in the marketplace.

vocal
consulting group

10:2:6

vocal revolution

private voice client

What does color say? The Vocal brand's logo comprises overlapping complementary colors, a design that works for a variety of groups within the organization. ELEMENT

Deconstruct color. A color's context matters and has a tremendous impact on the final result. In the jewelry category, Tiffany's classic blue sets the industry standard. It is registered under its founding date, 1837. In the construction category, Cemstone's robin's egg blue is a non-traditional color that grabs attention and stands out from traditional construction yellow. CEMSTONE

Color and Emotion

WHAT'S HIDING BEHIND YOUR SHADES

Many things can occur in the blink of your eye. When you look at something, you don't just automatically see it—although that's how it feels. The brain interprets images in stages. First the brain identifies shape, then color. Look at a banana, and you first see the oblong curve and the tapered ends. The shape helps you decide what the image is. Then you see the color. The color helps you decide how you feel about the image. A banana's yellow perks you up. Blueberries soothe. Red fire trucks spark aggression.

Color's influence runs so deeply into the subconscious that we have yet to map out all its wandering tributaries. But the things we do know have led us to respect color's practical purposes. Color can give clear direction when language fails to translate. It's a simple communication device that directs global traffic, helps establish status for everything from the Olympic Games to pie baking contests, and makes organizations stand out. Owning a color is one of

the higher achievements a brand can reach. In 1916, the Merchants Parcel Delivery, a young Seattle operation, adopted brown as its trademark color. Today, the firm still uses brown, but its name is now UPS.

The way to own a color is to choose one that no competitors in your category own. If there are a lot of established, visible brands in your category, this is tricky. Then again, don't get too worried. After all, the color spectrum is infinite. Step outside and identify typical colors. Then let your eyes rest on the atypical ones. Seek options that fit your brand and filter through them, to make sure there isn't a reason certain colors haven't been used before. Take the ones that make it through that filter and consider how well each will work across a variety of media. Considering all the media that exist now, and all that will exist in the near future, this is no small task. Don't worry if your color isn't comfortable at first. In fact, if it is, it may not be different enough from the rest of the existing category.

COLOR CONSIDERATION PROCESS

Find a color you can own in your category. It will aid brand recognition tremendously and add to brand equity.

Understand color's cultural connotations. Cultural meaning varies greatly. Weed out variations and any negative associations.

Identify a color that consistently communicates from chip to ink, toner, the Web, threads, signage, and standard paint.

Understand how electronic file formats affect color in the files. An .eps file won't treat color in the same way as a .jpg file made for the Web.

Color science is ever-evolving, due to new perspectives and discoveries about how the human brain reacts to colors.

Color impacts memory and contributes meaning to a brand. Proceed with thoughtful discretion and respect for its power.

GE Market Name
Solution Platform

unsteel

Ⓖ imagination at work

GE Consumer & Industrial

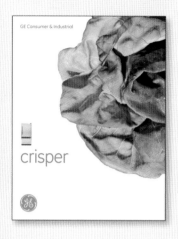

crisper

Ⓖ

GE Advanced Materials

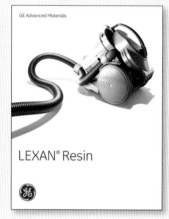

LEXAN® Resin

Ⓖ

GE Healthcare

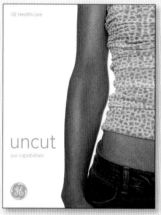

uncut
our capabilities

Ⓖ

GE Transportation
Aviation

power

Lorem ipsum dolor sit amet, consectetuer adipiscing elit. Sed orci
sapien, rutrum eget, hendrerit non, blandit et, massa. Pellen tesque
tempor metus sed purus. Quisque id mauris et urna hendrerit
molestie. Cum sociis natoque penatibus et magnis dis parturient
montes, nascetur ridiculus mus.

Visit www.ge.com for more details.

Ⓖ imagination at work

GE Advanced Materials

2005 product guide

Ⓖ

GE Consumer & Industrial
Lighting

DOUBLE BIAX
SPECIFICATIONS

Ⓖ

GE Money
Loans

6.6%=

Ⓖ imagination at work

---

no luce, no calore,
no elettricita',
ancora congelato.

GE imagination at work

Ⓖ

*Set a variety of tones. General Electric uses
color to convey the varied businesses and
perspectives it offers to the global economy.*
WOLFF OLINS

Memory and Meaning

TIE A STRING AROUND THEIR BRAINS

Long-term memory likes to keep a tidy cerebral cortex. Somewhere at this moment, it's rolling up its sleeves and tossing out the name of that B-list movie star. It probably figures you'll never need it again. Tomorrow, it just may tackle those high school fight song lyrics gathering dust in your medulla oblongata. When it comes to cleaning house, memory is fickle. If you want your logo to stay in people's memories, make it something that attaches to something in people's lives, something they want to remember and maybe even share with friends.

Essentially, make it mean something. Even if the client's line of business is completely uninspiring, find the meaning behind the service or product. Meaning manifests everywhere. Look around you. Think like Andy Warhol. He made soup cans arresting and provocative. Everything has potential. Know the brand, know the audience, and use the logo to connect the two.

Connect the audience and the brand through the brand story, but don't necessarily give it all away. A nice way to make people remember is to pitch out an unfinished sentence. Make them seek a resolution. Make them wonder why the logo for a computer company is a piece of fruit. People will try to make the connection, and when they do, it will have a good chance of sticking with them.

Smile! The treat for kids is sweet. The treat for parents is the smile the treats inspire. The Joy Co. logo creates a lasting impression with abstracted human faces. PENTAGRAM

The American Institute of Architects Fund Campaign for Open Our Doors borrows from a memorable icon, integrating the cityscape in an engaging way. PENTAGRAM

Wine from a hive, fancy that. WineHaven Winery and Vineyard is a family-run company with a unique history rooted in honey production. The bee logo is a simple mnemonic device that references the WineHaven story. CAPSULE

Typography

ALL EYES ARE ON YOUR FACE

Down on the floor. Up on the billboard. Type is crawling around everywhere. And most people don't even know it. Most consumers aren't able, even with some time and a lot of magnification, to tell the difference between Goudy and Garamond, or to begin to care about the implications of using Meta instead of Trade Gothic. Despite this, type can have as much influence as color when put in a designer's hands. To a designer, the difference between Goudy and Garamond is the difference between burlap and tin foil.

The number of typefaces currently available is hard to fathom. Think truckloads of telephone books. The major downside of this typeface overpopulation is that misused typefaces abound. Quite unfortunate, considering that type has a major presence and a subtle but potent ability to convey tone and personality. Consequently, an unreadable or inappropriate typeface has just as much potential to distract from a beautiful logo design as it does to enhance it.

Consider the subtle influences of type and spend time educating your clients. If you can defend the way in which a certain typeface reinforces a core brand message, your clients will value it well into the future.

HOW TO FIND A TYPE FOR YOUR LOGO DESIGN

▶ 1. Gather the largest library of available typefaces that you can access.

▶ 2. Consider what the brand needs to communicate and identify the brand's fundamental attributes.

▶ 3. Browse typefaces and select a few that communicate some of the brand's attributes.

▶ 4. Conduct type studies by examining how the type works with the letterforms of the brand name.

▶ 5. Consider creating a custom typeface or adapting a particular typeface to make it unique to the client.

▶ 6. Find complementary typefaces that work as a secondary typeface with the primary one.

▶ 7. Review the typeface with other designers and ask whether it is communicating what you had intended.

▶ 8. Integrate typefaces into the logo concepts so you can show them in the first presentation to the client.

Turn convention on its head. The Change logo design uses an ambigram to create a memorable moment of discovery when you happen to see the logo upside down. SUBPLOT DESIGN INC.

The simple type solution for the Dutch Presidency of the European Union in 2004 balances three colors and seven unique shapes. The elegant, calligraphic logotype creates a logo design that lives in a box, yet thinks outside of it. STUDIO DUMBAR

Take a little off the top. The logo type for Yosho evokes clever simplicity with an arresting visual edit. The cropped numerals refer to the Internet marketing company's number based solutions. SEGURA, INC.

Shape meaning with typography. The
elegant use of type in the CH monogram
for Chambers Hotel is a striking example
of typography and shape cooperating
seamlessly. PENTAGRAM

Hierarchy

LOOK BEFORE YOU CROSS THE UMBRELLA

Umbrella brands protect sub-brands from harsh market elements, casting long shadows of influence across them. In the brand hierarchy, they are the big kahunas. Sub-brands answer to them. If you're working on adding a new sub-brand to an established hierarchy, be careful where you tread. There is most likely a set way of doing things. It won't sit well with the other sub-brands or the umbrella brand if you don't consider how your new logo will get along with their logos.

Gather the umbrella brand and all its sub-brands on the couch for a heart-to-heart. Find out each of the sub-brands' express roles. Who's the leader? Who's the one with the good connections? Who's the rookie? Once you know everyone's place, you'll see the place your sub-brand, and consequently your logo, should occupy. Study how the sub-brands' personalities and roles are reflected in logos. The better you understand all the connected brands when you're designing, the easier it is for the audience to associate the new logo to the umbrella brand.

One sub-brand's logo may lead on the website, in brochures, and business cards. Another, however, may lead in other areas. Each logo has a unique strength, something it can say better than any of the others. In given situations, different ones jump to the front. Let the right brand lead when it should.

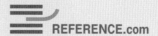

Hierarchy organizes. Structure and hierarchy are not new words to Lexico. Its sub-brands' logos live alone and also connect straight back to the source. SEGURA, INC.

City of Amsterdam

Within the chaos of a metropolitan area, logo design is implemented with great detail and attention to hierarchy. The St. Andrews' crosses come directly from the city coat of arms, harkening back to the city's heritage.

EDEN DESIGN

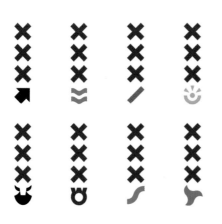

Three X's mark the spot. Amsterdam's brand comprises a variety of sub-brands under a larger umbrella brand. Each area of the city government has its own sub-brand. The design is ideal for a network organization, such as city government.

Protectable

IMITATION IS THE SINCEREST FORM OF THIEVERY

During the California gold rush, wagonloads of minors clamored to the Pacific Coast armed with homemade tin pan sifters and 24-karat dreams. These days, wealth no longer glitters from the shallow banks of sandy streams. Modern prospectors pan for wealth in the streams of their consciousness. Technology and service industries rely almost completely on ideas.

It's easy to overlook the legal side of the logo design process. Most designers don't consider legalese their forte or their responsibility. But it is—at least, to a point. You can determine this when you sit down with the client and explicitly talk through who is in charge of legal considerations. They may be completely new to the process, so walk them through what needs to be done. Talk to them about

preliminary trademark searches and decide who will contact and hire a lawyer to do the final, comprehensive trademark search. You should always take it upon yourself to search out redundancies with logos in your client's industry category. The Internet makes this a fairly simple process. But after your client decides on a final logo, a legally sound search will require a trained lawyer. Forgo a legal search, and two things can happen. One, your client gets sued by a competitor because the logo you designed looks too similar. Or two, your client's beautiful new logo gets ripped off because it isn't legally protected.

It's also important to remember that just because the client's brand name is trademarked doesn't mean the logo is as well. Competitors can use a different name and a very similar mark.

The rights of first use do offer some protection, but they often don't go far enough to protect your design in a global marketplace. This is important, because the global logo black market is growing. Online dealers are cropping up, repurposing logos, and selling bootleg versions to cash-strapped start-ups at a fraction of even freelance prices.

No matter where a logo design is sold, it runs the chance of sharing traits with other designs. This doesn't necessarily require a global comprehensive search, but it does require at least some foresight from the designer. Because if you don't know whether your logo is infringing on another's design, you'll find out when you get a fancy invitation to "immediately cease and desist."

Fly-fishing, anyone? The Fly Fishing logo design is deceptively suggestive. It offers a great example of a unique shape and form that might be descriptive, but also borders on suggestive. PENTAGRAM

zango

On the Internet, a logo design can be copied in the blink of a mouse. The Zango logo design adds protection to an already protectable name, building a large brick wall around its intellectual property.

HORNALL ANDERSON DESIGN WORKS

DE BEERS

De Beers is already facing product copycats that manufacture diamonds. Therefore, its logo design needs to be protected from knockoff brands. THE PARTNERS

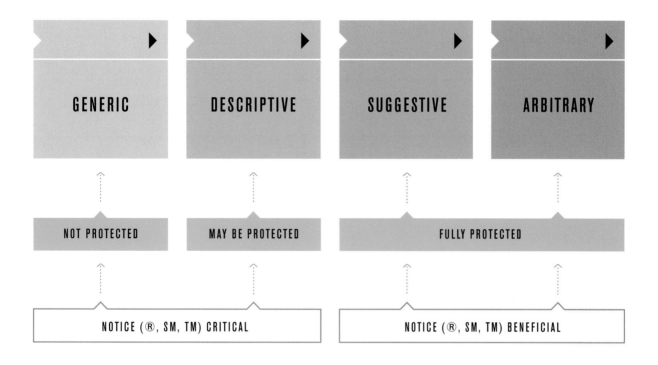

GENERIC   DESCRIPTIVE   SUGGESTIVE   ARBITRARY

NOT PROTECTED   MAY BE PROTECTED   FULLY PROTECTED

NOTICE (®, SM, TM) CRITICAL   NOTICE (®, SM, TM) BENEFICIAL

The more generic the image, the more necessary it is to protect it legally. The descriptive side of the chart requires some form of ™ or ® to identify logo ownership. The suggestive and arbitrary sides require less protection, because the logos are distinct.

Technical Considerations

JUST PUT YOUR ZIPS TOGETHER AND BLOG

For some, technology is a treat. New software launches are hailed as "events" worthy of the kind of anticipation and excitement others reserve for bat mitzvahs and rodeos. Not everyone feels this way, however. Every day, thousands of poor souls are brought to their knees by nefarious fax machines and diabolical copiers. Technology and its broad band of cohorts now run the world. Follow these technical considerations to avoid making simple mistakes within complicated media.

1. Any logo worth its price should work just as well on a golf ball as it does on a billboard.

2. Avoid using gradients or complicated techniques in the logo design. They may excite clients, but such garnishments wilt quickly under the harsh light of implementation.

3. Produce alternatives for different situations or contexts—a toolkit of pieces.

4. When it comes to using clip art or a third piece of art, as Nike's pessimistic cousin would say, "Just don't do it."

5. Design the original in vector graphics to ensure scalability without distortion. Then convert the original into all other required file formats and sizes.

6. Design a logo that works first in black and white—then add color. If a logo requires four or even five colors to convey the original idea, it is not a logo. It's a circus.

7. Never lock the brand's tagline to the logo design. Advertising campaigns and taglines generally change more often than logos. Keep the logo design and tagline separate to avoid unpleasant refinements when next year's advertising campaign launches.

8. The logo should retain its integrity in a variety of media. We design in a world in which logos show up on fabric, billboards, and even space shuttles.

9. Avoid using photography. A picture is worth a thousand words, but when it comes to logos, they're worthless. Photographs are very difficult to reproduce in challenging media.

10. Be careful when using culturally sensitive images, shapes, colors, or other visual language.

Technology has a lot of toes. You'll have plenty of opportunities to step on them. Just take some time to consider the implications of each step of your logo design.

Calling the media jackals may not be smart, but organizing a golf tournament just for media is brilliant spin. Former Minnesota governor Jesse Ventura needed a logo to work on golf balls, shirts, television, and the Internet. CAPSULE

Too busy bee or not too busy bee? That is the question. The Bloom logo's black and white design is decidedly simple, comprised of monochromatic lines that are easily adaptable to varied applications.
THE PARTNERS

This logo for WhiteStar Financial Services makes the grade. The gradation works in both black and white and in color.
OCTAVO DESIGN

experienceengineering

The shadow of an E reflects what isn't always visible to the consumer–the brand experience. Experience Engineering is an experience-management consulting firm.

CAPSULE

RESTING ON THE SHELF, STANDING TALL FOR THE PASSERBY TO SEE. SETTING A STANDARD FOR THE CATEGORY OR HOPING TO BE NEARLY AS GOOD AS THE LEADING PACKAGE. HAVING CRITERIA TO JUDGE A PACKAGE, SETS THE BAR AT THE RIGHT HEIGHT.

Essential Criteria

Keeping up with the Joneses can be exhausting, especially when the Joneses continually redefine their style.

High jumpers set high bars. Low jumpers, well, low bars. What standards do you set against your work to judge it before the world does? Criteria are essential marks against your own expectations, those of the client, and most important, the final consumer. Set your bar low and consumers will respond with the same sad look given the lowest jumper at the end of an Olympic event.

The four criteria of a successful package are identification, functionality, personality, and navigation. Identification speaks to how well the consumer can identify the product from the package when shopping the category. Functionality relates to the usability of the product and increasing the product's purpose and efficacy. Personality is how the brand comes to life on the package. And navigation refers to how the consumer finds and uses the category and specifically, your selection of packages. All four criteria may not be amplified on one package, as some criteria are set higher depending on the strategy agreed upon by the brand management team.

The result is a package that is in balance with the strategy and, if well executed, has an increased chance to contribute to a successful product launch. Set your own standards, communicate them clearly, and then design a package to exceed those standards.

Criteria 1: Identification

TELL ME WHAT YOU SEE, DR. RORSCHACH

Seeing is believing, right? Wrong. Seeing, feeling, hearing, smelling, and touching are worth believing. What is the first thing you see when you glance at a product on the shelf? What does the package say about the product inside? Depending on the category, there are many elements that help identify the product within the category. These identifiers can be long-established conventions in a category or new revolutions in an ever-changing marketplace.

Conventions, like color or bottle shape, are used to identify wine bottles in the U.S. market but are not required by law. The shape, along with the color, tends to follow the grape variety. These "laws" of the category might as well come with a prison sentence when considering the career implications if they're disobeyed.

But what's with boxed wine? Old rules need not apply. Put wine in a TetraPak package, provide individual serving sizes, offer it to a more youthful consumer, and you've broken away to create a new category. The good news: With success you get to write the new category rules. The bad news: First you have to achieve success.

Identification sets the foundation for a good package design. If this criterion is misunderstood or not used appropriately, the first step into the marketplace will be a big misstep.

Understanding category conventions requires a talent for keen observation.

Shape, color, type, materials, and many other aspects of packaging can hold identification conventions that are essential to the category. Knowing these and why they exist gives you permission to bend the conventions that need bending. Permission is key. Just bending rules because

get bent. Consider laundry detergent refill bottles that remind us of all the ways to get soiled, but still look clean and almost clinical. This package design walks a fine line on the edge of the category and will therefore stand out on the shelf. Although each package contains the same ingredients, the multitude of refill packages tells a novel of a story instead of the abridged version usually told on laun-

Great package design takes a leap within the category, not completely out of the category and over a cliff.

it's fun would be akin to child's play and certainly irresponsible design decision-making. For instance, what comes to mind when considering laundry detergent? Clean, bright, disinfected clothing—hence, clean, bright, lively, colored packaging. This is a category norm that deserves to

dry detergent packages. The package engages consumers first with novelty, and once the environmental story is told, they have the first of many reasons to be loyal. If you're tired of the sanitized, edited, and narrow story told by most laundry detergent packages, then this is your next purchase.

The same product packaged in a variety of bottles tells a visual story and engages consumers with the brand.
KINETIC

By identifying a new, more youthful category of wine consumers, boxed wine can be cool and successful without conforming to the rules of the category.

CAHAN & ASSOCIATES

Criteria 2: Fuctionality

HELLO MR. FUNCTION CURMUDGEON

When does a package become an integral part of the product? When the functionality of the package reaches or exceeds that of the product it contains. The moment when the package adds emotional rewards or unexpected benefits to buying the product is when the line between product and package is blurred.

The functional package design contributes to how the package will be accepted by essential audiences: the channel—distributor, buyer, and retailer—and the eventual product consumer. Because the function differs for the channel and the consumer, these two interests often conflict. The channel desires ease of transportation, restocking, efficient use of retail footprint, and many other operational efficiencies vital to cost containment. The consumer has vastly varied—almost too many to list—interests depending on the product category and their lifestyle. Highly functional design for a consumer is typically not in alignment with the interests of the channel participants. Intuitive designers should be able to find the overlaps and create exceptional design functionality for the essential audiences.

Understanding function means seeing dysfunction and being able to confidently identify it as such. You know it the moment you try to pick up a package without handles or open a container that takes three hands and a sharp tool. That's called dysfunction. The next step in educating your eyes is gaining the ability to identify exceptional function. Great functional design naturally becomes part of our life, as if it were meant to be there all along.

Seeking a competitive advantage to keep a pesky entrant out of your category? When done right, the packaging function will deliver on measurable business objectives. Functionality in a package can be stronger than changes to the product because it can alter how the product fits into someone's life. It can change behaviors, which a veteran marketer would say is like reaching the Holy Grail. Change how the package functions and you change how the consumer functions with it.

Having properly trained eyes and then a properly trained team to create function requires multiple disciplines. Designers, engineers, anthropologists, buyers, operations managers, and anyone who has passed the threshold of recognizing dysfunction and entered the world of articulating an elegant function should be included. Creating a new function or changing what exists needs to be handled by the properly experienced group—approaching it casually will likely result in casualties.

Pop the top, and pop your vitamins. Water infused with vitamins is finding its way into our lives. This package adds the functionality of enhancing your water just before you consume it, retaining the integrity of your vitamin consumption.

FORMATION DESIGN

Integrating a tray into the paint container is both convenient and a simple reduction in resources needed for that weekend paint job.

FLEX/THE INNOVATIONLAB

EXERCISE: FOLLOW THE PACKAGE

In order to find new functional design possibilities, you need to see where the current package is functioning. So, follow it through its entire life cycle. Follow each step, without exceptions and without skipping. Have at least three people do this exercise at different times and journal as they go, taking note of what they see and any ideas that may have popped up.

The first thing you should acquire following this process is a large number of notes taken during the package's journey from origination to final disposal. Each stage should have notes from the three participants, whose ideas can be analyzed and findings summarized using all three in a pseudo-triangulation of results. Dig deep into the results and you'll find the places where additional functionality may serve a relevant and valuable purpose. Dig into frustrations and places where consumers got stuck with the package, and you'll likely find additional functions worth exploring.

In the end, you're not looking for a competitive advantage. You're looking for ways to surprise a consumer with additional function that eventually leads to a competitive advantage in packaging.

Convenience and function are much the same idea. For example, when does the package contribute to the convenience of the product? When the paint can becomes the holder and strainer for the paint roller, the convenience factor is amplified. This is where the idea of context becomes essential.

STANDARD PAINTING TOOLS: ▶

- ▶ One roller
- ▶ One gallon (3.8 L) paint
- ▶ One tray

STANDARD PROCESS OF PAINTING: ▶

- ▶ Open paint
- ▶ Pour paint
- ▶ Apply paint
- ▶ Repeat until finished
- ▶ Clean up tray and brush

FLEXA: PREMIUM PAINT BRAND: ▶

- ▶ Quality of any paint is hard to judge
- ▶ Private label brands are infringing
- ▶ Customer experience has seen little innovation
- ▶ Existing packaging offers little additional functionality

The discoveries to be found in contextual research are amazing. Seeing your package in the world where it lives will reveal many possible improvements to functional design. Evaluating which improvements are worthwhile is up to you and your team.

INNOVATIVE CONCEPTS DEVELOPED: ▶

- ▶ Solutions generated
- ▶ Technical requirements met
- ▶ Quality and durability met
- ▶ Logistics requirements achieved

CONCEPT REFINEMENT: ▶

- ▶ Ergonomics considered
- ▶ Environmental challenges addressed
- ▶ Visual language designed
- ▶ Functional specifications further defined

IMPLEMENTAION:

- ▶ Logistically sexy
- ▶ Functionally elegant
- ▶ Less waste of paint
- ▶ Less waste of trays
- ▶ More happy homeowners

Criteria 3: Personality

PRINCESS CONSISTENCY WILL RULE THE KINGDOM

Sell a boat, car, house, or any other high-ticket item, and you'll finish with a handshake. Sell baby cereal or a cell phone accessory, and the only personal interaction may be the package itself. When this is all you have, it is essential to deliver on brand personality.

The brand personality comes to life and delivers its largest impression the moment someone picks up the package. From this point, we have to think of the brand personality as an actual person. Now, who is this person? It can't be ten people, but it has to appeal to tens of millions of people. Just like a shrewd person can see right through a shady character, consumers who spend time with brands feel the inconsistencies between a brand and its package. And feel is the operative word. They may not see it, be able to articulate it, or even know it exists, but they know something is rotten in Denmark. Therefore it's less about having the right personality than being true to that personality. Consistency is where strength is built.

Knowing the personality requires clear definition before conception and then ongoing research as the brand matures. Because the brand is neither born nor will live in a vacuum, and because the world around it constantly changes, it will require additional knowledge and continued refinement. As a person ages and becomes more mature, you can see and feel the experience he or she has gained over the years. It's the same with a brand. Not with gray hair, but it gains the maturity to know when and how much to change to remain culturally relevant.

Brand personality can be defined by human personality techniques such as archetypes, profiles, Myers-Briggs, or a litany of others. Multiple definitions provide a variety of perspectives on the brand. Limiting it to one method is easier, but it risks leaving some aspect out. Once it has been defined, how much you push the personality depends on your place in the history of the category. If you're first to market, you have a greater obligation to identify the category and

set standards for how brands should behave in the newly formed category. This doesn't mean your personality has to come with a pocket protector, but it does lessen in importance relative to the other criteria. If you happen to be forty-fifth to market with a brand of water, you'll have to push beyond your comfort zone on personality, unless your water happens to cure cancer as well.

If your brand has been around for a while, understanding the difference between how you define the personality and how your audiences define it is valuable. The differences will reveal potential areas of inconsistency that should be considered as the brand and package evolve. Using the same methods or tests internally as you use externally will identify the gap and the potential for inconsistent brand messages.

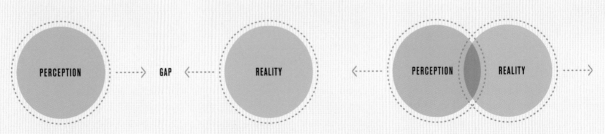

The more overlap between audience perceptions and the intended reality, the more consistency and strength in your brand. Brand personalities created and managed in such a way that creates distance from perception and reality will weaken the brand as audiences discover the inconsistencies. Strong brands are true to who they are.
SOURCE: CAPSULE

Cell phones have continued to advance the technology while also realizing the consumer desires a brand that reflects their lifestyle. The ROKR phone package offers a glimpse at the phone but more importantly, a glimpse at the personality of the brand.

TURNER DUCKWORTH

"Kiss it, I dare ya. Go ahead, soul smack my slick, amphibian cricket hole. C'mon, tingle me. Just don't get your humanoid hopes up, pal, I ain't changin'. I like my slippery self just the way I am. Enough of my croakin', I've got stuff to Yank. Sure, I can impale flies all day long, but I'm after bigger thrills. Set out some fresh DVDs and CDs and let the Yankin' commence."

COPY TONE
Copy tone is very important when designing for a particular audience. For Yank, it's the antibranding Gen Yers.

TOUCHPOINTS
Adding personality to the expected creates a memorable touch point.

PACKAGING REQUIREMENTS
Personality does not need to be restricted by packaging requirements.

FEATURES AND BENEFITS
Instead of a typical list of features and benefits, a humorous pictograph system was used.

GET YOURSELF A PERSONALITY, PLEASE

Industries evolve, categories coalesce, and every package in a category starts to look the same. Going to a party where everyone looks, talks, sounds, and smells the same—whom do you want to hang out with? The one who isn't the same as all the rest? If you walk down store aisles today, you'll pick up on the personality attributes just by viewing and reading the packages. If you start to see common patterns, it's because many personalities follow others who have got there first.

Leaders take the chance of having personality attributes that are not commonly seen in the category, but this is risky. If an attribute isn't common in the category, might it be because it has already been tried and failed? Or has no one thought of it before? And could that really be the case? It depends on the radical nature of the category. For instance, when Healthy Choice frozen meals chose green as their primary color, they had to face the food category

fear of that color. Green can be associated with rotting food, making it an uncommon color and a risk for the Healthy Choice brand. Bending or breaking with conventional wisdom is a hallmark of break-out brands, those brands that leave the others behind with their mouths gaping open and whispering, "How did they do that?"

Taking risks requires an understanding of what the real risks are in any situation. For instance, when something is uncomfortable, we chose to avoid and perhaps remove the discomfort instead of allowing ourselves to become comfortable or even analyzing our discomfort. This gut-wrenching emotional response can be a good contrast to the banal personalities likely to be shelved directly to the right and left of your brand. It can be a joy for the consumer to find something unique on the shelf, even if it was the result of a highly uncomfortable decision-making process. Translated, this means no emotional pain, no emotional gain.

Many times the biggest hurdle is getting your team (both client and design) to see the real risk. Making comparisons to other categories can be hugely instructive. By looking at other categories, you can zero in on products and packages that break away from their conventions—and draw valuable conclusions from the results. For instance, if you're in the food category, pick a category that's opposite (or least not similar) to food that you admire. In other words, looking at the peanut butter category isn't helpful if your product is honey (another food). Find something at some distance from your category— perfume, perhaps. As your team starts to review packaging, you can draw correlations to the categories you've studied, and you will find a team that's more comfortable with pushing personality boundaries.

As the breakfast cereal industry matured in the 1950s, cereal brands created characters like Tony the Tiger to infuse personality. In a world where impersonal technology is often the center of attention, seeing a bullfrog named B. Shizzle on the box cover for this DVD burner is an example of pushing personality.
CAPSULE

Criteria 4: Navigation

WHO MOVED MY PEANUT BUTTER, DAMN IT?

Walk into a retail environment and look around. Now, start counting the brands you can identify and those you cannot. If you begin to feel like you're counting stars in the sky, only less romantic, then you're getting it. Navigation in the age of pirates and treasure chests involved the challenge of crossing vast oceans. Today, consumers face the overwhelming task of navigating vast megastores stocked with brands and packages from all over the world. So if you want to help the pirates reach your treasure trove, you have to consider the importance of navigation when packaging a product and sending it out on the open market.

What happens when a consumer walks down the aisle? Exactly how does your package happily end up in his or her cart? By using design tools, consumers are given navigation clues to reach the destination you set out for them. There are navigation ele-

ments that help move them through the category of options. And there are elements that get them to the exact SKU within your display of options.

Navigation, like identification, relies on visual cues like type, colors, patterns, words, shapes, and anything else that's visible on the package. Some parts of a package serve to connect it to the larger family of products, while other elements make the package utterly distinctive. The full effect of these elements can only be understood by looking at the category as a whole. This means either you have to have a keen ability to see something in context or the ability to create context in a digital environment. Either way, it's what matters when understanding a package's contribution to navigation.

Limited navigation reduces the impact you can have on the category as your own personal billboard. It can also

limit how someone shops your brand and the knowledge he or she gains about how connected your products are to one another. The extreme of no navigation is a missed opportunity at best and a drain on sales at worst.

Navigation can also work too hard and drown out the personality of individual products, flavors, or variations. This can leave the consumer feeling like an individual product is generic or lacking a unique touch. Imagine ice cream that identifies its rocky road flavor using only words and missing the tummy-tingling photo of peanuts, marshmallows, and chocolate. Not that enticing anymore, huh? Extremes are valuable teaching tools, but finding the right balance is what you need in practice. It's harder to teach and is left to be intuited and understood. Balance just feels right—and it feels right next to mint chocolate chip.

An illustrated approach to navigation, the Dr. Stuart's tea box gives shoppers many subtle clues to help navigate their way to the right choice. Colors may vary but Dr. Stuart's tea logo does not. Illustrations tell a more nuanced and metaphorical story for those willing to spend a little time with it.
PEARLFISHER

Dry Soda beverages are designed to match specific meals. These unique bottles contain similarly unique flavors like lemongrass, lavender, and kumquat. The package design sets the product apart from the cluttered beverage marketplace.

TURNSTYLE

Balancing what changes and what stays the same is key to packaging with high navigation. The Neutral line of products creates a simple navigational tool to follow by using icons and color. The consistency among all the packages gives Neutral a larger presence on the shelf, while facilitating navigation.

MUGGIE RAMADANI DESIGN STUDIO (MRDS)

With a dizzying array of options on the shelf today—especially when it comes to personal care products—sometimes it is all about a number. Find your way through a crowded field by choosing the product you desire and all you have to remember is one number. This illustrates navigation at the shelf made easy while still infusing personality into the brand.

BERGMAN ASSOCIATES

CONSUMERS MISBEHAVING: NAVIGATING THE AISLE

Consumers behave in apparently irrational and erratic ways. That is, until you spend time observing and analyzing why they do what they do. It may be highly emotional and it may not be what you want to see and hear, but it is their behavior. The package design can either contribute to navigation or just get in the way.

Spend some time in an aisle, any aisle. You'll start to see subtleties of consumer behavior. Record and question everything you see. For instance, you might find yourself in the nail care aisle watching women paint any flat surface of the display with nail enamel. What does this say about the package design? Perhaps the bottles are too easy to open, and women like to paint things. Or, more likely, the bottle doesn't show color accurately so these women use a dab of the color to see how it will look when they get home. It might also lead to an idea for paper nail samples to give these aisle artists a reason not to open the product. It may also lead to a bottle that represents color more accurately in the cap and to a product that gains an advantage at the shelf. Consumers' behavior may seem irrational until ideas surface that address the behavior, and then the consumers are rational and valuable to the brand manager who achieves this greater understanding.

Decision-making modeling and behavior modeling goes far enough back that it should be on the tongue of any marketer with a degree today. Unfortunately, this is often not the case. They are simple tools used to map out consumer behavior and then to perform experiments to achieve the desired reaction. Perhaps in an effort to get someone to purchase your brand over another you spend zillions of dollars getting the consumer to recognize your brand name and be able to talk about it at parties. Then, what happens in the store? Can they remember?

Decision-making diagrams: consider them a framework but not the finite evidence of how consumers shop a category. The examples used are for nail care items, enamels, and implements; each offers a different perspective on how a shopper navigates each category. For those of you, 49 percent of the population, who may never purchase these items, you'll have to relate it to items you would buy.

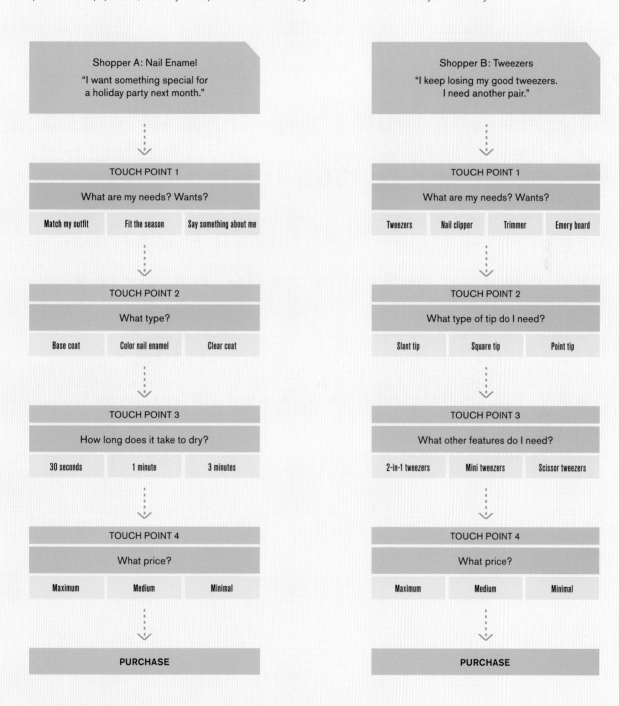

Shopper A: Nail Enamel		
"I want something special for a holiday party next month."		

TOUCH POINT 1

What are my needs? Wants?

| Match my outfit | Fit the season | Say something about me |

TOUCH POINT 2

What type?

| Base coat | Color nail enamel | Clear coat |

TOUCH POINT 3

How long does it take to dry?

| 30 seconds | 1 minute | 3 minutes |

TOUCH POINT 4

What price?

| Maximum | Medium | Minimal |

PURCHASE

Shopper B: Tweezers		
"I keep losing my good tweezers. I need another pair."		

TOUCH POINT 1

What are my needs? Wants?

| Tweezers | Nail clipper | Trimmer | Emery board |

TOUCH POINT 2

What type of tip do I need?

| Slant tip | Square tip | Point tip |

TOUCH POINT 3

What other features do I need?

| 2-in-1 tweezers | Mini tweezers | Scissor tweezers |

TOUCH POINT 4

What price?

| Maximum | Medium | Minimal |

PURCHASE

The tweezers are more of a task-driven purchase and therefore more focused on need (rational) and making the right decision faster. In contrast, the nail enamel decision, which is more driven by want (emotional), allows for exploration by the purchaser.

SOURCE: CAPSULE

THOUGHTFULLY CREATED FOR A MOMENT IN TIME. THE MOMENT A HAND REACHES OUT TO GRASP IT, PICK IT UP, TURN IT OVER, AND THEN PLACE IT IN A BASKET. DESIGN THE PERFECT PACKAGE, START WITH THE CONSUMER, AND WORK BACK TO A SPECIFIC MOMENT WHEN THE POWER OF DESIGN IS REALIZED.

Designing Packages

Design in the field of packaging is where the worlds of two-dimensional and three-dimensional design come together and shake hands. The typical package has a minimum of two sides and often many more. This combines the domains of product design and graphic design in an elegant merger that embraces the product itself.

Design is a discipline that is developed much like any craft, over a period of years under the right guidance, study, and tutelage. From materials to shapes and forms, to graphics on packages to openings and handles, there are many aspects of packaging design to understand. And just when everything seems crystal clear, an innovative new material or closure comes along.

As a package is often referred to as the salesperson on the shelf, the design process brings that person to life. And unless you want to bring another Frankenstein to life, a design team should aspire to create something people won't recoil from or reject out of hand. So the next question is, "Who would you like to have selling your product?"

This section covers how much the package contributes to the convenience and accessibility of the product it contains. It covers the three levels of packages—primary, secondary, and tertiary—and their purpose and potential. Then shape and structure come in to lend dimension and a unique form. Lastly, color, type, and art are the essential utensils of the design practitioner.

Design Green Thinkers
LIVING VERSUS ACTING SUSTAINABLY

Recently there have been several large elephants jumping up and down on the environmentally responsible bandwagon: Wal-Mart being the most notable. With its Sustainability Packaging Exposition, Wal-Mart introduced 3,000 product suppliers to 135 alternative packaging suppliers. Although this might bobble the heads of those who originally built the bandwagon, the effort is commendable. If you know any wagon builders, ask them this: "If there were a large corporation in the world you'd like to have singing the praises of the environmental movement, which one would it be? Who could make the greatest impact? What stores contain the most packages? Who could make it economical to be environmental?"

Although talking can get the ball rolling, the real action happens when the rubber hits the road. Or rather, when the bio-fiber, corn-based substance that feels like rubber but biodegrades in three hundred days hits the road.

We, as a design community, have all the tools at our disposal to make an impact with every package we design. Small steps make for little carbon footprints when it comes to an environmentally sound package.

Just inches of packaging material saved, or an extra moment spent considering the environmental impact from each part of the package, can yield profound results. The answer can't be, "It isn't important to our customers," because it will be. Nor can the answer be, "We think it's just a fad," because it's not. Books like *Cradle to Cradle*, *Natural Capitalism*, and others deliver great insight into how to think about the packages we create. In addition, both books hammer out the economic factors and the potential financial and social rewards for adopting responsible behaviors and a green business strategy.

Although consumer recycling certainly has great merit, it is not what stands to help the environment most. The "holy cow" impact will come from innovative new products and packages that use fewer raw materials, make it easier to reuse or recycle, and reduce the impact from point of origin to final destination. So what would be a good example? Stop shipping water. Or ship as little water as we possibly can. Studies have shown that homes in the civilized world already have equal or greater quality water on tap.

Need another example? Consider what *Cradle to Cradle* advocates: Keep biological innovations and industrial innovations separate when designing a package. Simple idea. When you have something that decomposes, make it easy to separate from the parts that need to be recycled. This means blending cardboards and unrecyclable plastics isn't good, but blending cardboard and bioplastics is. Keep it economically simple for the consumer. The impact is less and the reward greater.

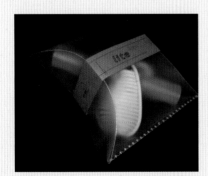 

Many packages have secondary uses, but few see the value of having their branded package carry on in the life of your customer. The lite2go packaging that becomes the light with minimal assembly is a highly creative articulation of how to reuse.
KNOEND

SUSTAINABLE PACKAGING CONSIDERATIONS

••• Beneficial, safe, and healthy for individuals and communities throughout its life cycle

••• Meets market criteria for performance and cost

••• Sourced, manufactured, transported, and recycled using renewable energy

••• Maximizes the use of renewable or recycled source materials

••• Manufactured using clean production technologies and best practices

••• Made from materials that are healthy in all probable end-of-life scenarios

••• Physically designed to optimize materials and energy

••• Can be effectively recovered and utilized in biological and/or industrial *Cradle to Cradle* cycles

website: www.sustainablepackaging.org

Sustainable Design Behaviors

"IF ONLY" IS BOLOGNA

We've all heard phrases that start with "If only" followed by some idealistic statement about saving the world with the flip of a light switch or the flush of a toilet. Idealism has its place, but if you want change, make it economic. Take a dollar from my pocket tomorrow and I'll turn off the lights early tonight. Oil prices go up and suddenly the environmental movement, sustainability, energy independence, and other related topics are part of virtually everyone's daily coffee conversation.

The same applies to packaging: Real change will happen when it makes solid economic sense. And it will make economic sense, unless it's trendy. Trends come and go. Hollywood likes trendy; environmental activists do not. If protecting the big blue marble we all live on becomes merely trendy, we're all in big trouble. Jumping out of your stretch SUV at an awards show and saying "I buy offsets" to the first reporter who asks a question should not, repeat, not be the standard behavior. Get your own behaviors in order first before buying offsets and bragging to your red

carpet fans. And for starters, make it a stretch hybrid.

But what are we doing about the box? Where will the package be when it stops moving or nears the end of its useful life? Will it need to be burned or buried to hide it from our fussy suburban eyes? Or will it need to be deconstructed in order to reintroduce each separate piece into a recycling program? Will it be used to fuel our homes? Could it be planted in the ground to grow a flower? These are the questions that Bill McDonough, author of *Cradle to Cradle*, posed to many corporate design teams long before it became hot to say, "Hi, I'm carbon neutral, how are you?" McDonough's efforts may not have led the consumer products environmental movement, but they have been recognized as important cogs in the system of sustainable design.

If your first thought is to use recycled materials when considering an environmentally responsible design, then you need to get current on your considerations because there are so many more factors at work.

Which is the more disposable cutlery, wood or plastic? If you choose wood, aren't you then cutting down the trees we hug? Not if they've fallen down already or if the wood is leftover from other sources. And what if we used wooden cutlery more than once because it is more durable and doesn't have the social stigma of hand-washed plastic forks? Thoughtful change leads to sustainable designs for Aspenware/Wun cutlery.

BLOK DESIGN

WASTE CREATION AND WHERE IT GOES

Country	Municipal Waste Per Capita	Percent Recycled	Percent Incinerated	Percent Land-filled
Austria	480k	38	14	48
Belgium	470k	14	31	55
Canada	630k	19	6	75
Czech Republic	230k	-	-	99
Denmark	530k	23	54	22
Finland	410k	33	2	65
Germany	400k	29	17	51
Greece	310k	7	-	93
Hungary	420k	-	7	93
Iceland	560k	14	17	69
Ireland	430k	8	-	92
Italy	470k	-	6	94
Japan	400k	4	69	27
Korea	390k	24	4	72
Luxembourg	530k	28	43	28
Mexico	330k	1	-	99
The Netherlands	580k	38	27	35
Norway	620k	15	16	69
Poland	290k	2	-	98
Portugal	350k	12	-	88
Spain	370k	12	4	83
Sweden	440k	19	42	39
Switzerland	610k	40	46	14
Turkey	590k	2	2	81
UK	490k	7	9	83
USA	720k	27	16	57

Source: Municipal Waste in OECD Countries, ARUP Drivers of Change, and AAAS Atlas

Figures based on available data

Waste not, want not. As the world breeds more consumption societies, waste needs to find its proper place in the economic cycle. These statistics represent current behaviors that will obviously not be sustainable behaviors.

Primary, Secondary, Tertiary

ONE, TWO, THREE; NOT IN THAT ORDER

The six-pack of bottles (primary) with a simple handled, collapsible package (secondary) and the insulated box that keeps your product cool and fresh while in transport (tertiary). These three layers of packages all contribute something important to the process of delivering a product from manufacturer to consumer.

Ever take a peek behind those plastic flaps protecting the backroom doorway at your local grocery store? Or better yet, did you ever have a job restocking shelves at a neighborhood convenience store? Remember all the boxes? Tertiary packages, also known as transport packaging, offer protection, transport, and some navigation for the participants in the channel. Because consumers rarely see the tertiary package, the logical result is a box with little or no brand messaging. But change is near as big box retailers have pallets of product displayed above or below the primary merchandise. Tertiary packaging's original and chief role was defined mainly by efficiencies obtained through manufacturing, packing, palletizing, shipping, storing, and unpacking. Today, tertiary packaging needs to keep its eye on function while looking toward a not-so-distant future with an emphasis on what it can do when it is sitting in bulk on a pallet.

Try carrying six bottles of beer from the liquor store shelf to your home, or better yet twenty-four bottles of water. Secondary packaging is the blending point between the function-driven tertiary packaging and the more brand-driven primary packaging. Secondary packaging often serves an important role in the display of a product on the shelf with such items as trays, display packs, and shipping packers. This means the secondary package has to be given nearly as much consideration as the primary package. Part of the consideration is based on what brand personality attributes should be conveyed on the secondary versus the primary package. Other considerations may include how the secondary package will stack, how it will contain the product while offering access, and how retailers will dispose of it. When the secondary package is successful, it balances function over form while offering a brand personality complement to the primary package.

As the anchor in a relay race from manufacturer to consumer, the primary package gets the attention and the rewards that come with being closest to the consumer. The primary package—i.e., the bottle that sits on your table or the can of soup in your pantry—is where most brands put their greatest investment and attention.

With this attention comes a storehouse of science and research surrounding what a primary package should accomplish. In the end, the primary package has the lead on a consumer relationship and needs to be designed to represent that leadership position in the array of packaging being leveraged. It needs to find that perfect balance of form and function and it must work hard in every context in which it will live.

Important, yes; overemphasized, maybe. With all the current changes in retailing, the primary package sometimes takes on the role as the only face of the brand, emphasis on only. This means that everything a consumer knows of the brand originates from the approximately six panels on the package. If this is true, the first issue is the missed opportunity to build a stronger relationship between the brand and a loyal consumer. The second issue is the consumer's desire to seek out knowledge of brands in their life—i.e., does the brand continue to live past the package? Be careful, because what they may find is not always good. For example, take an environmentally conscious brand with a primary package designed with every consideration for sustainability. What happens when the company's CEO is found acting environmentally irresponsible or a tertiary package is designed with little or no consideration for sustainable practices? The primary package definition should be given primary responsibility for leadership, but it should not take all the resources and attention away from the rest of the brand assets.

PRIMARY

SECONDARY

U'LUVKĄ
VODKA

FRIENDSHIP LOVE & PLEASURE

TERTIARY

From the moment it leaves its home, this brand of vodka is packaged in a stylish custom bottle (primary), which goes inside a tasteful paperboard box (secondary), and then gets shipped inside an elegantly designed corrugated cardboard box (tertiary). All three pieces of a premium vodka packaging experience done right.

ALOOF DESIGN

Convenience and Access

THE MASTER CHURCH KEY

Completely contained, safety sealed, protected, air tight, and ready to handle almost any shipping hazard. Now, how do we get this thing open? Access is all about making the product available when the consumer needs it, at the exact right moment. More easily sought after than accomplished.

Being able to open a bottle of aspirin while battling a searing headache can be a challenge. But that same package can't be accessible to chubby toddler fingers. The bottom line is that consumers, retailers, and the environment pay the price to restrict access while the product lives at the store. Once it leaves the store, the rest of us have to deal with the unpleasant task of extracting our new music CD, camping gadget, or pediatric thermometer. Access for the right person at the right time is one of many design challenges.

There's a frontier of possibilities when it comes to ideas that can be designed to give easy access to the right person. As a prototypical example, the blister lock provides a new way to look at the safety seal of a package.

Where will your package make itself useful? What tools will surround it and what purpose will they serve? These questions get to the context of use and create an ability to see the larger, slightly pixilated picture of the consumer situation. The design can then create a new value for the consumer by increasing the convenience of the product while adding positive attributes to the brand.

Due to the ever-increasing frantic pace of life for most people—go there, find this, do that, and get back as soon as possible—packages need to fit in and make a contribution. By understanding how your package melds with consumers' lives and integrates convenience, the package can contribute. Closures and convenience factors can be large contributors to this growing consumer demand.

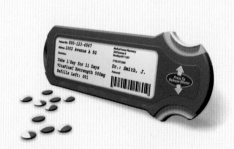

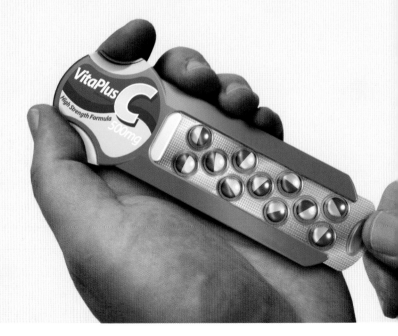

Making something convenient for parents but inaccessible to children is an elegant balance. Add to it a refill aspect and this design's achievement is impressive.

CHARGE INDUSTRIAL DESIGN

Convenience and access are fundamental. Each makes a sizeable contribution to product value by helping the consumer save time and effort, thereby streamlining some aspect of their daily lives.

Packaging slips into our lives and often makes a quiet impact on how we perceive the brand. The Carlo Giovani tea box packages entertain both adults and children and have proven to be a great example of the "packaging-as-toy" idea.

CARLO GIOVANI

Shape and Structure

THE SEXY NUCLEAR PHYSICIST

If you were blindfolded and someone put five similar products in front of you, could you pick out your brand of choice? The next time you're consuming a product right from the package, close your eyes and ask, "What do I feel?" Do you feel the shape, texture, and general structure of the package? Is it unique to this brand? Shape and structure can be made simple; put the product in a box that's strong enough to handle moderate damage during transport and you're done. Or, it can be more complex, innovative, and satisfying.

The shape of a package says something about a brand that graphics, colors, and typography cannot. At a minimum, it tells the consumer that someone spent time considering the shape of the package to make it unique and pleasing. Shape combines the sense of touch and sight to create a more lasting bond. Touch is a powerful sense, and yet it gets minimal consideration when it comes to managing brands. So, when a brand manager considers touch in package shape or texture, it earns an additional bit of attention from consumers. Think about the feel of a Coke bottle or the paper used

to wrap your favorite guilty pleasure, that dark chocolate bar hiding in the back of the freezer. Consider the items in your life that you touch and what the sense of touch communicates to you. With the sense of touch, accompanied by sight, the shape of a package can identify your brand on the shelf and offer the essential point of consistency in the brand's life.

Rapid prototyping technology advancements have given packaging designers the gift of seeing their work come to life in three-dimensional form. High-tech printers can build a model of your package design in a

matter of minutes by printing a layer of glue and then a layer of cornstarch. After hundreds of layers of each, the result is an off-white shape that can give everyone on the team a realistic feel for the final package shape and form. Then, take this prototype into consumer testing and you've got another level of knowledge that costs much less than it did a decade ago.

Structure, although most often considered for the purposes of protection and mere functional benefits, has other important attributes. The structure of a package determines its

The Vodafone brand owns the red quotation mark; this custom package design gives the quote dimension. The quote packages a phone card and more importantly shows us how a valuable brand asset can come to life in a package design.

MILK LTD

What does wealth feel like in your hand? If rose nectar happens to be your preferred liquid, this bottle would answer the question. Sence is a rare European rose nectar that originates from a harvested rose blossom. The package is designed to evoke an experience suggesting the opulence of the flower itself.

ADAM TIHANY/TIHANY DESIGN

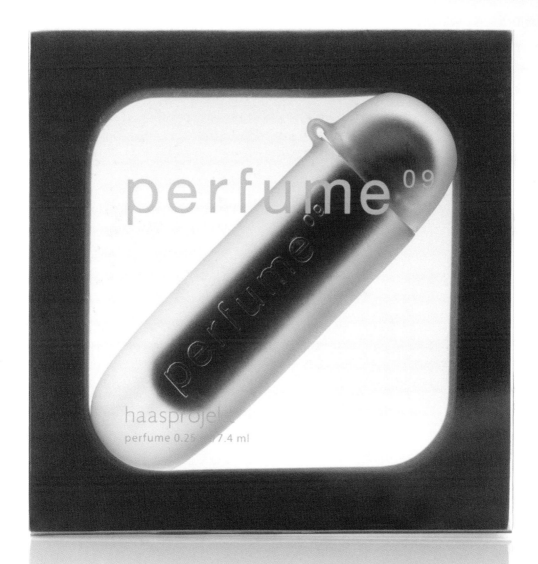

This package conveys the simple elegance of a perfume capsule within a stunning red box. Packaged to deliver an experience to the shopper with a desire for this perfume, it not only creates a sexy, alluring shape; it also merchandises nicely.

FUSEPROJECT

presence on the shelf but it also can determine how it fits into the hands of consumers. Structure in packaging design is best equated to building bridges, roads, and strong buildings. If the package doesn't have the proper structure, it doesn't stand a chance when faced with a forklift operator having a bad day. The trials and tribulations a package faces as it travels to market can be pleasant one day and terrifying the next. This is where structural thinking can help keep the product protected, contained, and uncontaminated during its journey.

Structure is becoming increasingly significant as we enter the current phase of the sustainable design movement. As new materials become available, they need to be structurally capable of performing at the same, if not higher, level as their predecessors. As the shape and form of packages change for the sake of sustainable design and greater efficiencies, the structure must be considered. With all the evolutions in materials, manufacturing methods, and sustainable design methods, packaging structure offers a great opportunity for design but also demands great responsibility to keep our standards at the highest level.

Respect must be paid to those who understand and consider shape and structure in the design process. And, for those who do not, the folly of a clumsy, poorly engineered and embarrassing package design looms on their horizon.

Shape and structure work together to form the foundation of a successful package design.

gloji
mix

100% JUICE
GOJI & POMEGRANATE
THE JUICE THAT MAKES YOU GLOW™
11 fl oz (325 ml)

Lower Tibet offers the world a gift of tranquil energy from the goji berry harvested for this juice. The package is as magical as the liquid it contains, looking first like art and then like a unique bottle of juice.
GLOJI, INC.

Many package shapes are unique enough to be recognized by their silhouette alone. Consider what owning a shape can do to prevent competitors from copying your product offering.

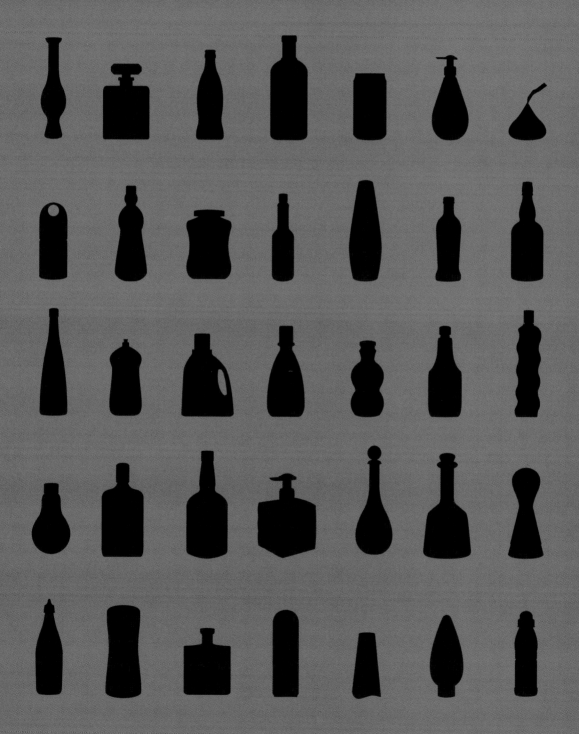

Color, Type, and Art

THREE ROADS CONVERGE IN THE WOODS

Designing a package today is made to look easy. Get a flat screen monitor, a Mac tower, some Adobe software, buy a library of typefaces and photography, teach yourself the basics, and you're on the road. Right? Some might say, "It's easier than flipping burgers." But then you start to make decisions. This typeface versus that one, red versus blue, this photograph versus that illustration. Where does it lead? There is a reason why design professionals apprentice for a period of time and a reason why they're constantly seeking greater knowledge and applying it to their work. Design isn't about pulling your stool up to the magical technology tap and adding three parts color theory, one part typeface, and two parts imagery.

Behind all three of these legs—color, type, and art—are theories, cultural norms, practices, and a host of other factors to consider. In color, the science of how our eyes see overlaps with color theory, which is connected more closely with art than actual science. Leave your country of residence and ask someone the meaning of a certain color. White is always an interesting choice as Western cultures see sterile and clean, purity and innocence, while many Eastern cultures see death and mourning. Then we have to travel down the road of color harmony to find which colors work well together and what they say together. This can seem entirely too complicated when all you want is a new package design. As programmers read code and see an application, designers read colors and see a contextual result. They design color combinations to be trademarked by brand owners. They use color to break out of category conventions or fit into them. And all the while they use it to convey the brand personality, leveraging all the emotion wrapped up in colors.

When it comes to type, with serifs and sans serifs, the number of options seems staggering. Are there thousands, hundreds of thousands? And what does a certain serif communicate and how does it read from three different distances? What typeface complements the serif but offers a smart contrast on the package? Type is a fertile area for making horrific mistakes on a package. For example, using a script typeface on something that needs to be legible from a few feet away is ill advised. At least we have regulations for ingredients and nutritional facts. A common mistake is using more than three—and what sometimes seems like more than ten—different typefaces

Color is often used to convey varieties and flavors of a product line. This package design uses color without hitting the shopper over the head with primary colors. The result is a highly functional package with a personality worth getting to know.

HORNALL ANDERSON DESIGN WORKS

on a single package design. If each typeface has a personality, doesn't the ten-typeface package suggest a multiple personality disorder? Type is core to the hierarchy of information, using bold to get attention, italics for product benefits, and all caps for functional information. But don't let the simplicity of type fool you. Dig deep into the nuances of type, and you may find yourself respecting it more and even becoming a type addict. Don't worry, there's a nine-step program available at your local art store, not that we recommend it.

Art isn't just for artists anymore. Here, art can mean photography and illustration, not just Monet. Art delivers a message and tells part of the brand story. If you know the brand story, you can focus your efforts around certain art forms that work better than others. Art conveys a feeling and like everything else, it can be interpreted and understood. It can range from fine art to illustration to photography. Each piece is created to communicate some form of meaning—attaching that meaning to the brand is what needs to be carefully thought out. Just picking art because you like it may give you a sense of inner joy but may do nothing for the consumer or the marketer of the product. Art can be debated just like any other part of the package: If you can defend it both rationally and emotionally, then your choice is probably appropriate.

As the package starts to come together, you've delved into type, art, and color, and what have you found? Consistency. The word that has all three of these parameters joined together like an old-fashioned ménage à trois. The goal is to be consistent with an unshakable understanding of what the brand means to the consumer who buys it. Introduce a color that doesn't make sense and you've got a mess on your hands. Do it right and there's reason to celebrate; do it wrong and the party's over.

The interaction between the color of the product and the package can be easily overlooked. But when it is planned for, the result can be amazing and amusing. The Jubes candy line uses contrasting colors to engage and entertain.

KINETIC SINGAPORE

How do fashionistas throw a party? Just like the rest of us, but with a lot more flair. Where do you find flair? Right here, inside this package of cocktails by Jenn. Using color-coding and iconography, the packaging is a welcome accessory at any party.

MICHAEL OSBORNE DESIGN

Il Fornaio olive oil is another nugget from Australia to be shared with the world. Referred to as a vessel, this package draws from all the visual and tactile cues of Tuscany, Italy.

HOYNE DESIGN

Engineering and Testing

NO PACKAGE IS AN ISLAND

Package design is integral to the entire manufacturing process that starts with creating a product and ends with delivery to the consumer. How the package fits into that manufacturing process is one part of the package engineering discipline. The other parts include food safety, tamper-evident closures, chemical interactions, cushioning, regulations, RFID, distribution, and testing for each. Some of these disciplines are covered by the packaging engineer; while other aspects fall under operations or quality control. Either way, they are essential to help your beautiful package become smarter. For you to become smarter, we touch on a few of the subjects, leaving you with the desire to find more through other sources.

Shelf stability doesn't refer to whether your package will fall on a small child, but rather, will the contents remain the same over time. Put another way, how long will it take to see chunks in your milk? Unfortunately it's not that simple, as the process to determine shelf stability is highly complex and factors in many variables. Because many consumable products will change properties and efficacy as they get exposed to air and light, their shelf stability is a critical timeline for the manufacturer and retailer. This shouldn't be confused with the "Born on" or "Enjoy by" date you find on your favorite malt beverage. This is the science behind those claims and much more essential to the safety and viability of the product.

Engineering a package requires the right education combined with experience to get a package to work

the way it was intended. It ranges from material tests to make sure it can handle all climate conditions to drop tests to make sure it will handle the average store clerk. The engineer of a package has many tools and resources, but the real talent is putting them to use creatively to find an optimal solution. This may mean numerous prototypes, molds, and mock-ups. It may also mean some hardcore predictive mathematics in order to insure that the package being built will live up to the promises we attach to it. And, of course, it needs to make it to the shelf.

Distribution or logistics is the science behind getting something specific to a specific location at a specific time in the most specific and efficient manner possible. Logistics is also the backbone and the intelligence supporting the largest retailer in the world, Wal-Mart. The relationship between packaging design and logistics can be challenging. If you're not careful, logistical requirements will work against what is most attractive about the original package design. Logistics can also be the largest constraining factor when it comes to

Does the juice market need another option? If you have less time in your day than disposable income to stay healthy, then perhaps there is a place for Wild Bunch & Co. This bottle has a simple resealing closure to extend the freshness of this organic juice.

SEED CREATIVE

creative solutions that fall outside the standard "box" design. This doesn't mean combating logistics with verbal abuse—it means learning all that you can about how your package fits into the logistics process. And then translating your learning into thoughtfully designed answers to logistics challenges.

Cushioning refers to how well your package protects the product inside from vibration and shock. Vibration comes from the perpetual movement a package endures on its way to market. Shock comes from the six-foot (1.8 m) drop by a lanky and clumsy warehouse employee. Although these are obvious, others include the impact from static electricity, temperature, and moisture. The engineering analysis turns to labor rates and manufacturing and material costs to arrive at a final outcome. In most cases it will include an expected damage rate because absolute protection is both cost prohibitive and presents a diminishing rate of return. In other words, it costs more to protect products from every possible injury than it does to lose an estimated number of units.

You can test almost anything to reach a reasonable level of confidence. The disciplines discussed previously have methods to ensure the highest level of confidence in each of the aspects. Testing can involve a focus group watching adults as they struggle to open a new child safety top on a pill bottle. More complex methods of drop testing, chemical interaction, and others lead to greater understanding of how the packaging will interact with the product inside or the environment outside. The broader objective of any testing is to reduce risk when taking a package to market.

Testing should increase or decrease confidence in one or more aspects of your package design. This doesn't have to destroy what's good about the package if the results are taken as a jumping-off point to make improvements or create a wholly new package design. Ignore the findings from testing and you may find yourself in a tight spot when the product hits the shelves and the results are more than disappointing. Understand the methods, embrace the results, and you may find new territory your design team has yet to explore.

In dangerous situations, we look to engineering to keep us safe. This package for LP gas is 50 percent lighter because it uses a polyethylene composition. The design team, however, didn't rely on material alone. They included a clean, elegant design with comfortable handles for efficient lifting. Now all men have something worthy of sitting beside our coveted gas grills.

BRANDIA CENTRAL

BE A BIG FISH IN A LITTLE POND. BE A LITTLE FISH IN A BIG POND. IN AN AGE WHERE "ANYTHING GOES," IT TAKES A LOT OF COMMITMENT TO DEFINE YOURSELF. LET YOUR LIGHT SHINE THROUGH. LET YOUR EXPERIENCE AND EXCITEMENT ABOUT YOUR WORK SHOW. BEHOLD YOUR COMPETENCY AND MAKE SURE YOUR PORTFOLIO IS ALL DRESSED UP WITH SOMEPLACE TO GO.

TAKE A GOOD LOOK AROUND.
WHAT DO YOU SEE?

Lather, Rinse, Repeat

To find work, you must look for it actively. This means promoting yourself. "I'm not a salesperson," you might insist. But the truth is, to grow your business, you're forced to wear a sales hat. You need to talk about your company and what you do. You have to be the walking, talking billboard of your company, with your portfolio in hand.

Experts agree that you need to structure your portfolio's content so that it is the most meaningful to those whom you have identified as your key audience. Strive for brevity, while also telling a story. For viewers who want more details, provide expansive case studies of your work.

Streamlined for Success

KISS–KEEP IT SIMPLE, STUPID

When evaluating your vision for your portfolio, ask yourself:

When your audience looks at your portfolio or self-promotion piece, do they quickly find what they are looking for? Are they engaged with what they see? In general, most don't, and they back out faster than they would when they leave a bad movie.

Here's where the tough part comes in. Engage with your audience and determine what is working and what is not. What information should you have in your portfolio and what can be omitted? Let's face it: every person is different and their response to your portfolio or self-promotion may be different from the next guy's. But if there is a consistent thread of discontent with your portfolio—such as not enough visuals or your copy does not meld with the visual creativity you espouse—pay attention. If you are repeatedly asked for clarifying information after a recipient has viewed your portfolio, take note and make the appropriate changes that will garner the response you are looking for.

Most expert advice on portfolio design can be summed up in a single word—simplicity. This may sound almost trite, but simplicity is key when it comes to developing a consistent, memorable portfolio or self-promotion.

In addition to simplicity, a well-thought-out portfolio strategy will go a long way. As in the early world of computing, it was often said that a computer is only as good as the programmer—"garbage in, garbage out"; the same can be said of portfolio design.

The bottom line? A focused, powerful portfolio will set you apart from the competition, break through the clutter, accelerate relationship-building, and dramatically improve your probability of success.

◄▲► 1977 Design created their portfolio showcasing nine case studies that demonstrate the skill sets of the studio. Instigating dialogue and engaging with the recipient was the drive behind the portfolio design, as they looked to use this as an opportunity to express the studio's personality and ethos. "An approachable tone of voice was created that used the logo as the lead-in for all headlines of the brochure," says Richard Stevens, designer at 1977 Design. The company name was given a variety of suffixes to create the headlines. "Client testimonials were featured next to each project, breaking down the barriers that design fluff sometimes creates," Stevens says. "This allowed us to communicate our design approach in a manner that wasn't arrogant or mundane, focusing on engaging the recipient. The '1977 Designed this' line is now used as a crediting logo for any work coming out of the studio."

1977 DESIGN

Portfolio Must-Haves

KNOWING WHEN TO STOP AND WHEN TO GO

Jeff Fisher, founder of LogoMotives and author of *The Savvy Designer's Guide to Success: Ideas and Tactics for a Killer Career*, provides insights for creating that perfect portfolio.

Be creative! That's now your job.
Don't simply present potential employers with a standard student portfolio. When portfolios from local schools are reviewed, many contain the same class projects and begin to look exactly the same. Incorporate some individual projects—perhaps some real-world work for a nonprofit organization in which you have a strong personal belief.

Keep actual book size manageable.
A large and unwieldy portfolio case is going to make for an awkward and less-than-favorable first impression with an interviewer. Keep it small, concise, and manageable so as to not knock items off the desk of a portfolio reviewer.

Be concise.
Maintain a limited number of pieces in your book and make sure the work is your BEST. Include unique pieces that showcase your talents and skills. Most creative directors and art directors will not have much time to review a large amount of your work. Showcase your very best work first, keep the number of included projects small, and make the most of the time you are given for the presentation.

Have a fine-tuned spiel.
Saying "and then I designed this, and then I designed this…" as you turn the pages of your book will not make a great impression. Clearly explain the brief, your process, and any defined results for each project included. Having a process or sketchbook available for review is a great idea. Practice your presentation with friends, family, or student peers before a presentation for a comfortable and polished presentation.

Be honest about your work.
Be up front about your participation in any collaborative project effort rather than claiming full credit for the job. Show only your own work in your book. You will be caught if attempting to misrepresent yourself. The design community makes up a very small world.

Make use of online portfolios.
The Internet provides incredible—and often free—resources for showcasing your work and creating easily accessible websites.

Social networking is your self-promotion/marketing friend.
Many of the current Internet social networking/media sites provide great opportunities to network with potential employers and showcase your work in a gallery.

Portfolio Expectations

TEST YOUR KNOWLEDGE

The Creative Group surveyed 250 advertising and marketing executives about what they expect in a portfolio. See if you know the answers.

① What is the percentage of executives polled who value overall creativity most when evaluating a portfolio?

Answer: ....

② What is the average number of items executives recommend should be included in a portfolio?

Answer: ....

③ What is the number of samples typically viewed before determining whether someone is qualified for the job?

Answer: ....

④ What is the number of people within a firm who typically evaluates a candidate's portfolio before a job offer is extended?

Answer: ....

⑤ What is the number of work samples that executives expect to see in an online portfolio?

Answer: ....

⑥ What is the percentage of executives who, on average, spent five minutes or less reviewing online work?

Answer: ....

Content Is King

LONG LIVE THE MOTTO: GARBAGE IN, GARBAGE OUT

When creating your portfolio, you need to find your niche and highlight the design components that fit your business and your experience. You know your product and you also hopefully know the people who need your product or service.

Do you embark on a treasure hunt of sorts, rummaging through every creative element you have ever developed? Certainly not. Determining the content of your portfolio should require deliberation and a fair amount of strategic thinking.

The first step in portfolio development is deciding which pieces warrant inclusion. Select items that are clearly representative of your skill base and expertise. Keep in mind that some clients require permission to promote work that you've completed for them, so get written approval prior to creating your portfolio or self-promotion items in which their work will appear.

Depending on your level of expertise; be sure to include enough elements within your portfolio that capture the breadth of your creative genius.

◀▲ *A fourteen-page concertina showcases the company's portfolio. The concertina is divided into two sections, "Work" and "Play." The Work section features corporate projects, while the Play section features personal projects and work for clients who specialize in fun products and services.*

CREATIVE SPARK

THE DO'S OF PORTFOLIO CREATION

••• Make it relevant. Your portfolio needs to be relevant to the audience. Include only those portfolio-worthy elements that really shine. Your portfolio should be streamlined, incorporating only the most pertinent examples of your work.

••• Make it timely. Ever walk into a doctor's office only to find an array of year-old magazines awaiting your perusal? No one wants to read old news. The same can be said for old portfolio content.

••• Make it understandable. There is no one standard way to organize a portfolio, but to be effective, it needs to be understandable and meaningful to your audience. Choose elements that provide a complete picture of your professional skills and abilities.

••• Remember that the documents in a portfolio are not meant to tell the whole story. Rather, the elements featured are intended to pique the viewers' interest and invite them to ask more questions.

Design Parameters

SHOWCASING YOUR CREATIVE CAPITAL

Artists, advertising creatives, designers, architects, photographers, fashion designers, and writers have been using portfolios as their primary promotional vehicle for centuries. Perhaps even Leonardo da Vinci had a portfolio of sorts when he was commissioned to paint the Sistine Chapel. A well-thought-out portfolio can be a very effective marketing tool—one that is imperative when landing that ideal job or next client.

According to Jeff Johnson, founder of Spunk Design Machine, today's high-end portfolios are efficient and very affordable to produce. That's because the advent of high-end, reliable, digital book printing and binding has really democratized the quality leave-behind portfolio options. "Companies like Bookmobile, Blurb, and others now provide excellent hard-bound, low-quantity, and low-cost book manufacturing," Johnson says. This trend is also sometimes aptly called "vanity books," as they allow an independent designer or design student the option of designing and publishing a great hard-bound portfolio that can double as a leave-behind.

"That's on the good side of the fence," Johnson says. "On the bad side is the sole reliance on online portfolios to represent one's work. I regret this trend. A big part of the job of any good designer is lending distinction to the work at hand. The options for creating a lively, honest, and distinctive portfolio are endless. A website, however grand, is still just a website. I really cherish the care for the artifact. We live, and choose options, in a real 3-D world.

"On the sunny side, the Internet has really done a lot for democratizing access for designers. Internet access to design media has allowed our Spunk Design Machine to compete and succeed on a global scale," he adds.

"For a small boutique like ours, having a diverse client base is a must. Our online portfolio allows our work to travel where we can't, or won't. We have clients in Mexico, Switzerland, Ireland, Japan, etc. The smaller, creatively focused studios have a distinct advantage, as the barriers for delivery of quality of work have been radically eliminated in less than a decade. It's been a real game changer. Last year, we opened our first branch office in New York City. I had experienced a really difficult, and ultimately unsuccessful, design office expansion from Minneapolis to New York City with another great design company. The technical ease of our current studio expansion is due, in no small part, to the maturity of remote digital media access. Our clients can see our work in any number of cities and decide if our work is a potential fit. The remote studio option is just one more decision maker for the potential client," Johnson notes.

THE DON'TS OF PORTFOLIO CREATION, BY JEFF JOHNSON

When I got into the design world after graduating, it was common to see some pretty mondo-crazy portfolio creations—mine being probably one of the worst and largest. The portfolio I brought to MTV, Push Pin Group, CSA, David Lance Goines, Duffy, etc., weighed in at 70 pounds—I'm not kidding. It even included a full 20 × 30-inch [51 × 76 cm] zinc plate,

and I manufactured my own carrying harness. I just had to have that hand-etched zinc plate, don'tcha know.

My second portfolio that I took to New Zealand was only slightly less stupid. This one was made as a metaphoric handshake. The portfolio was an old powder-coated electrical switch box with a ceramic hand bolted

to the box. The hand was an old rubber glove mold I found at a surplus store. One could flip open the switch box and review the work. It mostly looked like a Trent Reznor nightmare. Today's portfolio model is an easy leave-behind piece that holds a DVD of more expanded work.

▲► *Two of the portfolios that Jeff Johnson utilized during the early years of his career—albeit memorable, they simply didn't offer the streamlined approach of today's portfolios.*
SPUNK DESIGN MACHINE

DESIGN MATTERS // CREATING | PORTFOLIOS

It's a Digital World

LET YOUR FINGERS DO THE WALKING

Websites say a lot about a company, so their appearance and functionality is critical to the business they represent. We all know that Web use has grown at a phenomenal rate and projections are higher yet. Even your plumber has his own website. You see the trend and know where you need to be. But how do you use the Web as a portfolio tool?

According to Neil Tortorella, marketing consultant and founder of Tortorella Design, technology and, in particular, the Internet, has had a tremendous impact on portfolios.

"It's a 24/7/365 world now," Tortorella says. "Art directors, employers, and clients can view online books at their leisure, search for exactly what they need (medium, style, specialization, etc.), and create their short list faster than ever."

The Web has also significantly increased the competition. There are numerous portfolio sites with scores and scores of portfolios. It's tough to stand out. Competition is no longer local, regional, or even national. It's international. Designers now compete, daily, with others across the globe who can often work for a lot less, while still producing good design.

According to Laura Hamlyn, creative director at Clean Design, online portfolios are simply expected these days. Even PDF versions of designer portfolios feel a little "analog."

"Earlier on, online portfolios were purely for convenience's sake—to ensure your work is easy to access," Hamlyn says. "Today, online portfolios serve as a way to showcase Web design capabilities. Clean Design uses our online portfolio as a way to showcase fresh work. It does not cost a thing to post new work online as often as we can."

Tortorella agrees: "On the upside, technology has made it possible to have your portfolio available online all day, every day." Digital media enables designers to easily distribute samples of their work. Plus, enewsletters, blogs, the myriad of social networking sites, along with sites like Flickr and Google's Picasa, have given designers a host of mediums to display their work to a larger audience. These outlets can, in turn, point to a designer's website, where visitors can see additional work or larger versions, read case studies, and learn more about the designer or firm.

Marketing and promotion via the Internet is easier and much more cost-effective than in the past. Sites such as Jigsaw.com and Spoke.com make finding targeted prospects a snap. Online press-release distribution services get a designer's news out to a broader audience, often for free. Business networking sites, such as LinkedIn.com and Biznik.com, keep people connected and offer them a vehicle to obtain introductions to prospects and promote themselves through their profiles, articles, answers to member questions, and such. Social networking, when used correctly, can also be a promotional tool. There's more to Twitter and Facebook than telling the world you're having a bad hair day.

"Add blogging into the mix and there's more opportunity," Tortella says. Blog topics can be case studies, how-tos, tips about working with a designer, or other design- and marketing-related content that would be helpful to both clients and prospects.

Beyond this, website and enewsletter traffic statistics help designers determine what content is important to prospects. This enables them to place promotional messages within a page's content or sidebar or help to drive traffic to other pages, as needed.

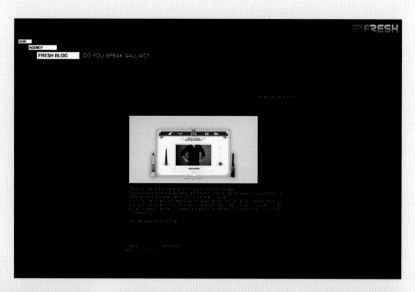

◄▲ *The website is one of the most essential tools of 2Fresh's self-promotion—especially while expanding to a new market like London. It provides a better format to express themselves and give in-depth information while maintaining the user's interest.*
2FRESH

Showcase Showdown

MAKE YOUR PORTFOLIO REALLY SHINE

Creative professionals have one thing in common—they strive to capture the attention of their potential audience through powerful visual messages. They want to make an impact on a viewer, to entice them to buy their product, attend their theatrical production, or simply marvel at the architectural prowess of a building. And for many, using digital elements can inform, delight, and inspire their audience like never before.

With each new day, technology brings exciting opportunities for growth and success. As businesses grow, designers encounter tough decisions regarding how to best use the technology available for portfolio development and self-promotion.

◄▲ Housed in a beautifully etched metallic case, this promotional portfolio is where technology and traditional portfolio strategies meet. The metallic case contains a personalized metallic covered notebook, promotional CD, and a Velcro-enhanced folder, which includes a series of portfolio postcards.

FACTOR TRES COMUNICACION

► When sending email introductions, Monderer Design attaches a twelve-page promotional PDF. The PDF presents a mini portfolio of print, branding, and interactive design work.

MONDERER DESIGN

Spring 2009

MONDERER DESIGN
OVERVIEW

> SolidWorks   Conference Branding

WORK
PRINT

> Thermo Fisher Scientific   Advertisements

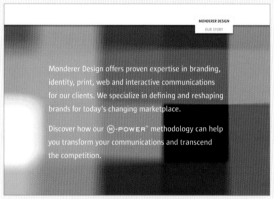

MONDERER DESIGN
OUR STORY

Monderer Design offers proven expertise in branding, identity, print, web and interactive communications for our clients. We specialize in defining and reshaping brands for today's changing marketplace.

Discover how our ⓜ-POWER™ methodology can help you transform your communications and transcend the competition.

WORK
BRANDING

belmont media center

> Belmont Media Center   Corporate Identity

> Ember Corporation   Literature System/Branding

> Informio   Literature System/Branding

MONDERER DESIGN
OUR STORY

For more than 25 years, Monderer Design has created smart, visually engaging communications that convey powerful messages and deliver measurable results. Our solutions help clients:

> **Gain** a competitive edge
> **Connect** more effectively with key audiences
> **Build** a solid brand through integrated communications
> **Increase** market share

Our business-driven strategies and distinctive design solutions form the foundation for building brands that communicate the values, mission, innovations, products and services that differentiate our clients in the only place that matters—the marketplace.

Discover what we can do for you.

WORK
INTERACTIVE

> xkoto   Web Site

> A.D. Makepeace   Web Site

> Stanley Rowin Photography   Web Site

> Language Weaver   Web Site

WORK
PRINT

> Northeastern University   MBA Viewbook

MONDERER DESIGN
CONNECT

Thanks for your time.
For new business, general inquiries or the weather/traffic report from Porter Square, please contact us at:

Monderer Design
2067 Massachusetts Avenue
Cambridge, MA 02140-1337

tel 617 661 6125
fax 661 6126
stewart@monderer.com
www.monderer.com

Interactivity at Its Best

TOSS A WIDE NET TO CAPTURE YOUR AUDIENCE

Creative individuals and firms are quickly seeing the Internet as an essential tool for handling the "meat and potatoes" of day-to-day operations—including generating new customers; communicating with vendors and suppliers; improving visibility among prospective clients; and following industry trends online.

A professional website helps potential clients develop confidence and trust in a business. Websites provide a platform to spotlight your creativity at its best, as well as testimonials, case studies, and press coverage. A Web-based portfolio can give a potential client the confidence to pick up the phone and call, or it can send her clicking away. An effective online marketing strategy can expose a business to the world and reach new customers that might otherwise not even know it exists.

"It is important to design your portfolio with some context," says Laura Hamlyn at Clean Design. "Nothing is more frustrating than work that is too small to read or understand, cropped in a confusing way, or delivered without context. It is helpful to let people know how you were challenged or what types of obstacles your work was forced to overcome. I also like to see work 'in the wild.' Show your work in the context of where it is used, when applicable. That applies to packaging, environmental design, etc. Even if you are not an expert photographer, you can link to the more casual or personal photos of your work on Flickr."

Obviously, there is no face-to-face connection online. You cannot establish that personal chemistry that is essential to winning new business, so make sure your personality comes through in the style and writing on the site. Browsers should get a sense

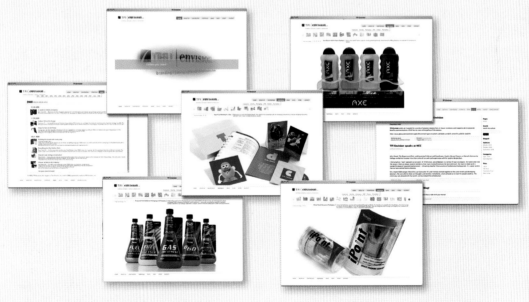

▲ *Simple, yet clearly defined imagery and straightforward project descriptions make TFI Envision's website one that is teeming with cohesive design and functionality.*

TFI ENVISION

of who you are or the environment in which your firm operates. People with compatible personalities tend to work better together.

Keep file sizes small or use pre-loaders to ensure that your load times are quick and people can focus more on the work and less on how hard it is to look at it. Average wait times are just a few seconds, and then viewers grow impatient and move on.

A website must not only look attractive and function well, it must be easy to find. The best website in the world that nobody can find is like a magic trick in the dark. That's where all of the latest online marketing techniques such as search engine optimization, email marketing, RSS feeds, blogs, and podcasts come into play.

And like paper-based portfolios, Web-based portfolios contain all the elements that show the world who you are as a firm or individual. But remember, electronic portfolios are not for everyone. Be prepared to supplement your electronic version with a handheld paper version.

While some creative professionals rely solely on their website to showcase their portfolio, others try to engage their audience with PDFs and other interactive delivery methods.

▲ This interactive PDF is an electronic exposé showcasing recent Spark Studio projects and success stories. The streamlined navigation system allows viewers to explore the interactive presentation via their own computer.
SPARK STUDIO

▲ From packaging to brand identity to
environmental graphics, this interactive
PDF document highlights Spark Studio's
most recent work.

SPARK STUDIO

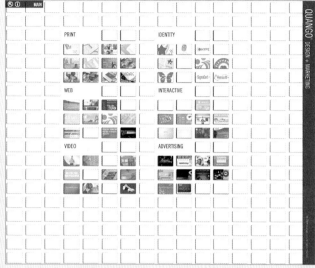

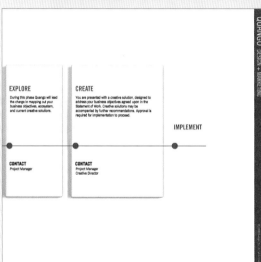

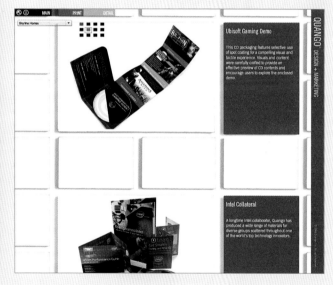

▲ Walk into the Portland-based Quango office, and you'll see them on the walls—a diverse photo collage on 6 × 4-inch (15 × 10 cm) wooden blocks arranged in a matrix. For Quango, these grids foster inspiration. In their interactive portfolio, they encourage a similar experience for prospective clients. Built on an XML database, Quango's portfolios are highly customizable—allowing images and messages to be tailored to specific viewer interests. Dynamically pulling database content greatly simplifies updates while helping to ensure a relevant presentation of recent work.

QUANGO

If updating your website or creating high-end interactive PDF portfolio presentations seems too daunting, why not try your hand at enewsletters—simple email blasts that are reminiscent of a press release, yet have the visuals and design elements to capture your audience's attention.

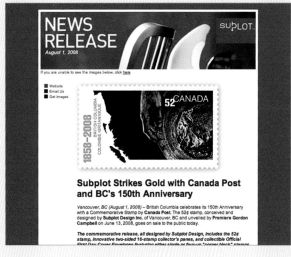

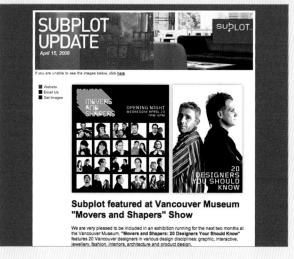

▲ Using an ongoing series of e-news updates, Subplot Design celebrates recent projects and news with clients and prospects.

SUBPLOT DESIGN

▲ *MMR Studio prides itself on ebrochures, both for their own marketing purposes and their clients'. To help support the firm's rebranding initiatives, MMR created collateral material including a CD presenter, business cards, and business card–size "flip folio."*

MMR STUDIO

Nontraditional Portfolios

GIVE THEM SOMETHING TO LOOK AT *AND* HOLD

Are you the type of person who likes to go with the flow, or do you prefer to chart your own course in life—going against the current of all things mainstream? Perhaps you were the kid who ate peanut butter and banana sandwiches out of your dad's old lunchbox rather than consuming cafeteria cuisine on plastic trays. Being nontraditional certainly has its advantages. And in the creative world, nontraditional portfolios and self-promotions not only get you noticed, but they add to the overall memorability of your creative genius in the minds of your audience.

SHOW YOUR TRUE COLORS

When you hand someone your capabilities brochure or latest self-promotion, do they say "cool" or just nod their head? You can easily measure your success with your portfolio by evaluating the response of your audience. Do they quickly flip the pages of your portfolio with thoughtless glances, or do they react with a "wow," or "that's impressive—tell me more." Be decidedly different.

That's exactly the mentality that Lawrence Everard, founder of Little Yellow Duck, espouses in his firm's portfolio strategies.

"There are a lot of tedious things in life, but top of the list has to be the traditional agency portfolio brochure," Everard says. "You know the sort of thing; '...a team of committed and experienced professionals... dedicated to the highest standards of creativity...results-focused and cost-effective...' and so it drones on, one earnest and completely redundant platitude after another."

Using humor and wit to create stories about yourself and your firm, along with a clever design, will draw potential clients in while demonstrating your creative abilities.

▶ "Little Yellow Duck and the Big Idea *was our attempt to show that charm, assurance, and a little wit would stand out from the crush of pompous agency philosophies that live out their short arc of life from drawing board to landfill via the client's wastepaper basket," founder Lawrence Everard says. "It was also a lot of fun to create, and that's important to us. Best of all, if you're the kind of client who likes the brochure, you'll like working with us, and if you don't, you won't. So it's not just a 'what kind of outfit are we?' brochure, but a 'what kind of client are you?' filter, too."*

LITTLE YELLOW DUCK

"Once upon a time, a young art director was waiting at a photographic studio for some products to arrive for a shoot," Lawrence Everard says. "The products were late; the camera and the lighting were set up, and while they were waiting impatiently, the art director and photographer were casting around for a stand-in object to check the light levels. Eventually, the photographer's assistant found a little yellow plastic duck in the ladies' room, which proved to be the perfect subject for the test shot. That young art director always remembered how the little yellow duck had helped him out on that stressful afternoon, and years later decided it would make the perfect name for his own agency. And that's a true story… good night."

To be cost-effective *Little Yellow Duck*'s initial (and only) print run of the book was 1,000 copies. The attention and recall the book generates has been outstanding—many of the firm's contacts report that they receive new business promotions every day, but *Little Yellow Duck*'s is the one that really stands out.

delivery, then we know we will enjoy working with them. And we have been proved right. Making follow-up phone calls to check that the book has arrived is a joy. People remember it (and our name). The books have usually been passed around, and if we can get the receptionist on our side our job is almost done."

Albeit childlike, the illustrations complement the single message within *Little Yellow Duck and the Big Idea*. With a little help from your friends, your business is sure to succeed.

"The book makes it very easy to engage in conversation with prospects and for them to think creatively about solutions to their own communications," Everard says. "As a result, we attract clients who are willing to be brave with their own activity. The bonus is that if they are the type of client who enjoys this method of

Some have been sent to existing clients to pass around to friends and colleagues, while others have been used for prospecting. And, as Everard explains, the book has more than paid for itself in terms of business generated, from both new clients and new projects from existing clients.

One day, the little yellow duck had a visitor.

"Sorry I'm late" said the businesswoman. "I was trying to get Japan on my Blackberry."

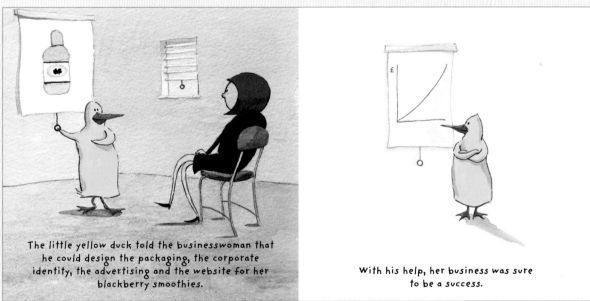

The little yellow duck told the businesswoman that he could design the packaging, the corporate identity, the advertising and the website for her blackberry smoothies.

With his help, her business was sure to be a success.

▲ This promotion was themed on Big Al's Farm Fresh Design—comparing the design industry to the chicken farming industry. The promotion included a screen-printed place mat; a wire spiral egg cup; a laser-engraved wooden egg, with teaspoon; plus a full-cover, French-folded booklet portfolio with a two-color plus white foil cover. All items were placed on a bed of wood wool (coarse, long wood shavings) inside a cardboard carton and finished with a custom-printed wrap.

LLOYDS GRAPHIC DESIGN (NEW ZEALAND)

▲ *Design Revolution in a can—themed around the Russian Revolution, with visual cues from that period of history, but some contemporary license in the design and typography—was an end-of-the-year promotion to thank clients. The tin included a candle, custom-wrapped chocolate cigar, and an A2 poster featuring various identities created by Lloyds Graphic Design during the previous year on one side and a call for designers everywhere to join the design revolution on the other. A printed tea towel features a tag that reads, "Unfurl this one-of-a-kind, custom-designed banner and show your true revolutionary colors to the world. Hold it high, walk tall and dare to resist the design despots who commit their crimes against our visual senses with impunity. Failing that, you can always dry the dishes with it."*

LLOYDS GRAPHIC DESIGN (NEW ZEALAND)

Magazine-style Promotions Educate and Inform

Worrell Design recently created *New: For Lateral Thinkers* to tell stories of design and innovation from around the world. "Our vision is to raise awareness of global concerns that affect the design of business and the new roles of designers," says Kai Worrell. "We want to be recognized as a thought leader. We want people to be able to gain from the valuable insights we have uncovered as a company over the past three decades."

With eye-catching, colorful graphics and rich, meaningful collages of images pertaining to the articles, Worrell Design wants readers to be able to flip through the magazine and get a quick sense of the depth of the material, while creating a cohesive visual impact.

Every issue begins with a Founder's Note from Robert Worrell, followed by up to three interviews. The first issue included James McGregor, author; Joe Ranieri, chief executive officer of Crocs China; and Yu Shen, secretary-general of Shanghai Design Center. Each issue also includes case studies and articles written by Worrell Design research specialists.

Approximately 1,500 magazines were printed for the first issue. "We mailed and labeled the magazines in custom envelopes designed exclusively for that particular issue," Kai Worrell says.

And the response?

"People were incredibly impressed by the relevant, third-party content and overall quality," Worrell says. "They expressed appreciation for the knowledge we not only gathered and shared from third-party experts but from the direct information compounded from Worrell Design researchers and designers."

WORRELL'S
EXCLUSIVE INTERVIEW WITH
THE ULTIMATE CHINA INSIDER

– JAMES McGREGOR

Background

James, you've been referred to as the "Ultimate China Insider" and your book has been referred to by many as the "Bible" for doing business here in China. Please tell us a little bit about your background and how you got started in China.

Somebody growing up 5 years apart from somebody else is growing up in a different China because **THE PACE OF CHANGE IS SO FAST.**

◄▲ *Worrell Design created a magazine to send to clients, featuring interviews and design case studies.*

WORRELL DESIGN

Self-Promotions

IN THE DRIVER'S SEAT

No one can afford to send out multiple portfolio pieces throughout the year. Nor do you want to. Rather, consider accenting your portfolio with over-the-top creative self-promotions that really grab the recipients' attention.

By coordinating a "wow" moment with each self-promotion piece you create, you can dramatically enhance your portfolio strategy.

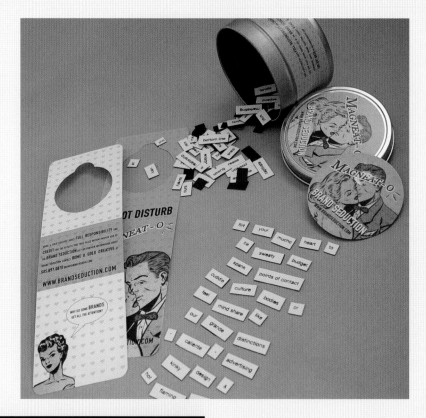

▲ *Based on the attraction and seduction of good branding, Rome & Gold creative developed a refrigerator magnet kit that served as a novelty gift for the recipients. The magnets had branding and seductive words such as* flaming, kinky, sweaty, *and* cuddle *on them.*
ROME & GOLD CREATIVE

◀ *This self-promotion was wrapped around America's favorite pastime—baseball and hot dogs. The gift included an invitation, along with a nicely designed package of ketchup, mustard, and relish. Rome & Gold Creative also rented a suite at the local A farm team stadium and invited everyone out for a fun, casual evening of baseball, allowing them to strengthen their current relationships and to develop new ones.*
ROME & GOLD CREATIVE

HOLIDAY MAILERS

An excuse to do anything impressive—simply put, that's the reason holiday mailers are such a worthwhile effort. "Any significant holiday, and even the insignificant ones, offer an opportunity to show your passion, creativity, and thinking," says Aaron Keller, managing partner at Capsule. "Holidays also represent times of the year when mail has a better chance of being opened, considered, and perhaps even saved." But don't go down the holiday mailer chimney unless you have the talent to get your piece noticed and opened; you might find yourself stuck with a big bill and not much recognition to show for it.

▼ *"Some assembly required" is annoying on Christmas morning, but a welcome distraction in your office mailbox. This promotional mailer packed a promise to amuse, entertain, and for some, challenge.* CAPSULE

▲ Seasonality can be a great technique when it comes to self-promotions. These seasonal coasters were designed and printed via letterpress as self-promotional materials. They were sent out to clients on a quarterly basis. They also serve as leave-behinds after each portfolio presentation.

2 HATS DESIGN

▲ This small cardboard box was sent by freelance designer Steven Swingler to a variety of design agencies in East Sussex, United Kingdom. "Christmas Wishes from Steven Swingler" is stamped on the lid, and inside are polystyrene balls used for packing. When all the balls are removed, the recipient is rewarded with the message "Snowed under?"

STEVEN SWINGLER

◄ This box of real fortune cookies contained fortunes only Capsule could predict. Telling fortunes like "You're going to get up in the morning and go to work" and "You may find yourself inside an office building soon" was a humorous way to reach out to their client base.

CAPSULE

face plot*

Every year we give
countless presentations, putting our
ideas and designs out there like
a lovingly-chosen holiday gift

And so
we've gotten pretty used to speculating on our
success by the audience reaction

It's in the small details
those that may otherwise go unnoticed
that you find the truth

You really need to scrutinise to get accurate results

Otherwise, you're just guessing,
aren't you?

With this easy-to-use pocket-sized set of flash
cards, you too can hone your expertise and
judge your own holiday gift-giving success rate.
Consider it your own little rosetta stone.

Go on, try your luck.
And see if you have the reaction-reading
abilities of a seasoned design team.

* Subplot's self-administered test
for gauging gift reactions
this Christmas season

euphoria*

* Pure, unadulterated joy.

The contented smile, the slight wrinkles at
the eyes that convey genuine happiness
at receiving the perfect gift. It's what we all
aim for. We see this a lot, but if you need
help discerning this one, look in the mirror
as you're holding this card.

feined gratitude*

* Don't be fooled by the smile
and seemingly genuine twinkle
in her eye.

She's too grateful. No one is that grateful.
You know she just doesn't want to hurt your
feelings. But that gift will never be used.
Ever. This is often followed up by an overly
polite email explaining why a custom die, foil-
stamped, engraved, embossed and laminated
origami business card isn't within the budget.
Or in your case, asking for the gift receipt.

wtf*
(what's the face?)

* Look at those glazed-over eyes,
the blank stare, the slightly
drooping mouth.

You can see it right? She is a virtual sphinx.
However, drawing upon our extensive
experience, we can tell you confidently that
this is the expression of elation. Or wrath.
It could be disappointment. There's a fair
chance that it's ennui. But more likely
exasperation. He's likely thinking "mmmm…
donuts." Or perhaps "is that guy's accent
real?" It's misery. Or potentially demoralization.
Irritation. Maybe heartbreak. Possibly revelation.
Or agony. Dashed hopes. Or repulse.
Pure wretchedness?

▲► *Subplot strives to design a holiday card
that's not only a festive greeting but also a
useful guide to help navigate life. One year,
it was* The Truth Behind Design Jargon:
An Illustrated Manual; *another year, it was*
Trash to Treasure: Learn to Turn Spam into
Treasured Gifts.

*It's in the same spirit that Face Plot was
created. Subplot drew on their many years of
experience in deciphering the cryptic and often
unintelligible reactions of clients and suppliers.
Armed with this indispensable, handy set of
cards, you will never be in doubt as to what
they're thinking again, whether it's in a design
presentation or on Christmas morning.*

SUBPLOT

▼► *Each year Real Art Design Group creates a unique gift during the holiday season, and one gift took personalization to a whole new level. A set of cards showcasing the puppet version of the Real Art employees invited clients, friends, and family members to log on to A New Year, A New You and create a puppet version of themselves. The Real Art team then crafted the puppets and shipped them to their new homes neatly* *packaged with instructions for completing the "new you" transformation. Keeping New Year's resolutions is never easy, but with the New You puppets, Real Art gave people the opportunity to accomplish their goals—even if it was through a puppet version of themselves. At the same time, Real Art was able to promote both their print and multimedia capabilities in a unique and fun fashion.*

REAL ART DESIGN GROUP

Portfolio Components

HOW YOU SHOW IT

"Curb appeal" isn't just for houses anymore. How you put your portfolio together—namely the materials used to house your portfolio—is often as important as what goes inside. Historically speaking, portfolios have traditionally come in two formats: books or binders. You know the ones—sleek black cases tucked under the arms or in the tight grip of creatives of all shapes and sizes.

Sometimes referred to as "show portfolios," these sophisticated renditions have garnered work for individuals and agencies alike. Remember, potential clients and employers get an immediate impression of you at first glance, so your portfolio format—both the exterior and interior—needs to be an extension of you or the company you represent.

Utilize a case that exudes professionalism and offers some distinction while reflecting the contents within. A custom case, albeit expensive, can be a perfect option. Local art supply stores also offer a wealth of innovative portfolio cases, binders, and boxes that may perfectly meet your specific portfolio needs.

Whether you mount your work or slide it into acetate sleeves, ensure that everything is clean, square, and without bent corners. "The substrate should be neutral and take a backseat to the work," says Neil Tortorella, marketing consultant and founder of Tortorella Design. "I've seen too many books with mattes and mounting methods that outshined the designer's work."

Make sure the case is clean and doesn't look like it was made in 1942, unless it's supposed to look like it's from 1942. The case is the first thing a prospect sees, and it sets the stage for the presentation.

Tortorella suggests you find a way to make your portfolio stand out. This is especially important for drop-off versions. That might mean a custom case or a clever, yet functional, way to mount the pieces. If it's mounted, be sure all work is mounted on a standardized board such as 16 × 20 inches (41 × 51 cm) or 20 × 24 inches (51 × 61 cm). Different-size boards are distracting and awkward.

DIMENSIONAL KITS

The physical act of opening a box has symbolic relevance to the start of any new partnership. The act of giving a box or kit to a prospective client reveals what you are as a firm or individual—giving a brief glimpse into how you do what you do.

Creating a box is a personal effort, and it really shouldn't be mass-produced. When a box is delivered, it should feel like it was created for that individual within that company. If it feels like a template and that you just dropped off three others around town, the resulting effect on the participant will be lessened. This requires a production and assembly method that balances personalization with efficiency.

Finding a stock box and making it your own is a place to start—or make your own. Whatever is designed, it should offer the chance to be consistently produced with the optimal efficiency in production and personalization. Not all boxes stay inside the box.

Capsule has created many forms of the box or kit idea in their experimentations to find the match for their brand. From a small metal box lined with green fur to a handmade wooden box with pencil holes, Capsule has found that these kinds of promotions make a lasting impression.

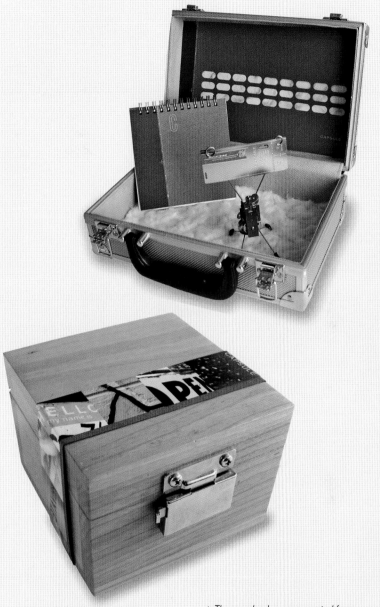

▲ *The wooden box was created for a multibillion-dollar toy manufacturer. Only two of these boxes were created, and they were hand-delivered to summarize a large presentation. The result was a significant amount of work from this toy manufacturer and a lasting relationship.*

The green fur box was created using leftover materials from two clients: The fur came from a client that produced stuffed animals, and the boxes were from a beauty supply chain. The results came together nicely, but offered a price challenge when replicating the idea.
CAPSULE

◄▲ Who says the way in which you house your portfolio has to be boring? WORKtoDATE uses an innovative packaging system for their portfolio, including an industrial-style plastic casing and a handy set of dog tags. These dynamic materials also allow for modification of the portfolio contents to meet the interests of the audience.

WORKTODATE

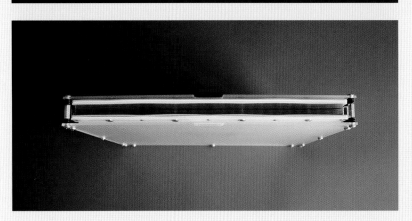

MAKE IT PORTABLE

Be sure to make your portfolio portable so you can always carry it with you. You can always supplement it with a promo kit—those leave-behind gems that are teeming with samples of your work, testimonials, client list, biographical information, and press materials.

"I see less and less conventional books in favor of more thoughtful/creative presentation formats," says Andrea Cutler, professor of design at Parsons School of Design and owner of Andrea Cutler Design. "There was a time when the standard black binder was ubiquitous and expected. Now when I do portfolio reviews, I see more and more unconventional containers, such as metal boxes and other custom portfolios. Of course, it doesn't mean the work inside is going to be better that the next person's, but it makes that presentation stand out and be memorable in another way, and they tend to be cleaner presentations."

One of the nicest books Cutler has seen was a horizontal 17 × 11-inch (43 × 28 cm) book the designer made himself, using simple binder scrapbook screws. The covers were rubber, the pages were teeming with white space, and the book was organized in a case-study fashion.

"The thing I loved most was the book came with a separate index and table of contents page," Cutler says. "So all the text about the clients, assignments, problem-solving specifics, and materials, were on that index/cover sheet and corresponded with the page number. That kept the pages clutter-free, but the viewer could read about each design project if they needed more info. And, of course, the design work was outstanding."

If you have both paper documents and small artifacts, you might consider using a large three-ring binder with work samples and artifacts slipped into plastic sleeves. Albums or scrapbooks make excellent holders for your portfolio if you want to create a more permanent collection and not return the artifacts to storage.

Most portfolio cases range in size from 8 × 10 inches (20 × 25 cm) to 11 × 17 inches (28 × 43 cm). But keep in mind that a portfolio becomes awkward to carry and to view if it is any larger than the sizes above.

▼ *Traditional leather albums are a perfect way to house some of your key portfolio elements. Soft to the touch, these versatile Lucca books by Kolo offer a luxurious design with wrapped sewn edges in accent thread colors selected to coordinate with the book's lining. Scratch-resistant, water-repellent, and expandable, the Lucca album is lined and offers Kolo's trademark self-contained cover window pocket for portfolio personalization.*

▲ Inspired by the beautiful design elements of classic premium cigar boxes, Kolo created Kolo Havana Photo Boxes using archival board, European book cloth, and archival bookbinding paper. These handsome boxes feature Kolo's trademark window to hold a photo or label, cleverly positioned on the front side of the box for visibility when displayed on a bookshelf. The large Kolo Havana Photo Box is perfect for portfolios or presentations and is sized to hold two 8½ × 11-inch (22 × 28 cm) albums in coordinating colors and fabrics.

◄▼ *Carrying your portfolio just became a whole lot easier. Oversize yet lightweight, these portfolio cases are versatile, sleek, and offer plenty of room for a medium- or large-size portfolio or laptop. To accommodate a variety of shapes, the cases are available in landscape and portrait styles. They also are fully padded and water resistant. They feature a removable padded shoulder strap, zippered front pocket, and clear ID back pocket.*

◄ *To dress up your portfolio and provide some extra depth to your presentation materials, this portfolio valise, which measures 15 × 12 × 3 inches (38 × 30 × 8 cm), offers the versatility of a laptop case while also housing samples to show to prospects, clients, or potential employers.*

▲ Portability is key for many portfolios. Bound like a book with linen covers, these small book-style portfolio binders include a sewn spine and accent ribbon tie. Their easy-load pockets hold 24 of your 4 × 6-inch (10 × 15 cm) portfolio images.

► For digital portfolios, more and more creative professionals are turning to portable digital photo albums. Featuring a slim design encased in a soft leather-like case for a convenient, elegant image display, this photo book offers more than 2½ hours of battery life and an easy and portable way to showcase portfolio images. Ideal for creative professionals to display their work, this photo book supports raw images as well as JPEG, BMP, GIF, and TIF image formats.

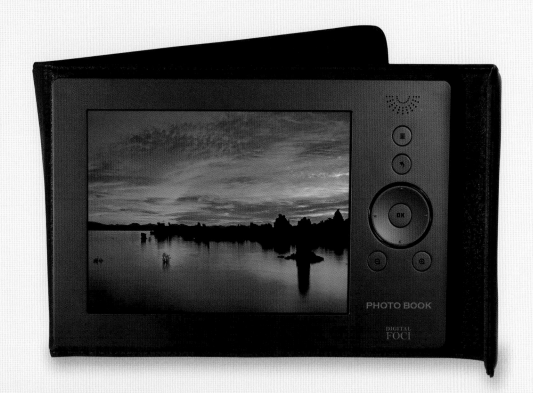

Promoting Sustainability

DEMONSTRATING YOUR SKILLS USING LESS

Turn on the television or open a newspaper, and you would be hard-pressed *not* to find information on living green. The sustainable design movement has embraced the global marketplace and captured the attention of consumers like never before. From sustainable building design to alternative fuels to water conservation, entire industries are taking notice and changing the way they're doing business. Even creative professionals looking for sustainable options for their portfolio development have reason to celebrate and can make their portfolio more sustainable.

The sustainable movement is receiving a tremendous amount of attention, so what goes into a portfolio is as important as what goes on it. Soy-based and low-solvent-based corn inks and UV-cured ink technology are very popular. Reclaimed materials—such as fabric and metal—are also being used.

For professionally printed portfolios or self-promotions, people are also minimizing the amount of virgin paper used and are selecting papers that are processed chlorine-free, or that even have seeds embedded in the paper, which can be planted in the ground later to grow flowers.

As for recycled paper, just about every mill offers a paper with at least 30 percent recycled material. Some mills also use alternative energy like wind power.

Today's portfolios and self-promotions run the gamut from simple to grand, from luxurious to subdued. But more and more creative professionals recognize that incorporating environmental elements into their portfolios is more than just green business—it's good business. In fact, for many creatives, sustainability is much more of a standard, as opposed to an exception—they understand the value, responsibility, and profitability of being responsible for the materials and processes they use.

In addition to using more earth-friendly materials, consider engaging your audience in other unique ways. Perhaps you can send a well-designed epostcard or small printed postcard that illustrates your creative genius, while pointing the recipient to your website or blog to learn more about your product, services, and experience. When presenting your work, consider using a portable digital portfolio rather than a printed one. All of these combined efforts can make a significant impact on your company's carbon footprint.

▶ *Larsen's monthly enewsletter, inSights, demonstrates Larsen's thought leadership via topics of interest to marketing managers, creative directors, and others who need ideas for communicating effectively to target audiences. It is also a wonderful sustainable approach to keeping in touch with client and prospects.*
LARSEN

Can't read this email? View as webpage.

LARSEN

DESIGN
BRANDING
MARKETING
INTERACTIVE

inSights

no. 32 | 16 December 2008

> forward to a colleague
> subscribe to inSights

Color
Five trends important to your business

Who's responsible for color trends? Who decides what the next hot color will be? Sometimes it seems as though a fashion designer in a Manhattan loft sits down with a Pantone book and determines for the rest of us what color is in and what color is out. Nothing could be farther from the truth. Color trends actually start from the bottom up — as a reaction to the world around us. Although the fashion industry unquestionably plays a role in color trends, it's also very reactionary, and one of the few industries where color choices change yearly.

Color has an undeniably powerful impact. It reflects and defines our world, and plays a large role in our behavior, emotional responses, and moods. Because of this, it's important for organizations large and small to pay attention to color forecasts and consider color carefully. Here are five trends that can help you make smart color choices for your business.

▸ read the full story

Color in motion
They asked for buzz. We gave them a brass band. This marketing promotion uses color to attract attention and generate excitement.

▸ view solution

news

New work, new clients
Larsen is pleased to announce new branding, design, marketing, interactive, and environmental graphics initiatives for clients including Best Buy, Catalyst Community Partners, Cold Spring Granite, College of Saint Benedict/Saint John's University, Core-Mark International, Fairview, Lominger International, Maple Grove Hospital, MTS Systems, San Jose State University, University of Minnesota, and Wausau Paper.

Larsen Design Scholarships: 2008-09 Awards
Larsen proudly announces three new Larsen Design Scholars: Elizabeth Berschneider, multimedia design, UW-Stout; Ben Moren, interactive media, Minneapolis College of Art and Design; and Sarah Mytych, graphic design, University of Minnesota-Twin Cities.
▸ read more

contact

Interested in hearing a Larsen speaker?
We have experts on design, branding, marketing, interactive.

▸ submit your request

IMPLEM

- BROCHURES
- LOGOS
- PACKAGING
- PORTFOLIOS

ENTING

"THERE ARE TWO KINDS OF PEOPLE,
THOSE WHO FINISH WHAT THEY START
AND SO ON." — ROBERT BYRNE

WHEN IT COMES TO LOW-BUDGET PROJECTS, THE RIGHT ATTITUDE IS ESSENTIAL. "GOOD DESIGN IS GOOD DESIGN," SAYS STEVE WATSON, PRINCIPAL OF TURNSTYLE IN SEATTLE. "YOU HAVE TO START WITHOUT GETTING BLINDED OR BOGGED DOWN IN THE LIMITATIONS A BUDGET MAY PRESENT TO YOU." IN FACT, THERE'S NO DIRECT CORRELATION BETWEEN HOW MUCH GETS SPENT ON PHOTOGRAPHY OR PAPER AND THE OVERALL QUALITY OF THE DESIGN.

A Positive Approach

Not every pricey project hits the mark, and there are plenty of head-turning efforts created on tight budgets. Strong ideas and concepts—rather than dollars and cents—are the true measures of success. In fact, the limitations of a budget can help bring a project into focus. For a Steelcase annual report, for example, Watson knew that the production constraints didn't make photography a viable option. But this restriction actually led the Turnstyle design team to a bold, graphic look that gave the company's report a distinctive quality. Silhouettes of the company's office furniture set against a bright blue background make the piece lively and engaging. It certainly doesn't look like a decision driven—at least in part—by cost constraints.

In the end, a budget is just one of the parameters that come with any given project. "I never let small budgets hinder my creativity," says Noah Scalin, founder of Another Limited Rebellion in Richmond, Virginia. "The challenge of graphic design for me is problem solving." He looks at budget as just one piece of a puzzle that might include everything from the message to the size of the print run. But Scalin does add one caveat: don't get too far into a project without knowing the budget. There's nothing worse than showing a client a great solution that isn't financially viable.

◄ Despite being printed on fairly modest paper at a financial printer, this Steelcase annual report creates an engaging narrative. The flood of color on this cover, for instance, immediately grabs attention.

► This text-heavy spread stays approachable with bold typography and color. The pull quote breaks up the running text, while changes in type color make the extensive copy less intimidating to read.

► Since photography wasn't a viable option with this project's production constraints, the designers at Turnstyle created silhouettes of Steelcase's products. "Their furniture creates very iconic shapes," says principal Steve Watson.

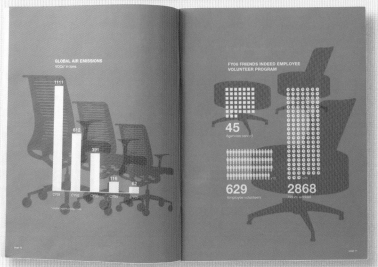

▲ *Noah Scalin, founder of Another Limited Rebellion, stretched a small budget by designing something with more than one function. This brochure—promoting a summer theater program—becomes a poster when unfolded. It's twice the marketing punch with a single printed piece.*

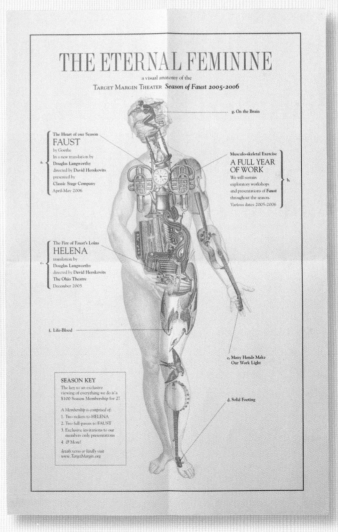

▲▶ *This unassuming mailer folds out into a striking poster. The strength of the concept—a woman depicted through an image collage—makes an impact without high production costs. Noah Scalin, founder of Another Limited Rebellion, also saved money by creating the collage himself from stock illustrations.*

KNOWING YOUR WAY AROUND THE PRODUCTION END OF A PROJECT IS A BIT LIKE FINDING A HUNDRED DOLLAR BILL ON THE SIDEWALK. WHEN THERE'S A TIGHT BUDGET, IT'S KEY TO THINK THROUGH HOW A PIECE WILL BE PRODUCED BEFORE YOU START DESIGNING. A SMALL CHANGE IN TRIM SIZE OR PAPER CAN MAKE OR BREAK YOUR BUDGET.

Production Strategies

Noah Scalin, founder of ALR Design, sometimes heads straight to the printer with his budget and print-run requirements, then he asks for advice about what is possible. A small change in the size of a brochure, for instance, might make it fit better on the press sheet and significantly reduce costs. Unfortunately, there's no magic formula to spitting out the most cost-effective print strategy for every job. One- or two-color printing, for instance, doesn't necessarily save money over four-color. The cost of any print job depends on variables ranging from the size of the print run to who provided the bid. But there are some general strategies to help stretch those production dollars. Justin Ahrens, creative director of Rule29 in Geneva, Illinois, offers these tips:

- BUILD STRONG RELATIONSHIPS WITH YOUR VENDORS. If you throw a lot of business to a particular photographer or printer, they're going to be more willing to work with you when you're trying to meet tight parameters.

- TALK TO YOUR PAPER REP ABOUT WHAT CHOICES ARE AVAILABLE. If you have a specific stock in mind, he or she might be able to point you to something similar with a lower price tag.

- ASK YOUR PRINTER ABOUT THE HOUSE SHEET. Typically, this is a paper purchased at a discount and may be a way to keep a brochure on budget.

- CONSIDER GOING WITH A LOWER GRADE OF PAPER. Depending on the project, a lower grade might work well and save money.

- BUY PAPER DIRECT FROM THE PAPER COMPANY. Though your printer may not be crazy about this choice—because it reduces his profits—it can cut costs when you're really struggling to meet a client's budget.

- EXPLORE DIGITAL PRINTING. Depending on the design specifics and print-run size, digital might be a more cost-effective option than offset printing. Just be sure you ask questions about the capabilities—and limitations—of any digital printer you choose.

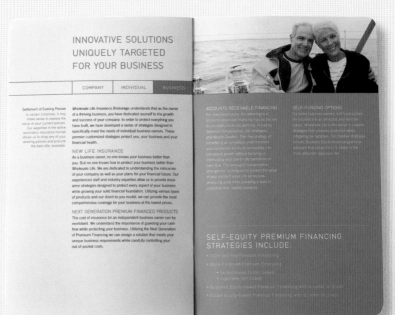

INNOVATIVE SOLUTIONS UNIQUELY TARGETED FOR YOUR BUSINESS

| COMPANY | INDIVIDUAL | BUSINESS |

▲ The Rule29 designers kept this brochure inexpensive by choosing a digital printer. They also gave it a more upscale feel with rounded corners. To keep this detail affordable, the corners were ground off rather than die-cut.

► When you're working with a charitable organization—such as this Food for the Hungry brochure—Justin Ahrens at Rule29 suggests telling the printer. They might be more willing to work with you on price when it benefits a good cause.

◄▼ *To maximize the budget, Rule29 designers reverse engineered this brochure's size with the printer to get the most out of the press sheet. An innovative fold—the brochure doubles in width twice as you unfold it—along with bold colors and graphics work together to form a lasting impression.*

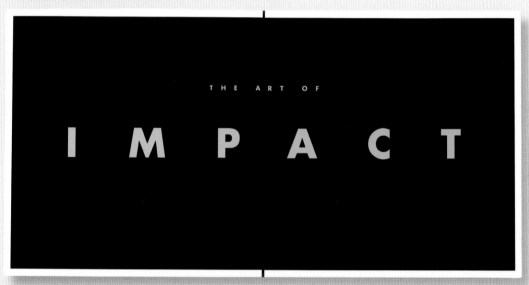

THE ART OF

IMPACT

Low-Cost Artwork

With a budget-conscious brochure, there's rarely enough money for original photography, but a little DIY elbow grease can put you in control of the artwork without breaking the bank. Scalin, for example, might create an illustration for a brochure he's designing—but only when his style meshes well with the client and project. He'll also shoot original photography for a brochure when the image needs to fall within his skill set. This approach simply adds design hours to a project rather than the high cost of an outside vendor.

There's also a wealth of inexpensive stock photography available when you can't hire a photographer. It's fairly quick and easy to search through any number of royalty-free options online. But the Web has also given birth to a new copyright model called Creative Commons (http://creativecommons.org). It allows everyone from photographers to scientists to share their work under a variety of alternative copyrights. Some, for example, allow use with attribution, while others restrict sharing to noncommercial purposes. On Flickr (www.flickr.com), some users mark their image sets to a Creative Commons copyright for various levels of sharing.

Depending on a project's subject matter, there may be other options for free, high-quality imagery. Donna McGrath, a design manager at Rand McNally in Skokie, Illinois, often taps the resources of convention and visitors bureaus for the company's travel-related projects. These groups often have great professional-quality photography available for the asking. A simple Google search may also turn up low- or no-cost imagery. One example is Stock.XCHNG (www.sxc.hu) where photographers upload their images to share with others for little or no cost, though sometimes small restrictions apply.

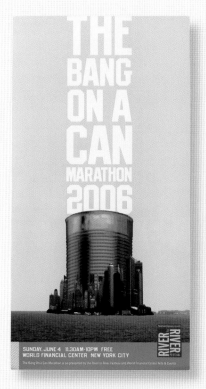

◄▼ *To get more mileage out of this music-event brochure, the specific scheduling details—likely to change—were intentionally left out. Instead, as event times and other details were finalized, a black-and-white photocopy was added. Noah Scalin, of Another Limited Rebellion, also kept the budget low by creating the cover photo collage himself.*

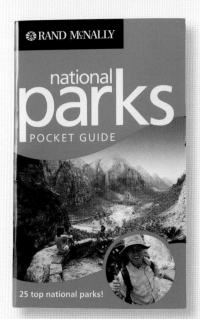

▲ *Since there wasn't a budget for original photography, Rand McNally's in-house design team needed to figure out how to make existing photography fresh for this National Parks Pocket Guide. Interesting crops—such as the circular one shown here—help keep the imagery engaging.*

▼ *Donna McGrath, a design manager at Rand McNally, put this travel booklet together on a tight timeframe and budget. To acquire free photography, she tapped convention and visitors bureaus along with specific attractions featured in the book. Museums and other tourist sites are often happy to provide high-quality imagery at no cost.*

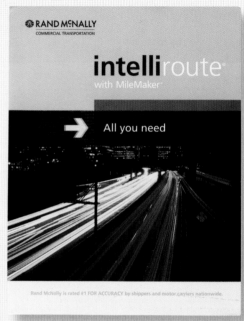

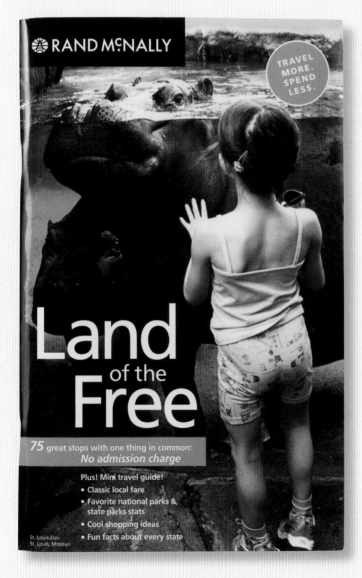

▲ *Rand McNally's in-house design team saved money on this brochure—handed out at a trade show—by picking up the same graphics used for the booth design. This technique also created a cohesive branding message.*

BE YOUR OWN STOCK AGENCY

It's a cringe-worthy moment: you spot the same royalty-free image you used for a client's brochure two months later on a highway billboard. But when there's no budget for original photography, it can feel like you're stuck choosing from the same low-cost images as everyone else. So what's an enterprising designer to do?

Become your own stock agency. Or, put more simply, start taking your digital camera with you wherever you go. Snap pictures of that funny sign at your favorite Chinese restaurant. Capture the line of cars in front of you when traffic is at a complete standstill. In fact, take a picture of anything that catches your eye—without giving too much thought to when or if you'll use the image.

With a little diligence, you can create a photography habit that turns into an image library that is thousands strong. You'll likely find yourself paying more attention to the details of everyday life and bringing those varied inspirations into your design work. Plus, your new image library will serve as a powerful idea bank. Scan through it to help you find ideas for texture or mood. And the next time there's a nonexistent photography budget, you may discover the perfect image living right on your hard drive, one you know won't unexpectedly show up on a billboard.

BOTTLE ROCKETS ARE A HEADY SOURCE OF DELIGHT FOR MANY YOUNGSTERS, FOR THE SAME REASON THEY'RE THE SOURCE OF ANGST FOR MANY PARENTS–THEY'RE UNPREDICTABLE. AS A DESIGNER, THERE'S NO TELLING WHETHER YOUR LOGO LAUNCH WILL SOAR, IMPLODE, OR SIMPLY FIZZLE. SCARY, CONSIDERING THAT NOW IT'S NOT JUST YOUR FINGERS ON THE LINE.

Logo Launch

The digits now on the line are connected to profit margins, not hands. And the person watching over your shoulder is the client, not Mom. So if something goes wrong, you will be held accountable. As with most things in life, the best way to avoid disaster is to read instructions carefully, follow them as best you can, then hope for the best. To that end, this section's intent is to serve as an instruction manual for brand launchers.

The ideas here offer a unique perspective, along with examples of logo launches, to set you on the right course. Read on to learn more about the stages of launching a logo, specifically how to properly set expectations, identify clear objectives, orchestrate everything, and then evaluate the outcomes.

Remember, launching a logo is like planning any wedding or event. Things will go wrong. Don't panic, just stay focused.

Potentials

THE LOGOS WHO LAUNCH

There are plenty of ways to fail at a logo launch—more than can be covered in one book. Just look over the past decade. Amusing failures run rampant. Get your chuckle, but also try to empathize with the people behind these efforts. Just imagine yourself sitting on the wrong side of the fan when the stuff hits. If only they could have seen it coming.

A successful logo launch is not that elusive. It just requires a serious effort to build appropriate expectations, identify potential outcomes, and map out a clear plan of action.

Build expectations from the inside out. Get to the most vocal and powerful individuals internally. Take some time to get them on board. If they accept the change in an early preview, there is less chance they'll undermine it afterward. Plus, these individuals can prove loyal allies if they get excited about its potential. When launching a logo, the more allies, the better.

Potential outcomes can be varied and fairly unpredictable. Find someone who has done it before. Ask that person to review your plans and give feedback on possible outcomes.

The plan of action includes a variety of contingencies. Offer a town hall forum or an online discussion room, so employees can express their concerns or feedback. Separately, offer the same idea to external audiences. If they don't need it, cancel it. Plan for success, but don't ignore the potential for failure. Potential outcomes can be varied and fairly unpredictable. Find someone who has done it before. Ask that person to review your plans and give feedback on possible outcomes.

TEN WAYS TO CREATE A LOGO LAUNCH BOMB

··· Launch a logo design to take attention away from or hide other issues in the business.

··· Launch the logo *on* the employees instead of *with* the employees.

··· Change the organization drastically, but make only small refinements to the logo design.

··· Change the logo design drastically, but make only small refinements to the business.

··· Change the logo design drastically, but fail to communicate the reasons internally.

··· Fail to set expectations with key people and influencers in your organization.

··· Change your logo design while facing bankruptcy protection.

··· Fail to give authentic or real answers for the change to employees.

··· Expect to have a logo design fix all your business problems and wait for the healing to begin.

··· Fight the change happening in your industry, and then play catch up with a logo design change and expect that to save your future.

3WIRE: LEVERAGING OPPORTUNITIES TO ENERGIZE

IMI Cornelius is a manufacturer of parts and equipment used in commercial kitchens. BEVCORe was a division of IMI Cornelius dedicated to beverage parts management. When BEVCORe acquired an outside food-service parts provider, Northern Parts United, the two entities were fused under the new name 3Wire.

During BEVCORe's transition, the management team went through a brand definition process to articulate the elements that made BEVCORe unique in the marketplace. It landed on one word: resourcefulness. The team then went through a naming process to identify a name for the new brand. The new name had to serve as the umbrella brand name for the original company; the first acquisition, Northern Parts; and any future acquisitions. The name 3Wire borrows a popular term used by fighter pilots to signal a perfect landing on an aircraft carrier.

The name 3Wire was absorbed into the logo design process, inspiring a logo that connected the precision metaphor back to the businesses' core focus. The 3 and W in the name alluded to 3Wire's parts capabilities. The logo also communicated a high-tech feel that is distinctive in an old industry not used to visible innovation. The 3Wire marketing team launched the new brand internally, and then externally, to customers a month later.

3Wire is an example of an umbrella brand successfully tying two current brands together efficiently. Existing brands that may have had equity in the marketplace are able to transition to meet the new brand, while room is made to welcome future acquisitions.

That's one hot metaphor. The 3Wire logo is actually two sides of a heating element, represented by wires in 3 and W. CAPSULE

The internal launch involved each and every employee. While everyone knew something was in the works, they were not all aware of the details, although the key individuals were made aware or were part of the original team. The launch was well received by Northern Parts employees and the core business partners. The launch party also garnered excitement and served to energize the staff and management team. Time will tell how all audiences adopt the new name and logo design, but early indications insinuate the changes will be leveraged with enthusiasm.

Gather internal steam. The internal brand launch can be a highly valuable way to energize staff and get them informed and excited about the logo and its connection to them.

Goals and Objectives

SING IT AGAIN, PLAN

Your action plan is like a steering wheel, directing you where you need to go. Measurable goals and objectives are your mirrors. Use them periodically to check where you are. Write your goals and objectives clearly and gain agreement among the important invested parties. If you do a careful job, your client's logo will benefit later.

Typical goals and objectives include signaling a change (internally, externally, or both); communicating a list of key messages; and making messages stick with intended audiences. An important part of establishing goals is also establishing specific successes. You'll need these analytics when a client wants to know what your logo did for his or her bottom line. Don't stutter or sweat. Just reach for your analytics binder and ask if they would like to talk about it in a nearby conference room. Analytics save the day again!

Don't lose sight of the long-term results or the immeasurable affects of this change. They may seem small now, but over time they build upon themselves. For example, say you change a logo's readability, and it now translates across media more consistently. Part of the immeasurable impact here is what consistency means to your client's brand over the next 25 years. What does it say about the trust people put in your client's brand if you can consistently communicate a clear message with a new logo design? A dollar amount could be attached, but the analytics are likely too hazy for today's knowledge base.

SAMPLE GOALS AND OBJECTIVES

··· Signal the change the brand is taking by having more than 95 percent of all internal audiences understand the change of direction.

··· Communicate the brand strategy to an energized staff and have them tell at least ten other people, internal or external.

··· Build brand equity by making sure everyone internal knows the brand promise, attributes, and personality, so they can represent the brand in our marketplace.

··· Build brand equity by ensuring that more than 60 percent of external audiences remembers the brand and associates it with the five key attributes.

··· Build brand loyalty by engaging external audiences with a new campaign started with the new logo design and communicated through an integrated campaign.

THIRST: A TASTE OF IMPLEMENTATION

What sounds are capable of grooving a global village? There's no definite answer. But it never hurts to be unique. Eclectic, diverse sounds are popular staples of youth culture around the world. DJs, MCs, and producers from Los Angeles to Istanbul all have the same goal: to fill clubs. The artistry comes in the pursuit. The Heineken music contest, Thirst, was created to uncover and reward a diverse trove of hidden talents in various cities around the world, from spacey techno mix-masters to funky retro popsters.

Music and beer pair together naturally. The promotion of one often leads to more consumption of the other. The Thirst contest flew from country to country—Denmark to Croatia to Indonesia—each stop a chance to showcase that city's unique talents.

The incentive for the talent was exposure to large audiences. Audiences, in turn, got to hear fresh sounds. Heineken, a popular brand of brewed hops, got the benefit of global exposure as well as the good will of consumers and artists enjoying themselves on its tab.

The Thirst logo is a modern, bold design, consisting of the word with a directional arrow. It flexes to meet cultural circumstances, but the type and color remain consistent. The surrounding layout is organic and fresh, exemplifying the brand coming to life.

Posters, passes, coasters, fans, and whistles were just a few implementation pieces that came to live together in a visual landscape of illustrations, photographs, and type. The result is an electric, vivid brand that works across many cultures.

The logo builds on the classic Heineken color palette, while creating a more contemporary language through the typeface and supporting hierarchy. CRUSH

A sexy, musical, illustrative style sets the tone of diverse surrounding materials and communications. The consistency and diversity in style is executed globally.

The brand lives in a variety of countries. The logo therefore represents more than what the word "thirst" means in English. The logo and name adopt other anticipated and unanticipated connotations as they travel around the world.

MOST CUSTOMERS HAVE TROUBLE COMMITTING. THEY'LL TAKE HOME A JAR OF PEANUT BUTTER ONE WEEK, THEN DITCH IT FOR A CHEAPER BRAND THE NEXT. STEADY CUSTOMER LOYALTY TAKES WORK. CUSTOMERS DON'T RESPOND TO A FLOWERS-AND-CANDY SPIEL—THEY RESPOND TO BRAND CONSISTENCY.

Consistent Flexibility

Logos are an essential part of this effort because they are part of virtually every interaction between the customer and the brand. And remember, a single message communicated seven times is always more memorable than seven messages communicated once. Beyond aesthetic and creative components, the bottom line is that logo consistency is critical.

If the devil lives in the details, then he parties in consistency. The more you explore what constitutes "consistency," the more daunting "consistent" becomes. The 3M logo is one example of consistency through color and placement. It's always a red 3M placed in a specified area of the package. Nickelodeon's logo color remains consistent, but the shape varies. Pottery Barn Kids switches out the logo shape within an icon system, but the colors (blue and gray) are always consistent. None of these is wrong. None is right. They are variations of consistency. Sounds funny, no? Nonetheless, it's an important concept to understand and consider throughout the logo design process.

If consistency equals details, flexibility equals the big picture. The amount of flexibility that lives alongside consistency is determined by the company culture. 3M's buttoned-up culture dictates that the logo has little flexibility, yet Nickelodeon's whimsical nature is reflected in a highly flexible logo design.

Flexibility

RUBBER DOESN'T WRINKLE

Remember Mosaic? During the Internet's spring tide from 1993 to 1996, young surfers got their feet wet with Mosaic, the first graphic Web browser. But, like the joystick and Pong, Mosaic sunk with little pomp, engulfed by the unremitting turbines of technological innovation. Few took it to heart when Mosaic folded in 1997, just five years after conception.

The moral of Mosaic is to heed change. As any surfer knows, you must adapt to the wave. Take control by giving a little of it up. Designing a logo is similar to surfing. Had Mosaic evolved as fast as the industry around it, perhaps it would still be riding high. Logos often struggle to keep pace with modern industries, especially the breakneck technology category. Prepackage flexibility into a logo design and, at the very least, it will enjoy as much longevity as possible.

A logo toolkit is a fine complement to any new logo. It's a family of options containing several logo versions that can be dropped into a variety of situations. So twenty years from now, designer John Doe Jr. will know exactly how the logo must adapt to swell onto a billboard, encircle a coffee mug, or shrink onto a pen cap.

No matter what you do, odd permutations occur and variations pop up, and there is nothing a client or design can do to prevent it completely. The toolkit is meant to provide options so this behavior is managed to a reasonable minimum. The options can cover most scenarios and then offer other options for the unknown, in the hope of covering all foreseeable situations. The key is composing a toolkit that is direct, available, and user-friendly, so designers will be more apt to use it than to gallivant off on their own short-sighted paths.

The logo for The Society of American Fight Directors has to represent several categories. The logo flexes for specific sectors of fighting.

CAPSULE

 winter

LUCINA spring

 summer

LUCINA fall

Balance color and shape. The use of color as a flexible variable is common and effective for both retail brands and others needing to evoke pre-planned changes. Lucina uses color to identify seasonal updates.

MORROW MCKENZIE

 BRIGITE BRIGITE BRIGITE BRIGITE

Use shape to communicate flexibility. This opens up plenty of creative opportunities in which the logo design can tailor the brand's tone to fit certain contexts. HARDY DESIGN

SEED: SPREADING FLEXIBILITY AND CONSISTENCY

Communication, like science, is the process of organizing organic elements. Seed Media Group, a publisher of scientific magazines, books, and films, sought an identity that would be conceptually deep and functionally flexible. Conceptually, Sagmeister Inc. needed to make sure Seed's new logo alluded to science and media, while, functionally, it had to adapt easily to new meanings and various media.

Phyllotaxis is used in botany to describe the arrangement of leaves on stems. The form is also found in seashells, Greek architecture, highway systems, and now, Seed Media Group's logo. It's a fitting metaphor for what Seed Media Group ultimately does: organize organic elements and information. It's also a symbol of the communication process as a whole: disparate components developing out of a central axis. The result is a logo that flexes dynamically while remaining identifiably consistent.

The Seed Media Group's logo exemplifies a thoughtful approach to consistency in tone and style without a strict structure of specific logo uses. The logo exemplifies Seed Media Group's philosophy, "Science is Culture," in a way that is beautiful to any observant eye.

Flexing the relationship between the seed icon and the logotype creates a visually stunning entrance.

seed media group.

Seed Media Group's logo is simple yet has an immense depth, beauty, and flexibility.
SAGMEISTER INC.

Don Hoyt Gorman
SENIOR EDITOR, EUROPE

Laura McNeil
DEPUTY EDITOR

Jennifer DiBlasi
ADVERTISING/PROJECT MANAGER

Christopher Carbone
MANAGING EDITOR

Headshots of Seed Media's staff create an intriguing mosaic on their business card and provide another interpretation of the Seed Media Group logo.

Style Guide

DO THESE MAKE MY LOGO LOOK BIG?

There comes a time in every person's life when it hits. For some, it comes at work. For others, at a party. You look around the room and realize you are not the style maven you'd always taken yourself to be. With the pill of a sweater and the fade of a cuff, your style has taken a turn for the worse. Who do you turn to? If your style is dire but your pocketbook is not, you hire a professional, a stylist who knows the secrets of the cut, the potential of the hem, and the importance of the color.

As a designer, you are essentially a logo stylist. You provide suggestions that guide the client toward better logo style. However, you won't always be there. That's when your client's logo may go through some awkward phases. Understand who will be implementing your client's logo in the future and create your style guide to work for that person or team. Use the style guide to ensure your client's logo is always stylishly implemented. That's the goal.

Your style guide can use the carrot method or the stick method. The carrot rewards: "Do this right, and you are helping us build strong brand." The stick threatens: "Do this wrong, and we may have to redo your work and show you how to do it right—that won't be fun." The best style guides assume everyone wants to do right but plans for those who like to get around the rules. Make it usable and quick to read, and the majority will comply. Make it hard to understand, unnecessarily long, and hard to navigate, and you'll hear plenty of excuses.

The example subject areas are by no means exhaustive. They offer a place to start.

BASIC SUBJECT AREAS

- ▶ Building our brand
- ▶ Product logo & versions
- ▶ Clear space & minimum size
- ▶ Colors & description of color usage
- ▶ Logo integrity & incorrect usage
- ▶ Complementary typefaces
- ▶ File name structure & color modes
- ▶ Descriptions & file formats

ADDITIONAL SUBJECT AREAS

- ▶ Signature
- ▶ Name usage
- ▶ Tagline & symbol usage
- ▶ Secondary logo signatures
- ▶ Glossary
- ▶ Production materials
- ▶ Stationery & forms
- ▶ Communication systems & brochures

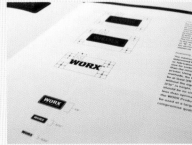

Some brands are not producing printed guidelines anymore because the Internet is so easy to update. But, printed match color chips and printed devices such as these are also accessible to anyone, anywhere.

CAPSULE

The opening line sets the tone for the Ford logo design manual. The manual uses the automobile manual as a metaphor for taking care of an important asset. The result is engaging and thoughtful. THE PARTNERS

The Personal Advisors of

Ameriprise
Financial SM

The Ameriprise Financial guidelines use a unique binding structure. It offers a simple, fast way to access the boundaries set up for the use of this new logo design. Designers enjoy using it, and others may find it interesting to browse through. LIPPINCOTT MERCER

Managing Assets

COVERING ASSETS IN A DIGITAL WORLD

You've spent months producing a highly memorable logo design. Now you need to let it go. Push it gently out of the design studio and into the big, scary world. It's an intimidating time. All your work and attention can be destroyed with a simple keystroke. Someone with a simple software package and good intentions can take your logo design and stretch it across the opening page of a presentation. Or add a drop shadow. The very tools that were necessary to create your beautiful design are the same tools that can bring it down.

The logo design's digital assets can be delivered in a variety of formats to meet specific scenarios. The key is building a structure that works for the novice user. Say a client just started to use Microsoft Word or PowerPoint and now wants to drop your new logo design into a presentation. What format does the client use? How easy is it to find that format? What size should it be? How does the client know the color will be right? Solve this confusion by considering all necessary formats available beforehand. There are formats that don't scale like .tif or .jpg, for example. Offer three size options for each.

Borders' online guide offers simple and intuitive navigation with three main sections: learn, design, and download. This format avoids overwhelming the user by condensing information. LIPPINCOTT MERCER

Also consider the ramifications when a professional printer or other technologically savvy user needs to get something fast—they have the ability to recreate the logo if they can't find what they need, making them more dangerous than a novice. The potential exists for these users to create a new logo design that is not authentic or authorized but becomes used in more contexts.

Have the logo design available when that happens. Most people will do the right thing when they see the path in front of them. It should eliminate most future variations. If it doesn't, hire a logo cop. Logo cops don't come with a badge. They do offer a stern look and the ability to intimidate the most stalwart CEO when the time is right. Give them the authority to enforce the rules.

Users can browse the Reuters site by medium: print, interactive broadcast, or display. Every time a user logs on, a brand-related message is displayed. REUTERS

WHAT'S THE WILDEST THING YOU'VE EVER DONE? WRESTLED ALLIGATORS? LIED TO THE NURSE ABOUT YOUR WEIGHT? FOR THE SAKE OF YOUR LIMBS AND YOUR SOCIAL LIFE, LET'S HOPE IT'S IN THE MIDDLE. WHEN CREATING A LOGO, OR ANYTHING FOR THAT MATTER, A SYSTEM OF CHECKS SHOULD BALANCE CREATIVITY'S WILD EBB AND FLOW.

Practical Considerations

For instance, be practical about the budget and timeline. Don't let things drag on, but also don't push yourself too hard. Set reasonable expectations. Designers often overextend themselves in their efforts to impress a new client. This often has the opposite effect, in the end.

It's also important for the designer to be practical, because often the client is not. Many clients have never seen the brand go through either a revolutionary or evolutionary change. You must steward clients though the design process by letting them know what is reasonable to expect. Remember, clients will judge the job you do by the expectations set forth at the beginning.

Overall, the most important function of practicality is maintaining balance between structure and creativity in the logo design. Successful logos mix beauty and information; they are artistic products that serve a practical commercial function. Make sure this is a theme of all your work.

Budget and Timeline

DESIGN ON THE MONEY

Managing your budget and managing your timeline are one and the same. The more time you have to work on something, the harder it is to stay on budget. The less time you have, the less budget you use. Ironically, when the budget is smaller, clients often offer you more time. The rationale is that time can make up for a deficient budget and vice versa. In fact, more time tends to strain budgets.

That said, try to get as much time as you feel you need. If you're not sure exactly how much, ask for a little extra up front. The logo shouldn't be something you rush to create. The typical timeframe for a full logo design ranges from two to eighteen months. If it takes less than two, you've likely skipped a few essential steps. If it takes more than eighteen, the world around you may have changed enough to warrant a complete restart. The time allotted for each of the steps between start and finish depends on the process you planned for your client and how the company makes design decisions. If you are working with a more democratic organization, you'll find a longer timeline is necessary to get decisions made. In the end match the process to the client culture and create a timeline that works with the process you've outlined.

The timeline is tied closely to the budget, so figure that out at the same time. Budgets can vary wildly and depend on the depth of the process: the number of people working on the design; the weeks allowed at each stage; and the number of hours in a day. A logo redesign budget can range from one or two million dollars down to ten or twenty thousand. Figure out what you need—and want. Once set, you can track results as you go. Remember, clients want to spend as little as possible. The best way to get them to spend a little more is to inform them about what they get for the money.

Now, here's the rub. Things change, as they always do. Imagine if you will: Your client finds the first round of concepts less than exciting—so you need to keep designing. How does this affect your process, timeline, and budget? Who should adjust expectations and dollar signs? You?

Your client? This depends on the process used up front and whether or not things changed on your client's side or on your side. Determine this with the client, and move forward with adjustments. Remember, the client is always right. Unless, of course, they're wrong. But if they don't admit it, you'll be left holding the bag. Getting someone to admit they're wrong is hard to do without admitting your own faults first. Open the gates of constructive communication by partly sharing responsibility for any problem. It may be hard on the ego, but it will be much softer on the process.

At the end of the entire process, it is important to go back and look at all the stages. Determine what sent the process down an alternative path. Your greatest learning will come from those challenging clients and situations that took rocky paths. Projects that go as planned are nice but are not always as satisfying, in the end. The steeper the mountain, the stronger the legs, and the better chance you'll be able to avoid the same trouble with a future client.

Proposal

▸ Determine budget

▸ Create project brief outlining goal

▸ Interview design firm candidates

▸ Request proposals

▸ Review and approve proposal

▸ Select internal team

Client: Getting a low price is not as valuable as finding a creative firm with a culture, process, talent, and experience level suited to your firm and objectives.

Designer: Demonstrating process and experience will get you to the table. Demonstrating passion and vision for the client's brand will go a long way toward getting work.

Planning

▸ Review project brief with design firm

▸ Gather current identity materials

▸ Confirm project components and deliverables

▸ Create project schedule

▸ Conduct research

▸ Define any missing brand attributes

Client: Include the design team in the planning effort, involving all individuals whom you believe will impact the final results.

Designer: When clients don't have design experience, you can help set direction by outlining the design stages and estimating time frames for each stage.

Creating

▸ Conduct logo design exploration

▸ Study applications

▸ Present logo

▸ Refine selected logo

Client: A constructive relationship is key to creative success. If you allow the firm creative freedom and demonstrate trust in what it will deliver, the relationship, process, and final product can only benefit.

Designer: Present the client with, at minimum, a couple of design options that you would be proud to implement. Once a design is chosen, refine thoughtfully, sparingly, and only when necessary.

Implementing

▸ Approve layouts for implementation items

▸ Approve printing and manufacturing costs

▸ Manage production schedules

▸ Oversee printing and manufacturing

▸ Create identity standards

▸ Prepare for launch

▸ Manage and assess identity (ongoing)

Client: Details are small but critical. During implementation, your ability to manage details will ultimately determine whether your project stays on schedule, within budget, and faithful to the plan's original vision and objectives.

Designer: If you don't have experience in this area, winging it won't do. Get advice from expert vendors, mentors, peers, and partners. Because though the details you know will keep you up at night, the details you don't know will haunt you after you're done.

Simple is the goal. The extreme complexities of a logo design process can always be simplified. Seeing the big picture is easier when you can simply see the plan, directly and forthrightly.

Logo Evolution

FROM MONKEYS TO LOGO SAPIENS

Evolution and revolution. Two terms for change. Evolution is a sedate form of change. Like sap, it seeps along in thick, lazy stammers. Revolution bursts. It whips down and detonates like a twister, tossing tradition, cows, and silos high up into the storm clouds.

Revolutionary logos are effective at hailing mergers or marking the complete renovation of a damaged brand. If a company experiences major change, it makes sense that the brand and logo follow suit. A revolutionary logo is capable of altering the audience's perception of the entire brand. It should grab attention and make a definite statement about the brand's future direction.

Sometimes, however, it is better to evolve. Evolve a logo if the brand is evolving. Pretty easy to remember, but it's a bit tricky to actually pull off. Evolutionary change is subtle, but if it is so minor that it goes unnoticed, it misses the point.

Logo change is a great opportunity to gain attention and renew enthusiasm about the brand. It can signal a bright future and reflect on where the organization is going, while respecting the brand's past. It can be used to energize the client's employees, from sales staff to management to truck drivers, if employees see results at the daily level. Change can be as simple as improving morale by refreshing the corporate fleet vehicles. Give the client's sales staff a reason to reintroduce themselves to past prospects and clients by signaling organizational change; they'll likely turn it into fiscal results for themselves and the organization. Change, if managed to your client's advantage, can energize and stimulate profit.

Evolutionary change can border on revolutionary. The change to the Wedgwood logo is significant from most perspectives. The connection between the old and new type is minimal, but the icon change is a major leap forward. THE PARTNERS

There are smart logos, and there are street-smart logos. The true test of any refinement is when the package joins the real world. The Wedgwood logo design hits High Street with modern appeal. THE PARTNERS

NURTURING GREATNESS: A ROLLING LOGO GATHERS NO MOSS

Every generation has its collection of bright starlets. Out of those, a handful of true legends emerge. They separate from the pack, meeting changing times with a fresh look while staying true to their essential beings. Is your logo a great one? Does it adapt with the times? As time passes, it's inevitable that associations get pegged onto your logo, for better or worse. And, as new mediums manifest, your logo design must not only deal with them but also must adjust to take full advantage of ever-changing surroundings.

Context changes for many reasons and can dramatically alter the logo's meaning. When the Nazis rose to power, the swastika, which had been a positive symbol in Asian, Native American, and Norse cultures for thousands of years, took on political connotations virtually overnight. The swastika is forever disfigured because the context surrounding it is as well.

Imagine if you were charged with evolving a symbol that was highly charged with negative connotations. How would you evolve the logo of a sullied company like a WorldCom or Enron to grow beyond public scandal? First, it's important to consider what is worth keeping and what should be thrown out. Approach the editing process by asking how people relate to certain components such as color, shape, and type treatment.

Then consider where the meaning manifests itself. Also, consider that changing strongly held meaning is expensive and takes time. Adopting a completely new look can be much less expensive and time-consuming for you and the client.

With any logo change, it's important to respect the equities that exist within the design. Start by understanding why the designer created it in the way he or she did. Changes to powerful equities can affect the core business if important audiences no longer identify with the brand as they did before the change.

Be sure you understand the equities that already exist in color, shape, and type or relationships between these three. Try to understand the components that are most identified by audiences and what makes the logo memorable. When refining a logo, tread carefully around equities and test results if the changes are significant enough. Although it may seem like a good idea to simplify a logo design or change it to convey a stronger metaphor, these changes may be overshadowed by what they do to existing equities. The best way to proceed is to continually look back at what was, to see how far you've come. When the distance is too far, step back. If you're not sure, test it with audiences who can understand the need for change and respect the nuances of the change.

Byerly's gourmet grocery chain in Minnesota, USA, enjoys a long history of devoted followers who like the brand just the way it's always been. But things change. The new logo retains loyal customers and attracts new ones. CAPSULE

The new logo now set in context makes a contribution to the communication device. However, most consumers never consciously notice evolutionary change. That is often the idea.

REFINEMENTS: SACRIFICE YOUR EGO AT THE ALTER

Refinements are not just a part of the business. They are what the business is all about. You are helping the client change his or her business, by either defining or redefining the brand. When clients want refinements—oh, and they will—don't take it personally. Instead, see where the client is coming from and understand how the brand is changing.

There are five principal reasons for a brand change. They include merger and acquisition, name change, revitalization, organizational change, and functional malfunction. Often, a brand goes through several or all of these stages simultaneously. It is good to differentiate between them, because doing so will give you an idea as to what truly is the client's overall objective.

During a brand merger, two brands fuse to create a larger, third brand. The design is thus a graphic integration of the two former logos or the design of a completely new logo to embody the newly created entity. The logo design takes center stage. It's the symbol for the uniting brands.

Name change occurs for several reasons. Sometimes a perfectly nice word in one language is a very bad word in another. A new name also might be due to changing contexts that alter the meaning of the name. Or the change may be due to an internal company change. Whatever the reason, the logo design is the visual translation of the name and should help connect the new name to the brand.

Brand revitalization is usually driven by changes in the surrounding industry or cultures. Industries can change quickly and can make a mature logo appear tired. Revitalization can breathe new life into the brand and signal fresh energy to important audiences, both internal and external.

Organizational change is a new brand direction. It is a core change that often takes place when the brand is entering a new global or domestic market. This kind of change requires significant resources and entails significant risk. It also requires a signal to the internal and external community that change is flowing outward from within the organization. A logo refinement signals this new direction. It is a rally point for internal audiences to begin the effort to set a new course.

In some cases, logos change not because the organization changed but because the logo just never really worked well in the first place. There is no special term for that. It's a common problem, especially among small-business clients. Startups with small budgets often initially invest little in the logo. As the business grows and becomes more sophisticated, a new logo suits the business better.

JOHN DEERE

1876

1912

1936

1937

1950

1956

1968

The evolution of the John Deere logo exemplifies change on a number of levels. Most notably, the logo is tailored to fit international audiences and is stylistically simplified. DEERE & COMPANY

Steward the Design Process

ONE PART MAGIC, ONE PART SAUSAGE

A lot of odd metaphors describe the inside of the creative process. Some people compare the creative process to the inside of a sausage factory. Others compare it to magic. Sausages are a bit too processed, magic is a bit too undisciplined. Neither represents exactly what the creative process is all about.

The challenge of any creative process lies in not getting discouraged or settling when ideas aren't flowing quickly. Sometimes it happens right away. Other times it seems to take an eternity. Often the problem is lack of inspiration. For instance, coming up with a memorable logo design for a name that is boring, descriptive, and five words long can be endlessly challenging. Coming up with a design for a product with a name like YANK can be less challenging, because the name is energetic, vivid, and unique. The better the inputs, the less time the creative process should take, and the better the output on the other side.

Managing a process with so many variables sounds about as easy as trapping excited worms in a can. It's definitely not for the faint of heart. It helps to find an approach that suits you. Some state the problem and ask for solutions. Others give creatives the facts and see what happens. However you approach it, keep your team inspired. Most problems have obvious solutions; eliminate those in advance. This sometimes creates constraints, which is good. Time, budget, and other parameters can also add constraints and can serve as tremendous motivation to achieving creative output.

These are some real, well-meaning quotes from clients who were attempting to keep the design process on track.

"Are you sure we couldn't use something that looks kind of like Disney's logo?"

"Can you add a drop shadow or a cool bevel to the logo?"

"I like this logo, but let me take it home and show my wife. She's the artist in the family."

"We'd like to run a contest where our employees come up with the design for our logo."

"I'd like to be able to see my logo from an airplane."

"Could you match the logo color to my bedroom walls?"

"I love them all…can you combine concept one and two with the type of concept three?"

"Can we put these logo designs in the Student Union for everyone to vote?"

THE ARMANI SUIT WITH A BLACK TIE, THE PLATE MAIL ENGLISH ARMOR, AND THE LEATHER CHAPS WITH A TEN-GALLON HAT. FROM LEATHER TO STEEL TO THREADS, FROM TOP TO BOTTOM AND SIDE-TO-SIDE, EACH PACKAGES AN IMAGE IN YOUR MIND.

Types, Materials, and Faces

From stock types of packages such as clamshells, bottles, cans, flexible bags, boxes, and tubes to an unimaginable number of unique types and hybrids, the possibilities reach farther than most people can imagine. Types of packages are constrained only by the current collective imagination of the global creative community.

A similar idea applies to materials used to leverage packaging design. Each material on its own has attributes such as weight, structure, strength, permeability, texture, colors, and many other aspects that either contribute to or contrast with the product being packaged.

Category conventions, manufacturability, and basic economics will drive much of the material decisions. This is the reason we seldom, if ever, see bread packaged in aluminum or peanut butter in polymer bags. The real contribution packaging materials can make is in the creative use of materials in between these examples. When a vodka bottle needs to feel just right in the hands of a bartender, or the rubber on the base creates the feeling of the super-premium vodka Effen.

The multitude of faces a package contains offers the opportunity to tell a dimensional story about the brand. Just following conventions would likely lead to the same information on the back of a package organized in much the same way. This might be interesting to a socialist engineer, but the rest of the world craves variety. The other faces of a package set a stage for showcasing the brand's ability to prove its uniqueness.

Package Types

PLEASE DON'T TYPECAST MY PACKAGE

Carton, box, tube, bottle, can, bag, clamshell, blister, label, and hybrids—walk around a superstore and packaging types start to categorize themselves. Walk a little further and you start to notice patterns in each aisle or category. And then just a bit further until you start seeing the rogue products, those that are packaged in a manner entirely different than the existing category patterns. And then there are those that combine types of packages to create new concepts of how a package type should function.

Bear Naked granola cereals in stand-up resealable bags. Frozen orange juice in a rectangular jug that you refrigerate for a few hours before use. Honey that comes in a beehive-shaped plastic bottle from Granja San Francisco of Barcelona, Spain.

Packages are in every crevice of our lives and can either complicate or simplify our lives.

Gourmet Garden parsley-herb blend in a plastic tube. All examples of packages that take an unconventional approach to their package type and offer a glimpse into how a new product can set itself apart on the shelf.

Now step into someone's home and you can see a package doing a hard day's work. Type of package can be heavily influenced by the context of use. If your package shows up on a pantry shelf and requires users to continually reseal the bag inside the box, they'll most likely look elsewhere for a similar product. Studies have shown that a vast majority of consumers are none too organized. We strive to be more organized but have limits on time, resources, and energy that keep us from reaching organization utopia.

Package types offer a variety of options that should be considered for the impact in the manufacturing line, distribution channel, retail environment, and finally, inside the consumption context.

Naked stock packages. There are many stock options available from a variety of packaging sources. This selection came from Comp24: www.comp24.com. Walk around your local retailer and you'll find many more examples of stock packages to source.

CAPSULE

Material Options

YES, MADONNA, WE DO LIVE IN A MATERIAL WORLD

Paper, plastic, glass, leather, fake fur, foam, cork, metal, wood, textiles, rubber, composites, and new materials are being developed every day. The possibilities are endless, intriguing, and sometimes a little scary.

What does it feel like to pick up a small wooden box? What is the message associated with each of the materials you use? If the medium is vital to conveying the message, paraphrasing from our studious Marshall McLuhan, the material used impacts your message. An area where packaging designers dive deep into the

abyss of possibilities is material, as it is derived from many sources, locations, and manufacturers.

Materials are most commonly paired with certain package types: Corrugated fiberboard boxes, glass bottles, and aluminum cans are classic examples. This is where the design mind can start reformulating to have corrugated plastic boxes, aluminum bottles, or even plastic cans. Start blending materials and creating hybrid combinations, and you may find some interesting results.

Ever have the moment when something makes you say, "I wish I'd thought of that"? TwentyFour Wine has a rubber band label, a unique material that keeps the bottle from slipping in your hand. Yeah, me too.

STUDIOBENBEN

Hugo Boss: Men's Skin product line is designed to feel like a German engineered automobile, something most men can't resist. Although the materials give it a sleek look, the full experience waits until it's in the hands of the consumer.

WEBB SCARLETT DEVLAM

Cabo Uno was made famous by the former Van Halen front man Sammy Hagar. Wood, leather, lead-free crystal, and one amazing liquid. Combined you can find it for $250 (£153). Materials blended like this add up to a genuinely unique experience.

MEAT AND POTATOES, INC.

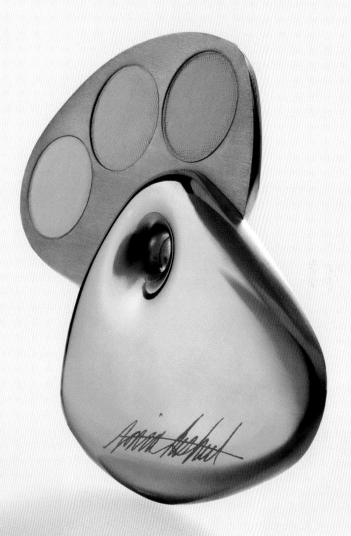

Everyday materials in unexpected contexts can provide a unique experience. This Sonia Kashuk design for fragrance packaging includes two products: a solid compact and a liquid bottle. The result is a product you can personalize to your individual preference. The bottle, if it can be called such, is made from aluminum to create a tactile sensation.

HARRY ALLEN & ASSOCIATES

MATERIAL OPTIONS

Within each of the aforementioned categories (glass, plastic, etc) there are many permutations and variations. The variations offer details like textured or heat-sensitive plastics or nonslip rubber or extra sticky rubber. Each detail can offer another element to build on the experience of the product and the package.

Keeping up on new materials can be done online (www.materialconnexion.com) or through other material sources in industrial design circles. Get samples, keep them around the office, and buy things you find that incorporate creative materials. Organize the materials by weight, feel, cost, and any other parameter that is important to your design process. You'll be surprised how oftentimes just having a unusual material nearby will lead to its being used in a package design.

KU-GREEN PACKAGING
Molded fiber packaging that uses tapioca starch. This patented composition incorporates nominally 90 percent cassava starch, 10 percent plant fibers, and a small amount of food-grade additives. As it is temporary in design, it's a great option for single-use food packaging, home delivery meals, outdoor food fairs, fast food restaurants, or catering packages.

BARK CLOTH
Moldable flexible surfaces manufactured from tree bark. Taken from Ugandan ficus trees, the material is transformed by mechanical deformation into a soft, flexible textile (like sheets) that has mechanical strength and good abrasion resistance. A beautiful and decorative accent material for luxury products of many forms.

NATURAL PLASTIC BY METABOLIX
Polyhydroxyalkanoate is the name for polymers that are produced from natural resources using a process of fermentation from natural sugars and oils. A possible replacement for many plastics used in injection-molded plastics and thermoforming situations. In other words, a more disposable package for disposable packages.

BIOXO BY CASCADE
Degradable polystyrene foam-molded parts designed to degrade in three years versus the hundred years for traditional polystyrene. Spend some time atop your local landfill and consider what it would be like if we had this thirty years ago. Possible uses include anything you've packaged with polystyrene in the past and any products where three years isn't an issue.

MEDGUARD BY COOLEY GROUP

Highly durable, woven or felted poly-ester is an alternative to PVC that can be incinerated without emitting toxic fumes. Useful for packages you know have or will have a high likelihood of being incinerated or used as fuel for someone's fire.

DEGRADABLE PLASTICS BY D2W

Imaging a time delay on the degrad-ing of the plastic bag designed for a bread company. How about eighteen months? The best part is that these polyethylene and polypropylene plastics don't need special conditions; just add air. The range of possible applications is endless—limited only by our collective imagination.

BIO PDO BY PIONEER AND TATE & LYLE

Fossil fuels are renewable; it just takes a mere hundred-plus years to produce more. Corn-based polymers have the benefit of less than one year to renew. Bio PDO is a polymer that uses 40 percent less energy to produce and re-duces greenhouse gas emissions by 20 percent. Applications are as vast as the number of packages that use plastics.

EARTHSHELL

Food-safe, biodegradable foam laminate packaging materials. Created by combin-ing potato starch, corn, limestone, and a bit of recycled fiber, which is then heat-pressed into shape. Immediate ap-plications include disposable meals and fast food; going forward, applications expand to many food categories.

CEREPLAST

This blended polyactic acid plastic comes from a variety of biodegradable ingredi-ents that keep the cost low and the ver-satility high. There are currently ten resin formulas that are optimized for injection molding, blow molding, thermoforming, and extrusion. This is an amazing material option for disposable and other packages in need of a balance between protection and environmental responsibility.

ABS / POM / PP BY KARELINE OF SWEDEN

All injection moldable resins that contain a large portion of natural fibers. Each has unique properties and applications. For instance, the polystyrene-based composites have a lovely surface quality that would add interesting personality to jewelry, cosmetics, or other beauty products.

GARDEN GREETINGS BY BOTANICAL PAPERWORKS

Looking to plant your package in consum-ers' minds and their backyards? Botanical Paperworks has paper products with embedded seeds. A number of socially responsible products—and certainly chil-dren's products—could benefit from this feel-good, earth-friendly feature.

INNOVIA FILMS

Heat sealable and biodegradable can be a tough marriage. Innovia Films pull it off by using 95 to 100 percent regenerated wood pulp. Biodegradable and worthy of your backyard compost heap, this mate-rial is terrific for food, household items, and personal care products.

SHEEP POO PAPER BY CREATIVE PAPER WALES

Not to be confused with paper made from elephant dung or reindeer droppings, this is Sheep Poo Paper from Wales, where they know their sheep. Forget your first worry: the odor has been eliminated with-out using intense chemicals. Sheep Poo Fiber from sheep with plenty of fiber is a great material for anything with a sense of humor and any clothing made from wool.

TERRASKIN

Drawing on the chemistry of eggshell material, this polymer film has the unique ability to slowly decompose into sand when exposed to sunlight. The material is microwavable, recyclable, and is FDA approved for fatty or dry food items. Obvious applications include any number of food items and perhaps any number of items that trace their origins to salt or calcium carbonate.

Front, Sides, Bottom, Top, and Back

SIX FACES, ONE PERSONALITY

Consider the salesperson metaphor again when looking at the faces on a package and the hierarchy of information on each. If it all looks exactly the same, then ask if you've just created the shallowest salesperson on the team. Procter & Gamble calls it the first moment of truth when the consumer picks up the package. Compare it to your initial handshake with the individual selling you a Mercedes. What does the first moment feel like when a consumer picks up your package? Does it feel heavy or light, soft or hard, flexible or rigid, sticky or slippery?

Then as you walk around the sales lot looking at gorgeous cars, what do you notice? Is the salesperson wearing ratty old sneakers under his suit? What does that mean? Does this individual smell like tanning beds? You know that smell. When the consumer turns your package over to one side,

the consistency in personality should be there, literally and visually. Does the back of the package communicate truths about the brand? If the consumer gets to the bottom of the package, will he or she find dirt or scuffs on it? Does it matter? Did your last Mercedes salesperson have mud on his shoes?

As consumers become more marketing savvy, they not only filter more, but they also know when something is being "sold" to them, even when it comes to package design. Considering this modern consumer, the package front must do its best to set the first sale and then be consistent for any repeat purchases. The other faces of the package must offer a look inside the brand, so the consumer can sense the truth of the brand from how it's designed to how the information is organized on each panel.

When designing a package, consider context and creatively discover ways the package can insert itself into the situation or conversation. Consider method home's dish soap package: It takes package design to the level of a piece of art that might not be as readily shoved beneath the sink.

The other faces often offer great opportunities for design because the consumer must commit to the package by holding it in order to spend time looking at the other faces. In other words, once you've got them engaged, how are you going to keep them connected? If the front of the package works to entice a consumer to pick it up, the rest of the package needs to get it into the cart.

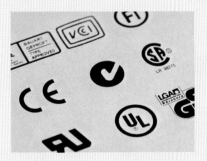

Regulations keep honest brands honest and keep dishonest brands on the run. Regulations are inherently not fun but always necessary.

CAPSULE

Standards and guidelines keep this part of a package design consistent across many product categories. Infusing a bit of brand personality requires a delicate touch.

TURNSTYLE

Barcode systems are nearly ubiquitous in nature, but with a bit of creativity and patience, the brand personality can be reflected in this part of the package.

CAPSULE

M.O.M. Knows Best

Maddy's Organic Meals (M.O.M.) is 100% certified organic. All of our meals are prepared shortly after harvest and then flash-frozen ensuring superior taste and nutritional value. Most ingredients are grown on Midwestern farms practicing sustainable farming methods. We keep it pure and simple. Easy for you and delectable for your baby. Healthy, palatable treasures created personally and lovingly just for your little treasure.

Heating Instructions

MICROWAVE : From Frozen, heat in 20 – 30 second intervals. Stir to distribute heat evenly, test temperature and serve with a smile.

STOVETOP : From Frozen, place cubes in saucepan over low heat.

THAWING : From Frozen, place in sealed container in the fridge and consume when reaches desired consistency. Use within 1 day of thawing.

*Always discard unused prepared meals that aren't fully consumed.

Ingredients

organic plums, water

maddy's organic meals™
maddysorganicmeals.com
©2007 Maddy's Organic Meals Chicago Illinois

BEST BEFORE :   LOT # :
MAY 2 1 2007   3 5

CERTIFIED ORGANIC BY MIDWEST ORGANIC SERVICES ASSOCIATION, INC. AVAILABLE : DO NOT PURCHASE IF OPEN OR TORN

* GRACIOUS GOODNESS *

FUNNEL: ERIC KASS: UTILITARIAN + COMMERCIAL + FINE: ART

FEATURES, BENEFITS, EMOTIONAL REWARDS

▶ Now that the shopper has picked up the package, how does your story continue? How do the features, benefits, and emotional rewards come to life on the package? This is where you go more in depth into why consumers should place the package in their basket, and where the body of your brand story comes to life and concludes with emotional and rational reasons to make the purchase.

MANDATORY ELEMENTS

▶ Depending on the category, country, region, or brand, mandatory elements vary. In the U.S. market, children's toys, food, alcohol, and electronics are subject to regulations meant to protect the consumer. The best place to start is with existing packages. Then regional, national, and international governmental authorities offer websites with exhaustive information on guidelines, regulations, and specific requirements.

INGREDIENTS AND INSTRUCTIONS

▶ When you can't see everything that's inside a particular product, it's good to know what you're buying. Inventory lists, checklists, and other specifics are comforting to anyone who may not fully understand the contents. The same goes for instructions: they can promote a clear benefit of one brand over another through simple installation and use instructions.

Weights, Measures, and Barcodes

STAND UP FOR STANDARDS

Locate something that requires standards and boundaries, and at a close distance you'll find those who bend the rules. Sure, bending is good, but knowing when you've broken them is better. The weights, measures, and barcodes required on a package are there for a legitimate and valuable purpose. For one, we don't carry a scale with us to the grocery. We also don't carry around measurement devices and it's difficult to analyze ingredients at home. Hence we have ingredient lists and other standards to guarantee a baseline of consistency by manufacturers for consumers.

Weights and measures (meant also to cover ingredient lists), nutritional facts, and all other highly functional language on the package provide consistency for consumers to compare their options. This means keeping to minimum type sizes and readability that favors grandma's eyes over little Billy's eyes. To the packaging world, this means regulation and additional time for government oversight. To the consumer world, this is another piece of trust they deposit in their bank account for that brand; break the trust and it gets withdrawn from the account. Do it too often and you'll find yourself with insufficient trust funds in that consumer's world.

Barcodes serve an obvious purpose at the checkout, but they also have an important role in inventory controls, just-in-time distribution, and many other essential phases in the product-to-market process. There, it's been said. Now how do we bend these unruly rules? Just like anything, bending without breaking is achieved through experimentation or knowing precisely where the boundaries

fall. With barcodes, be sure to do a scanner test numerous times if you're using a creative or constrained form of the standard barcode. The amount of time saved at the checkout counter and the fact that many retailers will fine the manufacturer for a barcode mishap should define your boundary. With ingredients, measurements, and weights, there are minimums, required formats, and placement prominence standards. Once you know these you can find ways to be creative with language and other aspects that don't have specific requirements.

Every once in a while, ask your team, "Are we being creative to be creative, or is there a greater purpose for our efforts?" You decide which philosophical path you'd like to take. If you need a reason, here are two: One, the more standard-looking something becomes, the less likely consumers will even notice it. Change it slightly and you create a small discovery for the individual handling the package. And two, never miss an opportunity to bring the brand personality to life.

There are plenty of creative ways to use the barcode as a
moment of discovery for the shopper. There are also ways
to make a barcode not work at all—a definite no-no.

ORCHESTRATING THE MARKETING MIX

Taking a product to market is one of the ultimate orchestrated events. There are reasons why some insist that the best marketing minds should be familiar with *The Art of War* by Sun Tzu. Taking a product from the thought bubble in the air to the final, successful product is akin to planning a war, hopefully without the death and destruction of real combat. The package is one element in a mix of communications materials with a variety of secondary objectives and a single primary objective: To get this product into the hands of people who will purchase it again and again. From an ad campaign (television, radio, or print) that hits on the key messages, emotional rewards, and key benefits, to a public relations

push to create buzz and have every noteworthy person talking about this new thingamajig, to a promotional plan with coupons, trial offers, and a variety of consumer and retailer incentives to push the product through the channel, to finally, an interactive presence so the brand can mingle with the virtual social world of our global online community—these elements all contribute to the success of the product.

Each of these elements requires a vast amount of specific knowledge and a director who can deftly pull it all together. Gone are the days when the "integrated" agency could serve as director or integrator. Today the management team on the client side needs to manage the brand and therefore has to serve as both director and integrator.

Once an orchestrated approach is understood, then beware of medium bias by the professionals you use or have as advisors. The best way to do this is to inquire into their backgrounds: If they come from advertising, they likely have a bias towards paid advertising in certain forms. If they come from public relations, from direct marketing, or from promotions, they will likely have the corresponding bias toward each of those professions. Now, ask yourself, if someone has a background in guerilla marketing, what then is the bias? It's probably that they prefer getting it done on a grass-roots level with a grab bag of creative tactics combining many of the available mediums. Not a bad bias, and this doesn't mean you avoid all ad people. It just means you should try to avoid having your promotions professionals doing advertising or your ad people doing packaging work. And if you need a good conductor to orchestrate it all, lean toward someone with an eclectic media background.

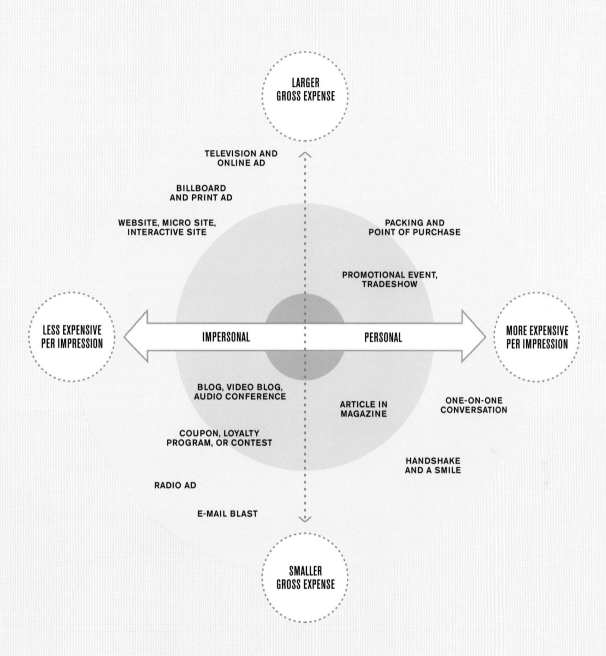

The tools you choose to use should vary by both gross expense of use, cost per impression, and effectiveness of the medium. Fully understand which mediums balance effectiveness (based on how you define it) and efficiency. And if you're not sure, experiment and keep score so you can repeat what works. All things being relative, this chart provides some perspective on the relationship between mediums and expense.

SOURCE: CAPSULE

Packaging Guidelines

THE FENCE ALONGSIDE THE ROAD TO SUCCESS

Spend days, nights, and weekends to create a unique-to-the-world package. It leaves your office, heads for the printer, packager, and then onto the shelf. Now what happens? It comes to life in ads, alongside other packages in product reviews, people talk about it, write about it, and the world starts to take notice. Now everyone wants to be attached to success and add it to their portfolio. The package starts to change. The line of products evolves as other designers find ways to "improve" the package even though it has seen amazing success. Change happens, whether good or bad, and it needs to be managed.

Setting up guidelines is much like designing a fence that runs along a dangerous stretch of road. The comparison extends to the type of car you're driving and whether you're insured to the extent you should be. If the process to create the package only cost a nominal amount, guidelines might not be necessary. If you're driving a new Bentley, you might want to build a strong fence to protect your metaphorical asset.

Now that you've decided to do it, what should be covered in a packaging guidelines document? Start with anything not covered in the corporate brand guidelines and everything important to the consistency of the package design. Start with colors, type, and art before moving to the proper use of the logo and all other intellectual property on the package. The depth of this document should correspond to the number of products in the line and the value of the brand as an asset of the organization.

ITEMS TO CONSIDER:

▸ Why following guidelines is important
▸ Brand attributes
▸ Audiences
▸ Packaging structure
▸ Imagery, illustration, and photography
▸ Language, tone, and style of copy
▸ Graphic structure and layout of packages
▸ Tools to use in packaging design process
▸ Contact person for answers to detailed questions

When the Honeywell brand is put in front of retail buyers, they know the product inside can be trusted to deliver on a promise. When consumers purchases a new product packaged under the Honeywell brand, they expect to trust the product. Consistent delivery with Honeywell means an innovative product and also means a package that delivers the same level of innovation and trust. Guidelines like these set the standard for anyone using the Honeywell brand.

CAPSULE

AIRCRAFT CARRIER IN TEN-FOOT (2.7 M) WAVES. PILOT APPROACHES AT 800 FEET (244 M). TAIL HOOK DOWN AND ARRESTER GEAR RESET. BREAK TURN AT 4G. WHEELS CONNECT; THE WIRE IS CAUGHT. 250 MPH (402 KM) TO DEAD STOP; SIX SECONDS. JUST AS COMPLEX WITH LESS PROBABILITY OF DEATH: GETTING A PRODUCT FROM A PRODUCER'S DOCK TO A RETAILER'S HOT SPOT.

From Producer to Shelf

What are your competitive advantages when it comes to getting a product from producer to shelf? The fewest products in the channel at any given point, the fewest human touches required, the least weight shipped, and finding your competitive advantage by how efficiently you manage the channel. Today's cost-accounting methods allow us to scrutinize every angle of the distribution channel and determine what parts are eating up margin. Then the ability to drill down into data affords managers amazing access to real-time data. Data, alas, is only a teaspoon in the recipe; creativity and leadership are two heaping cups each.

Creativity is the business term for intuitive design thinking. The sign of a creative mind in business is being able to float above the issues and see how one change in the channel affects any and all other aspects of your distribution. If eighty percent of the profit is in twenty percent of your customers, why do you still work with the other eighty percent? Because if you continue to apply the formula, how many customers would you have? One? How smart is it to use the eighty/twenty rule without considering other implications?

The value of leadership in channel management manifests in the ability to pull the trigger. If all decisions were black and white, the world wouldn't need leaders. Choices would be immediately apparent to anyone with enough book smarts to earn a bachelor's degree. Thankfully, our world is full of color and various shades of gray, and leadership rests on the ability to make decisions that are anything but black and white.

Detailed Delivery

FROM ALLIGATOR TO ZEBRA

Reaching the shelf is a process in itself. Depending on the category, the infinite number of details required to get a packaged product from point of origin to point of sale is astounding. The point A to point B metaphor just doesn't work unless you understand that points C to Z will require equal attention when distributing a packaged product.

If you're wondering how bad it could be, consider this: The way a fold on a box matches with the direction of the paper fiber determines whether the fold score looks cracked and unprofessional. These are the details that won't cause a product to fail on the shelf, but they will undoubtedly make it suffer in the hands of the retailer.

It may feel overwhelming, but when you break down everything, the process starts to feel manageable. Now consider the information flow running concurrently with the physical item in the distribution channel. It quickly turns overwhelming again until the idea of RFID (radio frequency identification) becomes a reality. It's the technological headache reducer you might consider as inventive and life-saving as aspirin.

STEPS OF THE EXECUTION PROCESS

Now you've done it. The brand strategy is defined. The name is identified and trademarked. The package concepts have been viewed and approved, and refinements have been made. The final package has been tested with consumers and they're ready to buy. The question out of their mouths is loud: "Where and when can I get it?" You are nowhere near the finish, but you are in the race. The appropriate phrase now is, "Bring it home."

Thinking of taking a new product to market? Feeling a bit intimidated? The good news arrives when you discover how many companies, firms, and individuals specialize in logistics/distribution.

The more you know as a designer about each step in the process, the better chance you'll have to influence the execution and delivery of your package. Leave it all up to someone else and you may be disappointed when your package shows up on the shelf. From the client's perspective, keeping the designer involved offers an eye for authenticity when the package and product hit each point in the process. Designers are problem solvers and visual thinkers. Their passion for quality will come through if they are intimately involved throughout the process.

Files to Printer / Proofs

▶ Digital files delivered

▶ Specification documents / Die lines

▶ List prints and color matching on materials

▶ Proofs reviewed by client team

▶ Proofs reviewed by design team

▶ Changes and review again until final

Client: The expense to make changes at this point is much less than when the product hits the shelf and your buyer doesn't like the typo.

Designer: Specifying every detail takes discipline and a fascination with details. You may not think you're responsible until the client comes back asking why you didn't have specific details for the printer. Now you are responsible.

Printing / Press Checks

▶ Material specs matched

▶ Quantities agreed on

▶ Color matching

▶ Photography / Illustration

▶ Match primary to secondary package colors

▶ Ink coverage / Faults in the plates or film

Client: You may not be obligated to attend all press checks, but you need to know who will sign the final approval. With responsibility comes cost, if you absolve yourself of responsibility you had better know to whom you've given it.

Designer: Now is a good time to go back to the original design approved by the client. Does the package reflect what they agreed to produce? Make changes now, don't wait until your client rejects it.

Delivery to Manufacturer / Packing Product

▶ Delivery timing

▶ Storage for inventory

▶ Integrated into manufacturing process

▶ Quality assurance checks / Safety sealing

▶ Just-in-time inventory

Client: Responsibility passes to other suppliers, but it doesn't mean you can't call upon the original designers to solve problems. Most designers are invested in getting a package all the way through the channel; so they have a good story to tell.

Designer: Although these are likely not your areas of expertise, the type of problem shouldn't be restricting. Use your intuitive nature and add valuable perspective to problems that arise.

Consolidating / Shipping

▶ Pallets

▶ Refrigeration / Climate controlled

▶ Truck sizes

▶ Locations

▶ Ship time / Unloading

▶ Pick, pack, and ship to stores

Client: Overlaying the brand meaning can impact the distribution channel. For instance, an environmentally responsible brand doesn't just consider the package; rather every aspect of the channel, product, and messaging.

Designer: Keeping true to the brand now can be challenging. This is where details and timing are essential while other factors fade. Help by keeping your eye on the original objectives.

Merchandising / Selling Through

▶ Unpacking

▶ Shelving

▶ Display adjustments

▶ Price adjustments

▶ Extra inventory

▶ Reporting

Client: Many of these details should fall into place if you've planned for product merchandising. If you don't have a plan, then pick up a magic wand at your local magic shop.

Designer: Checking in when the product is on the shelf can provide nuanced feedback on how well the original plan was executed.

SOURCE: CAPSULE

DESIGN MATTERS // IMPLEMENTING | PACKAGING

Review, Assess, Repeat
COMPLETE THE CIRCLE OF LIFE

The modern definition of insanity is endlessly repeating the same behaviors and expecting a different outcome. That said, change for the sake of change is not the answer either. The answer between these two options can be found on the back of most shampoo bottles—three simple steps.

After you've reached a milestone worthy of stopping for an assessment, review what's happened. Take an honest look at each piece of the process and identify the fault lines. If you don't see any and think you've achieved perfection, think again. Look at damaged product or packages. Look at returns and note what happened to your package. Devote some effort to observing how your package is being used, handled, and disposed of when it has reached the end of its useful life.

Assess the hot spots or what might be called "points of pain" coming from retailers or distributors. Not everything can be fixed at once, but fixing some issues may influence other problems. This is where net present value or internal rate of return can be factored in to determine what would result from changes to the package. Incremental change is the standard, but it all depends on how many issues come out of your assessment.

If your channel partners are important to your success, involving them in the process can build a stronger relationship for future product distribution. It can also give the partner more insight into how you do business. And, of course, you will likely be able to learn from their experience to take a leap beyond where the competitive set is lounging around at club complacent.

If your design team needs help seeing the changes, bring them closer to context so they can see how the package is being used and abused.

The visually intuitive design community can see it if it's there to be seen. What you may find is a design team capable of providing process improvement designs to surround a great package with exceptional distribution. At a minimum you'll gain a deeper appreciation for what the package has to endure from the road to the shelf.

Repeat what works and move away from behaviors that do not. Easier said than done, but there are ways to map out a logistics diagram and identify the weak points in the process. Just a simple diagram matched up with a discussion about where your package uses the most amount of energy, where it typically gets lost, or where it comes into contact with dangerous objects will light the way.

Even a priceless package is worthless if it never leaves the shipping box to feel the loving, yet greedy, grasp of a consumer.

PROCESS METHOD

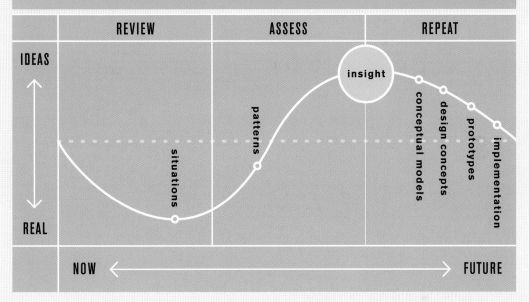

| REVIEW | ASSESS | REPEAT |

IDEAS

insight

conceptual models

design concepts

prototypes

implementation

patterns

situations

REAL

NOW ← → FUTURE

Seeing the finish line and working with that in mind is one trick. Seeing the next starting line gives an entirely new perspective on how iterative the process needs to be. If you're finished, you're done. If you're building an exceptional brand, you're never done.

SOURCE: CAPSULE

PENS FROM 1970, HARD CANDIES IN AND OUT OF THEIR WRAPPERS, AN OVERUSED LINT BRUSH, AND AN OLD CALCULATOR MISSING THE NUMBER TWO. THE FIRST REFERENCE POINT FOR ANYTHING LOST AND ALL THINGS HANDY. IT IS THE MOST RESOURCE-PACKED SPACE IN OUR LIVES, AND IT HUMBLY GOES BY THE NAME "JUNK DRAWER."

The Junk Drawer of Knowledge

When was the last time you dug into your junk drawer? Spend some in time there and you might find some surprising gems. Few of us go to our junk drawer seeking inspiration but we dip in often. When you need to get something done or you've lost something, this is usually the first place you look. Like the reference section of a library, it may not be beautiful or exciting, but it is brimming with helpful information. For our part, we have created this section to provide you with important reference points when you're deep into a packaging project. This is where you find the disciplines, professions, and requirements surrounding smart package design, including language translation, intellectual property, government agencies, and a few other parties interested in the safety and security of the person on the final receiving end of your package design.

Government regulations on the package of products touch on everything from fraudulent products to trademark infringements to the words required on a package entering another country. Languages can have governmental requirements but often the translation of meaning is more important to the success or failure of a package design. It is essential to understand, translate, and adapt to the meaning of language.

Intellectual property laws protect the soft goods like trademarks, copyrights, and patents in the same way that an outer box protects a package during delivery.

Created, expanded, and refined over time, this is the junk drawer that offers important artifacts of knowledge for that occasion when it's most needed.

IT'S 2015: DO YOU KNOW HOW YOUR COMPANY IS PERFORMING? PREDICTING THE FUTURE IS LIKE FORECASTING THE WEATHER. YOU THINK YOU KNOW WHAT'S GOING TO HAPPEN–THEN IT DOESN'T. UNFORESEEN CIRCUMSTANCES AND NONEVALUATED RISKS ARE INHERENT COMPONENTS OF DOING BUSINESS. BUT BY PROPERLY IMPLEMENTING YOUR PORTFOLIO AND SELF-PROMOTIONS, YOU CAN HELP USHER IN A PROMISING TOMORROW.

Schedule and Budget

Scheduling time to create a portfolio is probably the biggest challenge designers face because time is money. It's time to determine the resources it may require to create your portfolio or self-promotion. How much time can be allocated to developing your portfolio? What is your budget? Remember, you have to spend money to make money.

Look for the most cost-effective avenue for your portfolio development. List all of the methods and materials you would like to use within your portfolio. Break down the costs of each in terms of creating and implementing these materials.

Depending on your workload, formal portfolios, such as capabilities brochures, may be updated annually. Employability portfolios, aimed at landing a job or an internship, might be created throughout the year, and modified for a particular audience.

Utilizing a solid marketing plan, which includes a detailed schedule of upcoming self-promotions and direct-mail campaigns, can further ensure that the schedule, timelines, and budget parameters are being met.

Once you determine the approach you want to take in scheduling your portfolio distribution and self-promotion campaign, you can turn your attention to deciding how to promote yourself and to whom (that's where that handy-dandy database comes in).

According to the U.S. Small Business Administration, "Because marketing needs and costs vary widely, there are no simple rules for determining what your marketing budget should be. A popular method with small business owners is to allocate a small percentage of gross sales for the most recent year. This usually amounts to about two percent for an existing business."

At Minneapolis-based Capsule, creating, marketing, and distributing the firm's self-promotions, which include eblasts, portfolio presentation materials, and holiday promotions, are typically allocated 5 to 10 percent of the firm's revenues each year.

And while you certainly don't want to bombard your designated audience with all-too-frequent promotions, you want to make sure you avoid the adage, "Out of sight, out of mind." Blogs, eblasts, and newsletters can ensure that you remain "front and center." Determine what your clients and prospects positively respond to. For some, it may be graphic-filled eblasts, for others it may be a high-end portfolio brochure, mailed in a contemporary, costly vellum envelope. Whatever the method, choose an appropriate timetable for distribution.

TYPE	FREQUENCY			
	Weekly	Twice a Month	Montly	Annually
Eblast		×		
Postcard			×	
Newsletter			×	
Portfolio/brochure				×
Holiday promotion				×
Website update			×	
Interactive portfolio CD				×
Blog	×			

► *A translucent frosted glass portfolio features Organic Grid's logo identity etched into the glass cover. A screw-post binding system makes it easy to swap individual printed samples of the firm's work based on a particular client and their immediate needs.*

ORGANIC GRID

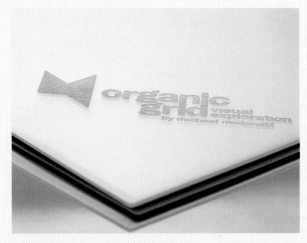

Presenting Your Portfolio

IT'S TIME FOR THE SHOWCASE SHOWDOWN

Bring your personality but check your attitude with the doorman. This is the time to show your confidence, but keep far from arrogance if you want to find a receptive audience. There's nothing more humbling than walking into a situation, thinking you know everything and finding out you know nothing. Start from a state of knowing nothing and let your portfolio speak to how much you know. Gain knowledge from each situation and either apply it right away or investigate further and add new tidbits of knowledge in the next presentation.

Presenting is theater: You are the actor, your portfolio is a prop, and the setting is your stage. No detail should be left unconsidered. Your audience will notice everything, even if they never say a word. From a broken seam to a weak piece of work, consider what they will see and what it will mean about you.

Now that you get the metaphor, put it to work. What happens if you spend the first 45 minutes of your hour talking, asking questions, creating some desire to see your portfolio before showing it? All the time leaving it on the table. Build drama instead of doing a portfolio "purge" on the table, putting it all out in front of your audience in the first 5 minutes. Not good theater.

Your portfolio becomes slightly less important if you consider the theatrical approach. Details, like where are your hands and eyes, are two critical pieces of any human communication. Do you let the audience touch your work? Do you create exclusivity by handling each piece with two hands? Consider the moments and you might find yourself spending some time at the theater to get some ideas. Avoid the Greek tragedies.

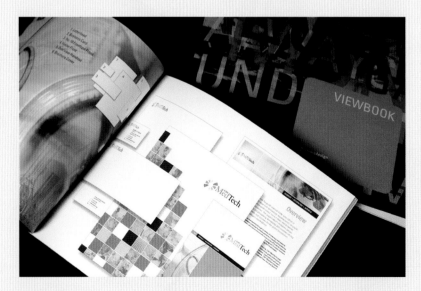

◄► *The StressDesign viewbook is used as an introductory piece for new and prospective clients. The sixty-page book is a showcase of the three main specialty areas at StressDesign: print, publication, and Web design. In order to present their portfolio of work properly, StressDesign clearly identifies the work completed and the overview of the project scope and solution.*

The firm also offers a smaller eight-page version of the viewbook. It is used as a stand-alone publication for new and prospective clients or as a leave-behind at job fairs or speaking events.

WHAT TO INCLUDE

When presenting your portfolio, be sure to include the who, what, how, and why:

··· Who was the client?

··· What was the "problem" that you were hired to solve?

··· How did you go about solving it?

··· Why did you use the design methodology that you did?

Never stumble on the basics. Who is your audience? What's important to them? Who was the client? What problems have you solved? How did you do it? Why did you take a particular approach? What were the results? Simple questions you can outline about each piece of work you are presenting.

Know the answers in your heart, and your passion for the work will come through. If you don't know, say so. Bluffing has many more risks than saying "I don't know."

▲ The well-defined elements throughout the viewbook offer readers a clear understanding of the approach StressDesign utilized with each profiled project.

Digital vs. Personal

WHAT'S YOUR STYLE?

As Michael Eckersley, principal at Human Centered, a U.S.-based team of affiliated designers, social scientists, and planners, explains, most design today involves plenty of teamwork; the portfolio presentation must be descriptive of that process and credit others on the project. He believes that portfolios today are most useful and accessible online. "Imagery must be contextualized as to project profile, role descriptions, and project outcomes," Eckersley says. "Effective portfolios I deal with today involve video and storytelling, not simply static imagery."

Dale Bohnert, manager of design and communications for 3M Brand Identity at 3M in St. Paul, Minnesota, says that while portfolio presentations have become more electronic or virtual in nature, he prefers portfolio presentations in person, rather than via email.

"The digital age has made it all too easy, too impersonal," Bohnert says. "I find it most appealing when someone says, 'Let's get together and think.' Sharpie markers and napkins—particularly on-the-fly—still impress me more than PDFs."

That said, strategic design, service design, and interaction design require different kinds of portfolio representation than traditional portfolios—say, for graphic design, industrial design, or interior design. "The purpose of the portfolio is simply to rapidly demonstrate competency and quality of creative thinking," Eckersley says. "It shouldn't be lorded over and turned into the equivalent of a fetish object. The portfolio should be shown and put away—not obsessed over. Then the conversation should be steered toward what the client or employer is looking for in the future—not what work has been done in the past in different situations, for different people."

Ask the Experts

Brett Lovelady, chief instigator at Astro Studios in San Francisco, sees his fair share of designers' portfolios cross his desk. So how do today's portfolios need to function to help land that "oh-so-perfect" job?

"I believe portfolios have taken on a stronger 'personal branding' approach," Lovelady says. "Design yourself a logo or 'logoize' your name with colors to create a more commercial 'you.' The portfolios should be full of process and philosophies in addition to polished results. Create a

Lovelady says that entertainment plays a large role in portfolios, including big, memorable ideas, headlines, unique bios, images, or videos with music.

book, brochure, mailer, website, reel (or some combination if not all), send them out, email a link or PDF, blog or tweet about all of it. Just make it about you, your personality, your point of view, and include your work samples, of course."

"But remember, I don't want to relive your whole project with you," Lovelady says. "Just give me the big ideas and insights—maybe a quirky inspiration image or statement along the way."

At Astro Studios, personal PDFs are appreciated, as are personal websites. Hosted portfolios are also helpful—just as long as they are easy to navigate and not overly "motion" indulgent. "I don't like just slide shows on image sites," Lovelady says. "This seems cheap and less unique—but better than tattered books in most cases. Most importantly, your portfolio is your image-based calling card for instilling confidence in people. It's your insurance policy or pulpit of expertise giving people a sense of who you are, what you can do, what you like to do, and possibly what you can become."

▲ *The use of innovative, contemporary materials helps Bohnsack Design's portfolio book stand out from the crowd.*

BOHNSACK DESIGN

Distribution Dynamics

THE KNOCK ON THE DOOR

Formally defined, distribution of your portfolio or self-promotion is the method you use to get your piece into the hands of your designated audience.

Some people feel that you should never leave your portfolio behind at the conclusion of a meeting. Once you let go of your portfolio, you lose control of a key communication tool. Others believe that a portfolio should stand alone and speak for itself.

Depending on the size of your portfolio, you may want to leave a smaller capabilities brochure that captures the core components of your portfolio—something that is a strong advocate for you in your absence.

Do a little recon. Determine what your competitors are doing in the area of portfolio development. Keep tabs on their website content and learn of any innovative strategies you can utilize to keep ahead of the pack.

Pay attention to your database. Okay, so maybe you don't have a database. Get one. To build a fan base, you must build a database of people or companies who may be interested in who you are and what you have to offer. If you create a phenomenal portfolio mailer but send it to the wrong group of prospects, you have completely wasted your time (and money) and theirs. Ignorance is not bliss. It pays to do your homework. Clichés aside, your mailing list should be those people who believe in what you do.

◄▲► *Akar Studios is a Santa Monica–based multidisciplinary design studio specializing in retail, hospitality, and branding design. They have created a small-size brochure specifically for marketing the retail and restaurant design services of their studio. Displaying an array of projects encompassing bars, restaurants, and high-street retail, the portfolio brochure provides an overview of the expertise the studio offers potential clients.*

AKAR STUDIOS

Making Connections

GET OUT THERE AND NETWORK WITH THE MASSES

Marketing executives use it as a key tool for their success. Financial consultants use it to obtain new clients and often make it a key part of their overall business strategies. Brand management consultants see it as a necessary effort to expand their business. What is it? It's networking, and in the world of business, people network to help smooth out the potholes on the road to success.

Whether you are the owner of a small design firm or a global firm with offices worldwide, networking with

your portfolio in hand—or at least a mini portfolio—will give you greater leverage than those without it. Those who get out there and flaunt their stuff *have* the ability to gain notoriety among prospects and clients. Those who sit on the sidelines, waiting for someone to notice them, *have not* embraced a "go-get-'em" attitude that can mean the difference between success and failure.

While networking can be beneficial, how and with whom you network are vital to the success of your

self-promotion efforts. People tend to cluster together based on education, age, race, professional status, and more. The bottom line is that we tend to hang out with people who have experiences or perspectives similar to ours. Often, most of our friends and associates are friends and associates with each other as well. The problem with this is that when we surround ourselves with people who have similar contacts, it may be difficult to make connections with new people or the companies we desire to do business with.

◄▲ *This portfolio was sent to various design companies worldwide from Changzhi Lee, a student at Nanyang Tech University in Singapore who was seeking an internship. Because these companies had environmental sustainability as one of their key philosophies, a pop-up book made out of leftover paper was the statement behind the package design. In addition to the curriculum vitae, each package also includes a CD containing samples of Lee's design.*

CHANGZHI LEE

NETWORKING STRATEGIES

So what are some of the best networking techniques as they relate to portfolio design and development? Try some of these simple ways to network and see where it takes your business.

- **Make a good first impression.** Look good. If you look good, you sell good. Your appearance and attitude do make a big difference, and this is what people see first.

- **Evaluate your surroundings.** Attend an organization's events and interview existing members. Ask them what they like about being a member and their strategy for getting the most out of their membership. Also, assess what benefits—both tangible and intangible—you will receive for your membership and event fees.

- **Diversify, diversity, diversify.** You need breadth and depth. Participate in different kinds of groups.

- **Work on those referrals.** Referrals are, and will be for the foreseeable future, all about relationships. Whether they're relationships built online or face to face, they're still relationships. People refer people they know and trust. They won't regularly refer someone just because they're listed on a website—that's called advertising, not networking.

- **Don't oversell.** Bring business cards only. Don't come with brochures, pamphlets, and gimmicks. People don't want to carry these materials around with them. They will most likely throw them away or just set them down and forget to pick them back up.

- **Learn how to "work" meetings.** It's not called "net-sit" or "net-eat," it's called "network." Learn networking systems and techniques

that apply to the different kinds of organizations you attend.

- **Develop your contact spheres.** These are groups of business professionals who have a symbiotic or compatible, noncompetitive relationship with you. In any networking situation, look to make two or three solid contacts whom you can learn from—both from a personal and business perspective. Do not just hop from one person to the next trying to collect as many business cards as possible. That is counterproductive.

- **Create a feeling of trust.** Experts agree that the approach to networking must be about building relationships based on providing value and gaining the trust of others. It is not about getting immediate business. Not enough business owners realize this, and they go into networking with the mind-set of getting business instead of building relationships.

- **Know your goal.** Perhaps most important, understand that networking is more about farming than it is about hunting. It's about cultivating relationships that can lead to productive experiences in the future.

- **Look at whom you know.** Ask your colleagues how you can better promote their business and if they would feel comfortable promoting yours. Join forces with other industry players and host an event. By coming together and presenting to prospects, you will all be promoting your own businesses.

- **Be specific about referrals.** Identify specific people to whom you wish to be introduced. Personal introductions can open doors for you that would've otherwise remained closed. If you don't know the name of the manager of another business you wish to meet, find out—then ask specifically for a referral to that person.

- **Meet one on one.** To deepen the relationships within your network, meet with each person away from the general networking session, to dial up the focus of your networking efforts.

▲ *A streamlined, well-defined portfolio system provides a cohesive message to your prospects and clients. Subtract Studio De Creation is a creative studio encompassing a full range of creative and technical needs in one complete package. This complete package of experience is housed within a succinct folder design with individual case studies highlighting the studio's experience.*

SUBTRACT STUDIO DE CREATION

Measuring Your Success

IT'S A NUMBERS GAME

The phone rings, your email blings—all with messages from prospective clients asking to meet with you to learn more about your core competencies. Perhaps they are interested in rebranding their corporate communications system, or maybe they are simply looking for an updated website. Whatever the reason, when a potential client walks across your company's threshold, what's the likelihood their "browsing" will result in a sale? For many businesses, improving their close ratio is key to a successful future.

In the simplest terms, a close ratio is the number of sales that are booked in relation to the number of opportunities that are presented. For example, if ten potential clients walk into your office and listen to your sales pitch and only five of them purchase your services, then the close ratio would be 50 percent.

One thing we know from talking to consumers of creative services is that price alone is rarely the primary motivator in the purchasing decision—in many studies it ranks as low as ninth or tenth. That's true whether you're in a high-, medium-, or low-price niche. So whether you're selling high-end packaging design or discount websites, the purchasing decision is part of a complex formula rooted in how clients know and understand your company, and the products and services you offer in terms of both quality and confidence—all of which should be carefully incorporated into your portfolio and self-promotional materials.

You should also consider tapping into your existing client base—many of whom may be more valuable than you realize. The beautiful thing about having an accurate database of existing clients is that these people know other people. Assuming you offered a gratifying client experience, there is no reason that your old clients wouldn't refer your offering to potential new clients. Perhaps you send out a dedicated mailer to your account base that offers up a small gift for any new clients that they refer to your business. This will give you more visibility and more opportunity for success.

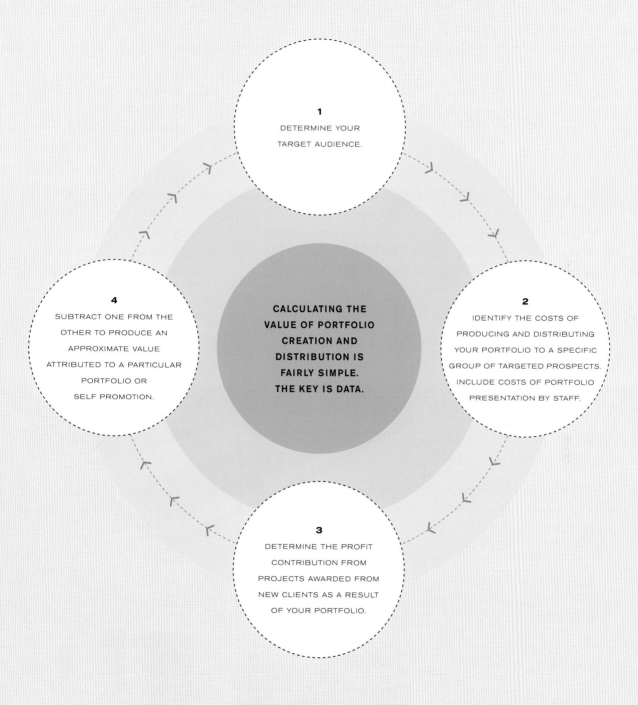

1

DETERMINE YOUR TARGET AUDIENCE.

2

IDENTIFY THE COSTS OF PRODUCING AND DISTRIBUTING YOUR PORTFOLIO TO A SPECIFIC GROUP OF TARGETED PROSPECTS. INCLUDE COSTS OF PORTFOLIO PRESENTATION BY STAFF.

3

DETERMINE THE PROFIT CONTRIBUTION FROM PROJECTS AWARDED FROM NEW CLIENTS AS A RESULT OF YOUR PORTFOLIO.

4

SUBTRACT ONE FROM THE OTHER TO PRODUCE AN APPROXIMATE VALUE ATTRIBUTED TO A PARTICULAR PORTFOLIO OR SELF PROMOTION.

CALCULATING THE VALUE OF PORTFOLIO CREATION AND DISTRIBUTION IS FAIRLY SIMPLE. THE KEY IS DATA.

Keep Them Coming Back for More

YOU GOT 'EM RIGHT WHERE YOU WANT 'EM

In the creative industry, it's all about getting people to remember your business, your products and services, and your brand. For many creative firms and individuals, portfolio design is the arena that puts the "big picture" perspective into focus and determines where a company takes and makes its future. It's the philosophy and core behind all business development for many creatives. With that said, more and more business owners are realizing the important role portfolios and self-promotions play in making immediate and lasting impressions on their bottom line.

While creating a solid portfolio and self-promotion program does not happen overnight, you can implement some simple techniques that will make immediate improvements to your clients' experience.

More and more creative professionals recognize that they need to make the portfolio experience as memorable as possible—to help them stand out from the crowd and compete with the big players. While many companies design great experiences, companies often lack the discipline to consistently execute them. To be successful, a company needs to define the experience, create the appropriate tools, train the staff to execute it, and measure its impact on the customer.

- **Create a memorable experience.** Creative professionals can make the experience memorable each time they visit your office or you present your portfolios by finding unique ways to roll out the red carpet, such as addressing each potential client by name, offering personalized parking if possible, and having a lovely room with coffee, water, and healthy snacks available for those waiting.

- **Commit to wow!** Creative firms can really stand out from the pack by coming up with strategies that will truly wow their potential clients and get them talking. Some ideas? Reserved parking, personalized gifts, overnight service, last-minute emergency service, personalized welcome signs for expected clients, and stress-release kits.

- **Partner with other suppliers.** Often clients are overwhelmed with the intricacies of purchasing creative services. Go beyond the business card table, partner with other suppliers, and be a resource for your customers for everything they could possibly need.

- **Survey former customers.** One of the best ways to improve your customer service is by surveying former clients. This means setting up a system to connect with customers and ask them two simple questions: What was your experience like? How can we improve our service? It can be done by phone, by mail, or online. The system produces a numerical rating you can use to measure how well your company is doing. It will also generate useful feedback about what you're doing well and what you need to change.

- **Write a handwritten thank-you note.** Creative professionals can mentally think through every little aspect of their client's experience and come up with ways to wow them at every turn.

- **Publish your customer service standards.** Make sure your employees and your customers know what your customer service standards are. Put them on wall posters, put them on the back of business cards—anywhere clients and employees will see them.

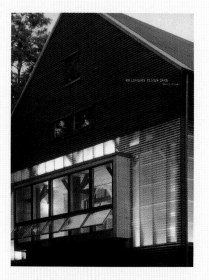

◄▼► *Willoughby Design utilizes two "lookbooks" to showcase the company's portfolio of work. The smaller lookbook is designed for first-time exchanges with potential new clients. The larger lookbook showcases the company's values, creative process, and the most relevant work. Each book is specifically edited to match a client's industry or particular needs. The modular format allows for continuous updating and customization.*
WILLOUGHBY DESIGN

The Quickest Ways to Kill a Sale

CAN'T SAY WE DIDN'T WARN YOU

Creative professionals are largely in charge of their own destiny. You've found the perfect niche within the industry, honed your creative skills, trained your employees, made your portfolio look perfect, invested in advertising, and are now ready for some serious sales. But sales mistakes can dramatically affect your bottom line. Here are some key mistakes to avoid during the portfolio presentation and sales process:

- **Not listening to a customer's needs.** Selling is more about listening than it is about talking. One of the inherent mistakes many creative professionals make is not listening to a client's request. Listening to and pinpointing exactly what the customer wants will help streamline the sales process and enhance your referral business.

- **Overselling.** We think the more a potential customer knows about a particular product or service, the more likely she will buy the product. In reality, though, information overload has the opposite effect: Instead of leading to a sale, it may lead to an exit—especially if a customer is overwhelmed with information.

- **Improper employee training.** Your best clients have formed an image in their minds of what you are, what you do, and how well you do it. But all of that can be quickly undone by a misguided employee. Your employees are the walking, talking billboards for your business. Every time someone in your company comes in contact with others—whether they are customers or vendors—he or she leaves a lasting impression of your company's brand on their minds. Be sure to train employees to conduct themselves in a manner consistent with your brand message and they will be goodwill ambassadors to your current and prospective clients.

- **Lack of follow-up communication.** One of the biggest mistakes creative agencies and individuals make is forgetting to communicate with their customers after the project has concluded. However, this is a key communication point and sales opportunity. Remember, your customers often spend a considerable amount of time and money with you—you owe them a "thank you" and you owe your company a chance to communicate with the client one more time.

After presenting your portfolio, take the time to write a handwritten thank you note. That's right, the good old-fashioned thank-you written on your company letterhead or personalized stationery. Be sure to thank your prospective client or employer for taking the time to review your portfolio. Don't waste time reiterating your exemplary talent and services. Rather, make it short, sweet, and to the point.

Again, thank them for the opportunity to present your portfolio and ask if they have any additional questions. The resulting conversation will give you a good idea if you made the cut. Of course, if you don't make it, ask why. Inquire about what your portfolio may be lacking and how it compared to others. Taking the initiative to improve your portfolio presentation will illustrate to a prospective client or employee that you take your portfolio seriously.

As Vince Lombardi said, "Some of us will do our jobs well and some will not, but we all will be judged by only one thing—the result."

If your prospect hasn't given you a timeline for getting back to you, give them a call about a week after your portfolio presentation. That way, your portfolio will still be fresh in their mind, and you won't appear desperate.

Keep developing your sales skills to ensure that you have done all that you can for your customer—your future depends on it.

Introduce yourself.

↓

Listen to prospective client's needs.

↓

Justify your experience.

↓

Show your credibility through visuals and testimonials.

↓

Discuss the specific project or job.

↓

Ask for the sale or job.

↓

Schedule the next steps.

↓

Send a thank-you note and repeat your request for the business or job.

CASE S

- BROCHURES
- LOGOS
- PACKAGING
- PORTFOLIOS

TUDIES

"IF YOU SIT IN THE MIDDLE OF THE ROAD, IT'S A SCARY PLACE TO BE. YOU GET RUN OVER." —PUM LEFEBURE, CREATIVE DIRECTOR AT DESIGN ARMY

DESIGN FIRM: GO WELSH (USA)

A Passion for Unique Portfolio Presentations

With dozens of projects featured in a wealth of different publications, Go Welsh has earned a reputation within the design community for creating innovative, inspiring branding and design initiatives for clients and for their own firm's promotional materials.

PLANNING

Go Welsh's main goal for their portfolio was to approach the design in a way that would allow them to cost-effectively create a series of themed promotional pieces. "We had talked about four-color offset printing but felt we'd be limited by production costs in terms of the final size (dimensions) and length (number of pages)," says Go Welsh founder Craig Welsh. "We really liked the idea of being able to work at a larger scale across many more pages than we'd realistically be able to afford on an ongoing basis with offset printing. We had also produced some newsprint-based pieces for a client and found that the tactile, low-grade quality of the paper and inks was a nice change from the slickened world of hi-def, screen-based media. It has an authenticity that's hard to find in other materials. It's the medium from which the masses used to get their news."

CREATING

According to Welsh, the most difficult task was to come up with a title for the publication. "We had many, many concepts we reviewed over the course of several weeks. However, every title we considered brought its own unique set of emotional and implicit messaging," Welsh says. "We didn't want the first issue to set a mood that would be challenging to address with future issues. So we finally started to seriously consider *Title* as the title with the ability to clearly theme each issue."

► *A treasure trove of sorts,* Title *01, the "Thanks" issue, was sent by Go Welsh to family, friends, clients, and prospects.*

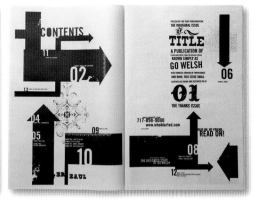

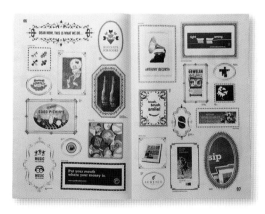
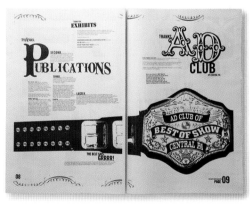

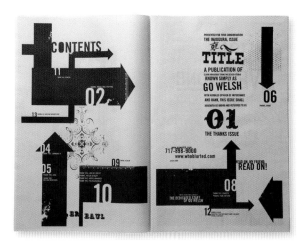

Title won, and the theme for the first issue was "The Thanks Issue." *Title* 02 was "The Giving Issue." The flexibility of theming is paramount, and the future issues in the works will include "The Alphabet Issue" and "The Contributor Issue."

Go Welsh also wanted to highlight the firm's writing capabilities in these promotions. "We're a design studio, which tends to make people think we only work with visual elements," Welsh says. "We expect our designers to also have solid writing skills, and *Title* has provided an outlet for writing. Each issue includes contributions from all of our staff, regardless of their role within the studio. The issues are truly expressions of everyone here. In fact, we had a high school intern contribute several elements to *Title* 02."

IMPLEMENTING

The goal of these newspaper-style portfolio pieces is to get people to stop and take notice. "To help aid in that, we do a few things beyond simply designing and printing each issue of *Title*," Welsh says. "First, we write all the addresses by hand. We have a total of about 900 addresses—our staff LOVES to do this. We like that it has a more personal feeling when it hits someone's desk, as so few pieces of mail are addressed by hand these days. Second, we create a rubber stamp that is applied to the outside of the envelope that is unique to each issue." The stamp for *Title* 01 read, "You Might Want to Open This in Private," and *Title* 02 included, "Give It Up for [arrow]" above the recipient's name.

Go Welsh sends *Title* about once a year, each issue costing about 25 cents to print. "We'd like to send them more frequently, but we've been busy with client work and we're so particular and picky with how we design *Title* that it usually takes a long period of time to complete," Welsh says. The firm sends issues to family, friends, clients, prospects, and pretty much anyone who asks for copies. After posting an image on their website of *Title* 02, they had people emailing from all over the United States and someone in London also requested to be on the mailing list. "We've also distributed several hundred copies at presentations we've given. They usually get grabbed up pretty quickly—funny how excited people get about newsprint."

Go Welsh has had two people call to talk about projects simply based on their reactions to the "Give It Up for…" stamp. "One has since turned into a new client," he says. "We also have a current client that has pinned the envelope to her office wall because she likes the "Give It Up for…" stamp above her name so much."

They also included a full-page puzzle in the last spread. There were 192 triangular shapes mixed up on the left side of the spread with a numbered grid on the right side of spread.

"We got this idea based on work from Norman Ives we had seen in an exhibit," Welsh says. "We like curious people and try to be curious about things when we work. We wanted to see if anyone would take the time to complete the puzzle. We thought it would only be fitting that 'The Giving Issue' of *Title* would include a prize for the first person to complete the puzzle. We set up a unique email address and waited. And waited. And waited. And around the thirtieth day we finally received an email from someone who had completed the puzzle. The reward for such curiosity was a brand new iPod."

The studio then posted an image of the completed puzzle on their website and began getting calls from other people who were frustrated that they hadn't taken the time to put the puzzle together. However, they also expressed similar reactions along the lines of "I should have known you would do something like that!"

"We had a client tell us a funny story about his teenagers arguing about who gets to sit in the front seat of the car," Welsh said. "Turns out his daughter had hopped in the front passenger seat, buckled in, and thought she had outwitted her brother. However, her brother had read through *Title* 02 and cut out the 'Calling Shotgun' coupon. He proceeded to knock on the front passenger window and held up the coupon to show his sister that he was now claiming shotgun. The dad had also read through *Title* 02 and knew what the coupon was declaring. Holding back laughter, he then honored the coupon and made the daughter get in the backseat so the son could have shotgun. The coupons have been much more fun than we anticipated."

◄▲► *Called* Title 02, *"The Giving Issue,"*
this self-promotion was distributed prior
to the 2008 holiday season. Go Welsh
reconfigured previous logo projects into gift
wrap patterns. The issue also included a
visual puzzle that, when completed, revealed
a hidden message with an email address
to claim a prize for the first person who
completed it.

THE CLIENT: THE WALTERS ART MUSEUM

DESIGN FIRM: PRINCIPLE

The Walters Art Museum

DESIGNING FOR THE RIGHT AUDIENCE

Sometimes the best way to kick off a project is by taking a hard look at its previous incarnation. When Principle started working with the Walters Art Museum on a brochure for its school programs, Allyson Lack, a partner at the design firm, studied the existing piece's primary colors and glossy paper. "It was very much what comes to mind when you think of young children," she says.

But for school programs, it's the teachers, not the students, who sign their classes up for outings at the Baltimore museum—a fact that meant the project's target audience consisted primarily of 25- to 40-year-old women. So Lack pitched an entirely different approach: "Let's make it more sophisticated." The resulting brochure feels more like a program handed out at the symphony than something found at a grade school.

The piece's white, uncoated paper gives it a refined feel, while the brown text and illustrations keep it soft. Interior pages pair copy about planning a visit with the gorgeous artwork that teachers and students might see at the museum. To make sure these rich, colorful paintings reproduced well, Principle chose a stochastic printing method—its randomized dot pattern results in a tighter image. The brochure also features stock line art, which Lack found to represent items in one of the museum's exhibits.

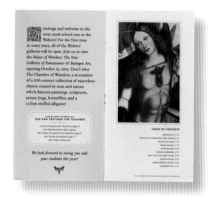

▲ *This brochure highlights school programs at the Walters Art Museum in Baltimore, Maryland. Since teachers make up the target audience, designers at Principle created a sophisticated—rather than kid-centric—design. Brown type gives this piece a warm feel without detracting from the gorgeous paintings.*

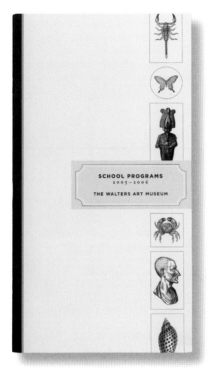

In the middle of the brochure, there is something just for students: a full-sized poster is folded and bound into the piece. Teachers can pull it out and hang it up in their classrooms for their students to enjoy. The poster is covered with line art that corresponds to objects at the Walters Art Museum, so it gives students something to get excited about before they step in the door.

▲► To give the brochure additional value, there's a full-size poster bound in the center. Teachers can take it out and hang it up in their classrooms to get students excited about visiting the museum. The front side of the poster features line art that corresponds with items students might see during a visit. On the back, they can read about each curiosity.

This piece went so well that Principle was also tapped to create a family guide for the museum. The new project needed to be equally fun and engaging for parents and their kids. After some brainstorming, the design team and museum staff settled on the idea of a deck of cards. This format makes a visit to the museum feel like a game designed for the whole family. A mom can hand a card or two to each of her kids—no fighting over a single brochure.

To keep things kid-friendly, Principle made the cards fairly large—8 $\frac{7}{8}$ x 5 $\frac{5}{8}$-inches (22.5 x 14.3 cm)—and printed them on sturdy 80 lb. stock. Each card features a different item for families to find in the museum and the entire set slips easily into a sleeve. There's also an introductory card in large type that explains how to use the deck, making the copy more accessible for young readers. Much like a deck of standard playing cards, rounded corners also give the set a friendly feel.

◄ *Each card features a different object for families to find together in the museum. To make them kid friendly, the cards are fairly large at 8 ⅞ x 5 ⅝ inches (22.5 x 14.3 cm) and printed on sturdy 80 lb. (36.28739 kg) stock.*

The outer sleeve was created from a lighter weight paper, so Lack needed to make sure the glue used to hold it together wouldn't seep through. It also features a thumb notch at the top for ease of use, which also serves as a subtle branding element with the Walters logo showing through from the top card. The front features a magnifying glass, which hints at the scavenger hunt nature of the cards inside.

For the cards themselves, Principle kept things bright and fun, choosing a different color for each one. These highlight a picture of an artifact on the front side along with a brief description of the item. The back includes additional details about the art along with questions for a family to discuss together. This approach allows different age groups to enjoy the piece together. Small children can simply look for the object in the picture, while older kids can read the copy and initiate discussions with their parents.

GO TO THE CHARLES ST. BUILDING,
LEVEL 2, 18TH- & 19TH-CENTURY TREASURY

FABERGÉ EGG

Given as an Easter gift to the former Czarina *(tzar-e-na)* or queen, of Russia by her son Nicholas II, this egg is decorated with gold and pearls and is one of only 56 imperial Easter eggs. It opens to reveal a perfect miniature replica of a royal palace in Russia.

THE FAMILY GUIDE
── FABERGÉ EGG ──

👁 **look**

As part of a family tradition, the Czar *(zar)* or king, had an artist create an egg shaped gift to give both his mother and his wife at Easter. See if you can find the cannon, the flag, the statue, and the trees. Look for other things you recognize and point them out to the people with you.

imagine 💬

Discuss some of your own family traditions with the people who are with you. For what occasions do you give gifts to friends and family members? What kind of surprise would you give as a gift? Why?

You act as an artist when you create something to give to another. You have the choice to make it large or small. Which is more difficult to create? Why do you say that?

🔍 **discover**

Decorated eggs have been a symbol of life and spring since ancient times. Ancient Egyptians and Persians dyed eggs in spring colors and gave them to friends as gifts.

→ **COLLECTION CONNECTION** ←

Henry Walters gave his entire collection of art to the city of Baltimore when he died. Everything in this museum should be considered a gift to the citizens of the city by Mr. Walters.

◄ *"Even if little kids can't read yet, they can still hold up a bright yellow card and look for a Fabergé egg," says Allyson Lack, a partner at Principle. For older children, the back of each card gives information about the item and questions to talk about with parents. Large, legible type keeps things accessible for young readers.*

THE CLIENT: KNOLL

DESIGN FIRM: GIAMPIETRO+SMITH

Knoll Space

A LITTLE PACKAGE PACKS A BIG PUNCH

"How can we make a piece as structurally interesting as the furniture itself?"

—Rob Giampietro, principal, Giampietro+Smith

Though it's relatively small in scale, this brochure needed to make a lasting impression: It kicked off a new brand called Knoll Space. The legendary furniture company wanted to make select pieces from its studio line normally sold through architects and interior designers available directly to the public. So the company turned to New York design firm Giampietro+Smith to help launch this venture.

The firm worked on everything from the name and attributes of the new brand to the look and feel of the introductory print piece. One name considered was Knoll Home, but ultimately, it didn't make sense to associate the line with a name that would limit the base of potential customers. Apartment dwellers might be just

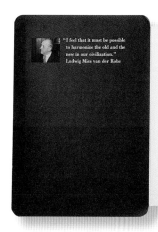

In 1927, Ludwig Mies van der Rohe designed a chair with a single concept in mind. His Barcelona Chair, created for the Barcelona World Exhibition of 1929, stood for the synthesis of old and new: it blended the comfort of home with the thrill of innovation. Nearly eight decades later, the chair is still a classic, and it's still available from Knoll.

Barcelona®
Lounge Chair
Ludwig Mies
van der Rohe

Knoll has always designed furnishings that inspire, evolve and endure. More than 30 of our classic designs are included in the permanent collection of MoMA, and our signature pieces number many more. This design leadership defines the past and future of Knoll, and we're adding new elements to our collection of modern classics every year.

Womb
Chair
Eero
Saarinen

With Knoll Space, Knoll has assembled the best of its past and present for the home and home office.

PaperClip®
Table
Vignelli
Design

▲ *New York firm Giampietro+Smith put together this brochure to help launch Knoll Space, a selection of Knoll furniture sold directly to consumers. Since they needed to work with existing photography, the design team created interesting crops with the cover imagery to help distinguish this new brand.*

as likely to splurge on a womb chair as traditional homeowners. Plus, the line includes office furniture as well as residential pieces.

But perhaps an even bigger challenge than naming the brand was creating a brochure that lived up to its contents. "How can we make a piece as structurally interesting as the furniture itself?" says Rob Giampietro, principal of Giampietro+Smith. It's a tough question to answer when you're working with furniture designed by such icons as Frank Gehry and Ludwig Mies van der Rohe.

The firm had recently finished another project with an accordion fold, so after some brainstorming, the design team decided to use the same technique for this piece. The accordion fold gives the piece a sculptural feel, one that makes consumers want to keep the brochure once they pick it up at a retailer such as Design Within Reach. This approach also gives a nod to the exquisite forms of the furniture featured in the line.

The spreads on the front side of the brochure pair furniture beauty shots with approachable copy that establishes the brand's personality. This section introduces consumers to Knoll's history and lets them know what to expect from Knoll Space with such lines as: "Surround yourself with beauty. Invest in innovation." On the back, the brochure becomes a mini product catalog with small, labeled images of the pieces offered in the Knoll Space collection.

◄ *The piece's accordion fold makes it feel like a sculpture—a nod to the exquisite forms of the furniture shown within the brochure.*

> "I feel that it must be possible to harmonize the old and the new in our civilization."
> Ludwig Mies van der Rohe

In 1927, Ludwig Mies van der Rohe designed a chair with a single concept in mind. His Barcelona Chair, created for the Barcelona World Exhibition of 1929, stood for the synthesis of old and new: it blended the comfort of home with the thrill of innovation. Nearly eight decades later, the chair is still a classic, and it's still available from Knoll.

Barcelona®
Lounge Chair
Ludwig Mies
van der Rohe

► *Interior pages are slightly smaller than the front and back covers, giving the piece a feel similar to a hardcover book. Die-cut from a single sheet of paper, the piece was folded at the printer.*

Since project parameters didn't allow for original photography, designers worked hard to make existing imagery create its own statement. They put an emphasis on individual pieces of furniture instead of beauty shots of a room and used both silhouetting and cropping to help distinguish the brand. In the catalog section, for instance, individual chairs face different directions to simulate how you might find them in a room. "We wanted things to feel like they're conversing with each other," Giampietro says. The designers stripped drop shadows out of the photos to make this approach work.

Overall, the brochure feels as deluxe as the furniture inside, but it's still afford-able enough to be feasible as a retail giveaway. The thick, coated stock gives the piece a substantial, upscale feel. It's also sturdy enough that the brochure can stand up on its own, creating something akin to a shrunken trade-show display. It's seductive enough to make a design lover splurge on some new living room furniture.

Knoll has always designed furnishings that inspire, evolve and endure. More than 30 of our classic designs are included in the permanent collection of MoMA, and our signature pieces number many more. This design leadership defines the past and future of Knoll, and we're adding new elements to our collection of modern classics every year.

Womb
Chair
Eero
Saarinen

With Knoll Space, Knoll has assembled the best of its past and present for the home and home office.

PaperClip®
Table
Vignelli
Design

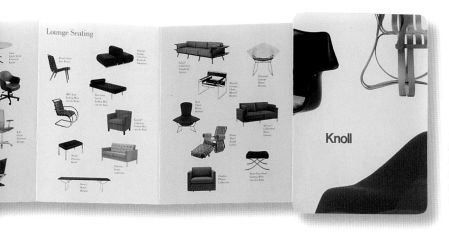

◄ The brochure's flip side functions as a mini-catalog, showing off the collection's furniture. "Knoll liked the brochure so much they wanted to add more pieces to the collection," says Rob Giampietro, principal of Giampietro+Smith.

Lounge Seating

Knoll

THE CLIENT: NEENAH PAPER

DESIGN FIRM: AND PARTNERS

Neenah Paper

WHAT'S YOUR COLOR?

▼ *And Partners created this book, which focuses on color and personality, as a promotion for Neenah Paper. The firm chose to use both a clear foil and embossing to help the N and speech bubble stand out on the cover. Inside the piece, the gatefold hides the back of the embossing and makes the perfect spot for the table of contents.*

"I'm a blue orange brown," says David Schimmel, president and creative director of And Partners in New York City. He talks about this three-color designation in the same lighthearted way you might discuss your horoscope, pointing out the personality traits—visionary and dreamer—associated with his color preferences. No, he hasn't been drafted into a new age movement geared toward graphic designers.

Schimmel referenced the Dewey Color System, a scientifically valid color-based personality test, as the subject of a small flip book that And Partners designed for Neenah Paper. The Dewey system was developed by Dewey Sadka, a former staffing agency owner, as a way to understand people through color. Think of it as a shorter, visual version of the Myers-Briggs personality test.

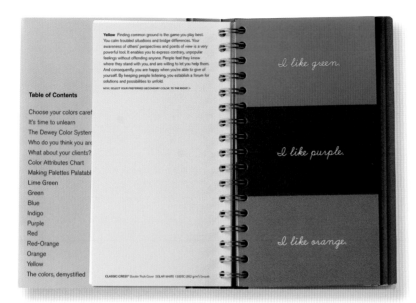

Table of Contents

Yellow Finding common ground is the game you play best. You calm troubled situations and bridge differences. Your awareness of others' perspectives and points of view is a very powerful tool. It enables you to express contrary, unpopular feelings without offending anyone. People feel they know where they stand with you, and are willing to let you help them. And consequently, you are happy when you're able to give of yourself. By keeping people listening, you establish a forum for solutions and possibilities to unfold.

NOW, SELECT YOUR PREFERRED SECONDARY COLOR. TO THE RIGHT. >

I like green.

I like purple.

I like orange.

CLASSIC CREST® Double Thick Cover SOLAR WHITE 130DTC (352 g/m²) Smooth

◄ *The beginning of the book leads readers through a simple personality test based on the colors they like most. These three colors—green, purple, and orange—are separated by perforation. This allows users to tear them apart and flip over the appropriate card to learn about their personality.*

As you browse the first few pages of the book, you'll be asked to choose your favorite color within several sets of three colors. Flip over the page or card bearing your preferred shade and you'll uncover a paragraph about your personality traits. Prefer yellow over blue and red? Dewey says, "You calm troubled situations and bridge differences." If you like yellow and purple, you're passionate and open to change. In his own informal poll of test takers, Schimmel found the descriptions to be uncannily accurate.

Neenah tapped And Partners to turn the Dewey system into a resource for the graphic design community—one that would be useful enough to stick around studios and help build the Neenah brand. Since Sadka had already put together several books on his creation, there was a great deal of material to pull from. "It seemed like they wanted everything and the kitchen sink in this book," Schimmel says. "It was very complicated information, and the application was difficult." His firm worked closely with Sadka as they pared down the source material and made it more relevant for designers.

To accomplish the latter, the firm added a section called "What about your clients?" that talks about applying the system's proven color attributes to brands. There's a foldout chart that shows which shades to choose if you're trying to convey stability, impulsiveness, or a host of other descriptors. It takes something subjective and makes it objective—a handy tool for any client meeting. The bulk of the book consists of foldout color palettes based on different base colors—a resource that a designer could put to use on almost any project. There are about 1,300 different colors in the book, and tabs labeled with the base color names make this guide easy to navigate.

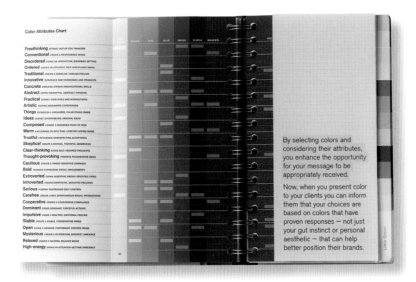

This color attributes chart folds out to help designers put the Dewey Color System to use. Creatives can scan down the sides of the chart to find the message they're trying to convey in a given project and then move across the chart to match the quality with the appropriate color(s).

The piece took close to nine months to complete, and as a result of this effort, it's highly usable. The designers chose a spiral wire binding for its practicality. This feature makes the book easier to use because it always lies flat as you go through the pages. Plus, the double-sided palette sheets are accordion-folded, so they can be pulled out to more than twice the book's width when in use. "This enables you to look at things side-by-side and play with them," Schimmel says. "If you go with these color palettes, you're not going to have what Sadka calls a 'color oops.'"

Another big challenge was recreating all the colors within the Dewey system; they're built colors rather than Pantone color formulas. "Once we got the design and concept worked out, we had to figure out the prototypes of the colors," Schimmel says. His firm went back and forth with a number of press proofs to get them just right. Then they included the six-color process formats for many of the colors in the back of the book.

The piece also promotes Neenah's Classic Crest paper and demonstrates how well solid colors print on this uncoated paper. Pages of vibrant red and blue make better testimonials than any copy. This book also helps position Neenah, in conjunction with Sadka, as a color expert and provides ongoing value for designers. "People seem to love it," Schimmel says.

▲ *A clever accordion fold means that palettes rest comfortably in the book until a designer unfolds them to compare color options. This approach allows for side-by-side color comparisons.*

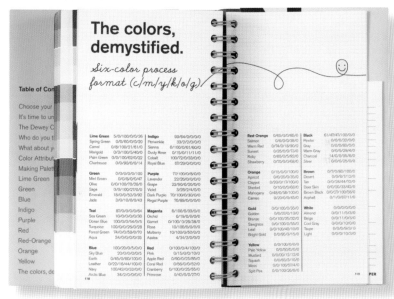

▲ *To make the book easier to use, the design team included color builds for key shades in the back of the book. Humorous, friendly headlines make the content more inviting and simpler to absorb.*

THE CLIENT: UNIVERSITY OF FLORIDA SCHOOL OF ART AND ART HISTORY

DESIGN FIRM: CONNIE HWANG DESIGN

University of Florida School of Art and Art History

CREATIVE FOLDING

Connie Hwang needed to figure out how to make the promotional brochure for the Workshop for Art Research and Practice (WARP) at the University of Florida School of Art and Art History stand out despite a relatively modest budget. The piece's ultimate form emerged from a two-hour meeting with the client and an oversized sheet of paper. "We just sat there folding and folding," says Hwang, principal of Connie Hwang Design and an assistant professor of graphic design at the Gainesville-based university. "We wanted something that could stand up."

◄ *A unique fold created from a rectangular sheet allows this brochure to stand up. This feature helps the piece attract the attention of young high school and college students.*

▲ *Besides allowing the piece to stand up, these two triangles represent the couple that teaches this art program.*

The piece needed to be eye-catching enough to attract the target audience of both high school seniors and current art students. And the client wanted the brochure to function as a template, so they could update the images with new student work. Hwang's solution is both simple and elegant. She folded the rectangular sheet in half to form a square, then folded the square on the diagonal to create a standing triangle. This process results in a form you immediately want to pick up and unfold to see exactly how it works.

The two triangles that allow the piece to stand up also reference WARP, which is taught by a couple. "You can't have one without the other," Hwang says. WARP, which is geared to freshmen, includes both classroom and studio instruction and encompasses everything from creative process to artistic integrity. It also covers a wide range of disciplines.

The brochure's cover uses the school's standard color palette, and the first spread gives a brief overview of the program. When the piece is completely unfolded, it features a range of student work intercepted by diagonal lines. Hwang started with roughly 200 images from the client. "We just found the most interesting ones that represented all the disciplines within the school," she says. These can be swapped out easily when the piece is updated. And the diagonal lines? They're a nod to the program's interdisciplinary research.

To make sure this unusual format would actually work, a fair amount of testing took place. Hwang mailed a blank version to make sure it wouldn't get mangled by the post office and worked hard to select the right paper—some stocks crack when folded. Additionally, Hwang ran her idea by the printer to make sure the unusual folds were possible.

► *This spread's design makes it easy for the program to update the brochure with new student projects for future printings.*

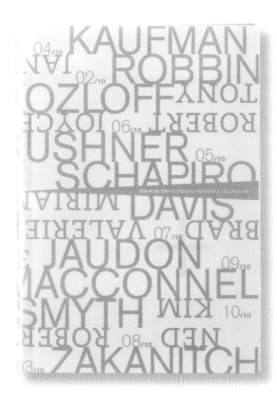

▲ *This exhibition catalog comes wrapped in a vellum cover with a metallic finish. The text is printed in metallic ink and features the artists' names in a pleasing pattern. Both elements are a nod to the metallic elements within many of the show's paintings.*

Hwang also incorporated folding into a small catalog she created for an exhibit at the University Gallery. The show, *Ten Plus Ten: Revisiting Pattern & Decoration,* featured works by 10 artists prominent in the pattern and decoration movement of the 1970s. There were two pieces in the show from each artist—one from the 1970s and one that was created fairly recently. Hwang wanted to reflect the show's key concepts—pattern and decoration—through the tools of graphic design.

"When I was brainstorming, the client said, 'Just take an image and put it on the cover,'" she says. "But the work is so diverse, it's really hard to pick one. I decided to create my own pattern." On the brochure's vellum jacket, Hwang uses typography as a pattern, while still keeping the names of all ten artists readable. For the actual brochure cover, she created a pattern inspired by the colors from the 1970s-era pieces within the exhibition.

In fact, many of Hwang's design decisions were driven by the desire to represent both pattern and decoration within the piece. The accordion fold—inspired by a piece in the exhibit painted on a Japanese screen door—creates its own pattern, while the numbers and lines embossed on the cover fall under decoration. "When I design, I really try to include all the traditional printing techniques I can to reinforce the concept," she says.

▲ This brochure is constructed from an accordion fold, but since the paper gradually gets higher from the front to the back, the tops of the folded pages create an interesting overlap.

► Individual spreads show off artwork from the show, while subtle lines at the top of the page reinforce the idea of pattern and decoration—key themes of the exhibition.

THE CLIENT: DAYCORP PROPERTY DEVELOPMENT AND
THE UNIVERSITY OF ADELAIDE

DESIGN FIRM: VOICE

Daycorp Property Development and the University of Adelaide

DIY TYPE

Though Daycorp Property Development has been around for 30 years, the company only recently started to develop a brand presence. A few years ago, they turned to design firm Voice in Adelaide, Australia, to create a new identity and, more recently, tapped the design firm to create a capabilities brochure. "When this document came up, we wanted to create a visual identity for the book through the type," says Anthony Deleo, a director at Voice.

The firm had created custom characters for Daycorp's logo and decided to expand them into a full set for this brochure. "We wanted to make sure the typeface felt strong and felt like it belonged to a big industry," says Scott Carslake, a director at Voice. Since the typeface is quite structural, it helps Daycorp project confidence—a quality that helps them partner with other companies on large developments. This typeface, simply referred to as Daycorp, appears in headlines and display copy throughout the piece, creating both compelling shapes and a strong visual thread.

▼ *Designers at Voice created the custom typeface that dominates this cover to help the client carve out a brand identity. The copy wraps from the front of the brochure around the spine to the back.*

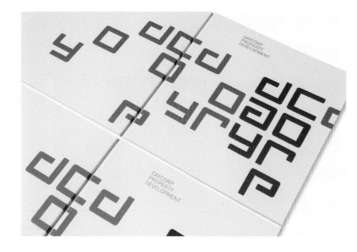

BULKY GOODS

◄ *The Daycorp custom typeface dominates section dividers, giving readers a strong visual cue that they're about to look at a different category of projects. Text blocks are set in an off-the-shelf typeface called Interstate.*

► *Since the projects featured in this brochure aren't all naturally beautiful, designers hired a fine art photographer, rather than an architectural one, to help capture each location in its best light. "He brought a lot to the table," says Anthony Deleo, a director at the design firm Voice.*

In addition to building brand awareness, this piece needed to highlight some of Daycorp's projects—a task that wasn't as easy as it sounds. "We knew some of their sites weren't very attractive," Deleo says. "We really had to sit down and figure out how to approach the photography." To help solve this problem, the designers hired a fine art photographer rather than an architectural one. Digital shots came first, and then the team brainstormed about how best to capture each site. What time of day? Which angle works best? Does it need people or movement? The photographer was an integral part of this process.

Overall, this brochure has a simple, elegant feel. It's an approach that starts things off on the right foot for Daycorp, which had never created a sophisticated print piece before. The layouts are uncluttered and let the emphasis fall on the photography and display type. One or two images on most spreads, along with ample white space, allow Daycorp's work to stand out. The piece definitely takes a big step toward establishing a visual identity for the developer.

To make this piece compelling within a limited budget, designers created handwritten notes on many of the photos. These teasers help draw people into the main copy by quickly telling stories.

Voice also created custom typography for a fundraising brochure designed for the University of Adelaide, although it was somewhat less formal. In addition to traditional type, there are short, handwritten notes and doodles scrawled across the piece's full-page photos. And these casual elements play a key role in the brochure's concept. "It's a way of making people aware there's a different message on the page," Deleo says.

The brochure hinges on the stories of amazing people connected with the university, including both individuals who donate money and those who benefit from those funds. There's a ninety-three-year-old who earned her masters in anthropology and a young woman who researches Alzheimer's disease using zebra fish. Carslake's hand-penned notes quickly highlight each person's story and help forge an emotional connection with readers. This helps to draw people into the main text to learn more about these extraordinary people and various fundraising efforts.

To create the handwritten text, Carslake printed out each photograph on laser paper and put it on a light box. He laid another piece of paper over the top and started handwriting the type. Once he was satisfied, he scanned his creation into the computer. "It was a very low-budget job," he says. "We had to find ways to make it interesting."

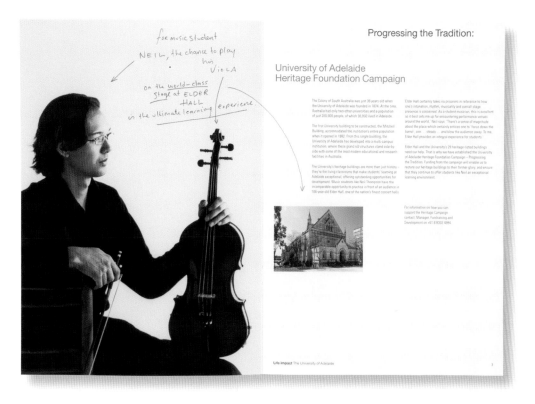

Each of the portraits was shot specifically for this brochure, though there wasn't enough room in the budget for styling. The subjects just showed up at the shoot in their own clothes and were photographed without much fuss over their appearance. Since most of the university's brochures are quite colorful, designers decided to lower the saturation of the photographs to differentiate the piece. This approach also gave the brochure a softer feel.

▲ To make the brochure engaging, the design team put the focus on people who participate in and benefit from the university's fundraising efforts. This approach helps forge a strong emotional connection with readers.

► Many of the university's printed materials use photos from a preexisting photography bank, so designers shot the oversized portraits featured in this brochure to help set the piece apart. Smaller images were pulled from existing imagery.

THE CLIENT: ARENT FOX

DESIGN FIRM: DESIGN ARMY

Arent Fox

SELLING GOOD IDEAS

"It's not about B.S.—it's about telling the truth. I tell the client, 'I'm in this with you. If you fail, I fail.'"

—Pum Lefebure, creative director at Design Army

Law firm brochures tend to be a little too starched around the collar—in fact, you can probably describe the typical formula. Two men wearing suits and shaking hands. A buttoned-up layout and muted color palette. It's all a little too predictable. So when the team at Design Army revamped Arent Fox's brochures, they wanted to avoid the visual equivalent of legalese.

To help this law firm stand out from the competition, the Washington, D.C.–based design shop decided to run with the client's tagline: "Smart in your world." This brief phrase helped inspire the concept for a capabilities brochure. Rather than emphasize a client list and case wins, the piece focuses on the people and stories that make the firm unique. You can read about an unusual lawsuit against building owners whose tenants sell fake Louis Vuitton bags or learn about a racial discrimination settlement with the Library of Congress. They're the kinds of tales you'd find more readily in a magazine or newspaper than a piece of marketing collateral.

To enrich these stories, all the copy is presented in a narrative style and paired with original location photography. The firm's lawyers come across as warm and intelligent, the kind of folks you might like to invite over for dinner. In addition, Design Army made the piece friendly, with a clean layout and liberal use of blue and red—two of the firm's brand colors. The third color, gray, serves as a complement throughout the book. There's also another important way the brochure makes its mark: instead of a typical 8½ x 11–inch (21.6 x 27.9–cm) or 9 x 12–inch (22.9 x 30.5–cm) piece, it measures an intimate 5½ x 7½ inches (14 x 17.8 cm).

◄ This capabilities piece stands out from other law-firm brochures with a friendly, engaging design and strong storytelling. "If you sit in the middle of the road, it's a scary place to be," says Pum Lefebure, a creative director at Design Army. "You get run over."

Sounds like the perfect solution, right? But it didn't come to fruition without its fair share of obstacles. Creative director Pum Lefebure spent a lot of time on the phone with Arent Fox's chief marketing officer, giving her the rationale behind concepts and design decisions. Those conversations sometimes stretched as long as an hour, but they provided crucial information for selling ideas to the law firm's fifteen partners. "It's not about B.S.," says Lefebure. "It's about telling the truth. I tell the client, 'I'm in this with you. If you fail, I fail.'" This allows her to stand up for ideas without becoming an adversary—and since the firm doesn't have account executives, the creative staff is able to present the thinking behind their work with genuine passion.

► Each case study in the book starts with an engaging, first-person lead-in. This copy is presented on a page flooded with a solid color to signal a new story to readers.

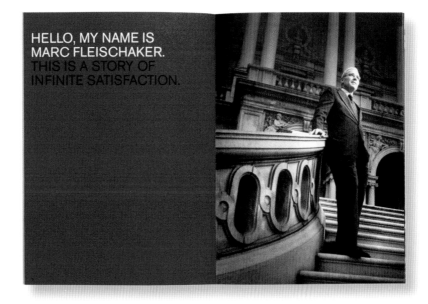

THE CLIENT:	RED WING SHOES
TIME FRAME:	SIX MONTHS
DESIGN FIRM:	CAPSULE (USA)

Red Wing Shoes

THE MOST AMAZING THING YOU'VE NEVER SEEN

INTRODUCTION

Red Wing Shoes' identity is a logo heard around the world. What is now Red Wing Shoe Company, Inc., began with modest means and grew to become an international brand of handmade work boots and fashionable footwear. The classic work boots brand has widely become a fashion boot as well.

Capsule, a brand development and design firm based in Minneapolis, USA, redesigned the brand's logo. The effort had to tie into a larger brand evolution that was taking place simultaneously. This meant the logo required extensive planning aimed at transforming the logo's functional elements and retaining its existing brand equities. Red Wing Shoes' authentic American style is based on its decades of heritage—Norman Rockwell immortalized the brand in a series of drawings from 1960 to 1969—and its role as a figurehead of old-fashioned quality.

PLANNING

Planning included the exhaustive research and study of similar changes implemented by brands such as Shell, Harley-Davidson, John Deere, and many others. At this stage, research suggested much of the logo's equity resided in the black type over the red wing. Moderate variations lost the authentic American feel that attracted consumers in Canada, Mexico, Europe, and Asia. This planning process set the foundation for the design's direction and exploration.

EST. 1905
**RED
WING
SHOES**

*The Red Wing Shoes wing logo, with an
overlay of the Red Wing Shoes name, was
originally designed in 1904.*

Remove the type from the wing, and it morphs into a "box of pork chops" that doesn't offer an ideal solution.

The revised Red Wing Shoes logo varies from the original, but the untrained eye is challenged to see the difference.

CREATING

The process of visualizing and creating change was driven by both client and design teams with an ability to flex the design process. It began with an exhaustive exploration of possibilities that helped the group visualize change. Studies were conducted to observe the shapes of various wings. The original swan wing was the model. Type studies were also conducted to ensure that the style remained similar enough to the original. The new design improved readability and other details, such as consistent thick and thins. A toolkit was also designed to provide a variety of options for use in specific contexts. The design was refined, and the wing was hand-drawn more than ten times throughout the process.

IMPLEMENTING

An exhaustive online site was created for vendors to source the redesigned Red Wing Shoes logo and toolkit. The new logo was implemented on everything from signage and advertising to shoes and other clothing accessories. The result was a logo design that offers a multitude of options with a logo toolkit and design that retain original brand equity.

A redrawn wing spurred the creation of a toolkit of Red Wing Shoes logo designs. Each solution makes a connection back to the original but offers flexibility for specific media.

THE CLIENT:	ROYAL TROPICAL INSTITUTE
TIME FRAME:	FOUR MONTHS
DESIGN FIRM:	EDEN DESIGN & COMMUNICATIONS (NETHERLANDS)

Royal Tropical Institute

BRANCHING OUT

INTRODUCTION

The Royal Tropical Institute (KIT) is an international center of knowledge and expertise focusing on international and intercultural cooperation. The organization contributes its energy to building sustainable development, alleviating poverty, and preserving and promoting diverse cultures. Though KIT has roots in the Netherlands, its reach is global.

PLANNING

Eden Design & Communication used nature as inspiration when designing the Royal Tropical Institute's new logo. The result is a visual expression of KIT's mission and core values conveyed in a bright, organic form. At the heart of the design process was KIT's brand promise: knowledge, choices, and opportunities.

KIT needed a logo that would inspire others to provide their support. To do this, the logo needed to express KIT's mission—assisting people in developing countries—while also conveying its most essential values of equivalence, diversity, sustainable development, and good government. The goal was to strike a non-Western, worldly, dignified, cooperative, sharing, and respectful design tone, one of an ambassador with the welcoming cadence of a friendly, trusted acquaintance. The logo also had to engage others on a fundamental level so the audience would become curious and motivated to learn more.

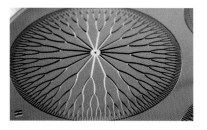

The designer gathered tree images from all over the world with the goal of creating a universally recognizable, relevant, and organic image. The influence of these initial tree images can be seen in the final logo.

The Royal Tropical Institute's logo organically blends people and trees into a unique, simple, and memorable design.

CREATING

Eden Design went through a thorough planning process to build a strong and clear foundation; it then used this foundation to leap into the organic creative process, which followed many paths. By conducting an exhaustive visual image study, the designers found the right metaphors to convey this complex and sensitive message.

Because the Institute increases choices and spreads a broader worldview, contributing to the odds of a better life, one design inspiration was the tree of life, an ancient symbol with many iterations and interpretations. In the search for the correct tree form, the design team explored many variations. In the end, however, Eden's innovative and visually compelling design integrated human forms, which reflect the organization's worldly focus. For color, Eden chose a non-Western, worldly, and respectful color palette.

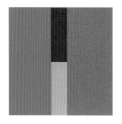

To develop the identity's color palette, the design team collected art and imagery from specific world regions as inspiration.

Refinements to the logo illustrate how the two elements gracefully come together.

IMPLEMENTING

The Royal Tropical Institute's goal was to generate and disseminate specialized knowledge in the areas of sustainable economic development, education, healthcare, and culture. This information would be distributed through a variety of channels, meaning the company needed tailored logo variations for different groups and initiatives. The new logo also needed to reflect the organization's values by creating a flexible, structured hierarchy. There were many challenges in this project, but careful research and attention to every element, as well as understanding how the overall program held together, paid off.

Eden Design's implementation of the larger visual language was impeccably detailed, and the logo beautifully reflects the organization's mission, personality, and brand promise. The resulting logo design is aligned accurately with the organization's vision and executed with flawless detail.

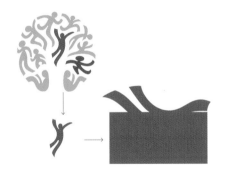

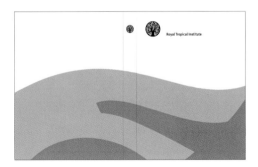

The logo design is the center of an elegant, efficient, and global design system.

THE CLIENT: LONDON SYMPHONY ORCHESTRA

TIME FRAME: FOUR MONTHS

DESIGN FIRM: THE PARTNERS (UNITED KINGDOM)

London Symphony Orchestra

AN INSTITUTION CHANGES ITS TUNE

INTRODUCTION

The London Symphony Orchestra logo was redesigned to reflect recent organizational changes. The redesign represents the elegant and delicate balance between the orchestra and the conductor. It's a visual depiction of the two parties working in concert to create a memorable musical experience.

The Partners, a design consultancy based in the United Kingdom, designed the new logo for the world-renowned institution. The firm's process included three distinct stages that eventually brought vibrant life to the combined vision of the organization and the design team.

PLANNING

The addition of a new performance venue, LSO St. Luke's, was the most notable of several new changes that impacted the London Symphony Orchestra, its employees, and its patrons. It therefore seemed like the appropriate time to signal the changes in a substantial way. When The Partners took on the project, they began by gathering research and inspiration about where the organization was heading. The team delved deeply into the world of classical music, gathering firsthand research from behind the curtain. This work informed the creative brief for the new visual identity.

The establishment of a new performance venue, LSO St. Luke's, London, is a significant change that propels the logo redesign.

The line between letters and image blur together in a new logo. The illustration of a conductor is also a monogram, lending warmth and humanity to the London Symphony Orchestra.

CREATING

The design of the LSO logo blended an elegant, casually handwritten version of the organization's acronym with a subtle reference to the conductor. This final identity was the product of an exploratory design process that led designers down a number of paths pointing to the past, present, and future history of the organization.

The new logo signaled changes, including the addition of a new location that would be the new home of free public lunchtime concerts, new community events, and a variety of other concerts. Beyond this, the new identity set a tone for the orchestra's future. The final test was the presentation of the final logo design to the full orchestra. The musicians' collective tapping of their instruments symbolized approval and hailed the beginning of a new era.

Orchestra players are a key audience that the design team needs to impress. The symbolic tapping of their instruments signals approval, a key element of future success.

IMPLEMENTING

The new visual identity was implemented on a variety of media and communication tools. It was executed on vehicle sides, on the organization's website, in campaign advertisements, on programs, on live concert CD covers, and throughout other supplemental materials. The final product heralded change while paying homage to a rich history.

The integration of the new logo into a seasonal campaign can be a good test to see whether results show up in the fiscal column. In this case, online ticket and CD sales went up 200 percent.

THE CLIENT:	SPRINT
TIME FRAME:	TWO MONTHS
DESIGN FIRM:	LIPPINCOTT MERCER (USA)

Sprint

ELEGANTLY MERGING TWO BRANDS

INTRODUCTION

When Sprint and Nextel planned to merge, the focus was on creating America's premier communications company. Nextel benefited from public awareness of the Sprint brand, both its history of innovation and asset value. But the new logo design also had to represent Nextel and its brand equities. Design firm Lippincott Mercer created a new logo for the new telecommunications brand.

PLANNING

The merger of two highly recognized and respected brands required thoughtful planning and strategy. Because of the competitive nature of the visual land-scape, extensive research was essential. Each existing logo's equity had to be measured carefully and then carried forward, with one name and style taking a dominant position.

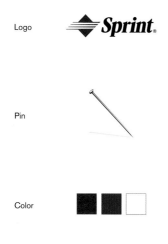

Logo

Pin

Color

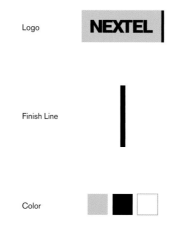

Logo

Finish Line

Color

It's red, yellow, and abstract all over. Both brands have equity in their names, color, and visual shapes. The design team chose to leverage the yellow of Nextel and the pin drop of Sprint.

Sprint's new logo flies high. It's a simple, beautiful, and memorable design, representing both the classic pin drop and a new wing in flight.

Sprint ·· Nextel

Exploration has many faces. After the company decides to keep the Sprint name, designers look at a variety of ways to integrate the equities of both brands through shape, color, and typography.

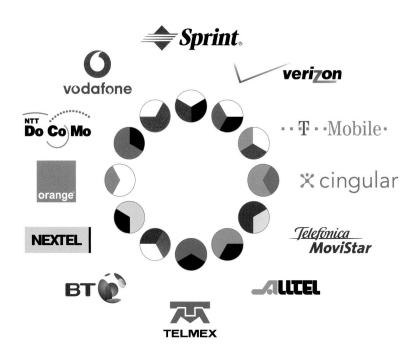

The communications category is chock full of color. Designers conduct a thorough and simple audit to clearly identify what color palette the new Sprint logo can own in a crowded marketplace.

CREATING

Creativity rarely escapes a corporate board meeting without a few substantial bruises. The new logo design for Sprint defies most expectations for a large corporate logo design. It is not only an effective logo on a functional level; it is also inspired in form. The metaphor of the pin drop, a trademarked sound for Sprint, elegantly matches the shape of a wing taking flight. The logo design sets Sprint in the only open spot on a cluttered map of competitors in the telecommunications industry, which many suits said couldn't be done at this point in the history of the category. Most important, it positions Sprint in the minds of consumers in a far more effective manner than most of the competitive set.

IMPLEMENTING

Some logo designs almost execute themselves. This often occurs when they've been designed carefully from the beginning. The new Sprint logo went through an efficient implementation in a variety of media, crossing over into signage, the Web, advertisements, and even backpacks. The new brand vision is refreshing on many levels, alluding to better customer relationships and a bright future.

When you are Sprint, the launch of a new logo turns a few heads. Whether it's a topic of conversation, confusion, or it's an afterthought, the new Sprint logo touches millions of consumers.

Kinderarzt, Dr. Uhlig

MAKING KIDS SMILE

INTRODUCTION

Dr. Uhlig's practice is concerned with healing children and helping children feel comfortable in an unfamiliar and discomforting situation, such as in a doctor's office. The logo plays an important role in this effort.

Factor Design, of Hamburg, Germany, worked with the doctor to create a logo that would convey a cheerful tone. The challenge was to make the logo welcoming for young children without going over the top in the eyes of parents or older children.

PLANNING

Doctors can be intimidating, instruments can be intimidating, and the combination can make a standard checkup a traumatic experience for many adults, let alone children. The planning process, also called a "launch," for Dr. Uhlig's new logo design focused on comforting a very specific section of his practice: his youngest patients. Success required equal participation from the client, Dr. Uhlig, as well as the design firm. The new design needed to reflect a medical professional and also needed to engage and welcome children. The team was set to create, brief in hand.

KINDERARZT
Doktor Uhlig

The logo for Dr. Uhlig's medical practice, Kinderarzt, reinvents the tone of both his brand and his stethoscope. The medical device that is traditionally used to listen to patients' heartbeats appears in this context as the personification of cheer and happiness.

Factor Design lets research inspire. The design team has children draw images of doctor's artifacts and the surroundings at the doctor's office. The result is a better understanding of their perspective. Copies of original art are used on a variety of communications.

Certain applications require a fresh outlook. Stationery is used and seen almost exclusively by parents. Therefore, it must address their needs while remaining true to the original kid-friendly concept.

CREATING

The design process absorbed inspiration from children's drawings, industry artifacts, and a variety of other inputs. Out of this, the design process homed in on one concept: creating a smiling face with a stethoscope. The idea garnered rave reviews from the clinic and the rest of the team. After that, colors were chosen to convey warmth while still communicating professionalism. In the end, primary colors were chosen to appeal to the young audience.

Many children's practices pepper waiting rooms with teddy bears and clowns that distract kids momentarily but don't lend warmth to the environment at a fundamental level. Other practices simply approach kids in the same way they would adults. The results can feel cold, sterile, and intimidating. The new Kinderarzt logo conveys friendliness and care in a light, unique, and clever way.

IMPLEMENTING

The logo design inspired the rest of the project, from the kids' waiting area to a variety of other communications. Childlike energy bounced out clearly from the patterns created from original kids' drawings. The color palette was simple, playful, and never intimidating.

When kids are involved, there is extra incentive to create something inspirational. The new logo is an effort to do just that. The final logo achieves this in many ways, becoming a popular conversation piece that the audience also uses functionally and values aesthetically.

The logo design and surrounding language have to communicate in a digital world– a place where some children may be more comfortable than their parents.

THE CLIENT:	(RED)™
TIME FRAME:	TWO MONTHS
DESIGN FIRM:	WOLFF OLINS (USA)

(RED)™

THE COLOR OF COMMERCE, EMERGENCY, AND SOCIAL CONSCIOUSNESS

INTRODUCTION

Conceptualized by Bono, (RED) is an idea—an idea that connects brands with conscious commerce, by making the idea of "doing good" real and fiscally rewarding. It provides a financial impetus for prominent brands to lend their clout to bettering humanity.

PLANNING

The design team was given the direction to create a brand that would exemplify "doing good is good business" and bring to life this idea. The design needed to entice big, powerful brands by standing apart from the myriad other organizations requesting financial support. The concept of (RED) needed to build its own equity by borrowing from the equity of iconic brands. According to (RED)'s lead strategist, Sam Wilson, "(RED) is an extraordinary union of business, people, and ideas, a twenty-first–century brand that inspires individuals, drives positive commerce, and advances the world. All profits go to the global fund to fight AIDS, tuberculosis, and malaria in Africa."

The direction and inspiration were set. The next task was to create a logo design to exemplify the idea: a design that created urgency of attention and also provided enough exposure to partner brands to interest them in joining the cause.

Just as (RED) borrows equity from famous brands, it also borrows equity from culturally valuable words.

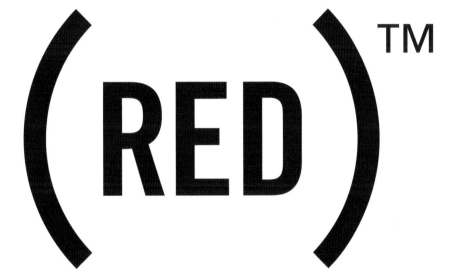

(RED) is a brand created for social good. It's a brand designed for global advancement, blending commerce and charity.

CREATING

The challenge was how to unite two brands visually. The traditional method of bonding two brands—simply placing them side by side—didn't seem to live up to the aspirations of the brand. The brand needed to covet the generous partner brands but not lose its own individual equity. Striking a balance between the two was difficult.

The design explorations led the team to a simple, elegant idea. Two brackets surround the word red. When shown with a collaborative brand, the mark is embraced "to the power of (RED)." Minimalist in visual and conceptual form, the design is metaphorical. As you dig, it tells more of the brand's story. Further, the design is naturally unique. All three criteria are not just met but exemplified with a logo design destined to become a force of economic and social inspiration.

(PRODUCT)RED™

DO THE (RED) THING™

By surrounding other logo designs, (RED)'s logo creates a visual relationship that is both comforting and clear. The result is a brand relationship that creates curiosity in both the new and existing brands.

IMPLEMENTING

If you have earned airline miles in the past twenty years, you've interacted with a loyalty program. Designed to buy loyalty, these programs have grown up to become ugly beasts, creating large corporate liabilities and disillusioned consumers. The implementation of (RED) marks the beginning of something new, a method of earning consumer loyalty instead of attempting to buy it—earning it by proving loyalty to customers, to the Earth, to employees, and to the global community.

By surrounding existing brands with the (RED) brand, the implementation should provide the inspiration and even provide the vehicle for leading brands to take ownership of a new philosophy around earned consumer loyalty. Implemented and accepted by the marketplace, this new brand aims to breed more conscious consumers.

The card is designed to use everyday transactions to purchase a piece of global responsibility. The (RED) card paints a brand with the passion surrounding responsible living without the guilt.

This generated image sets the (RED) logo in context, showing how the brand would look dropped into global media hot spot Times Square.

THE CLIENT: FOX RIVER SOCKS

DESIGN FIRM: CAPSULE (USA)

Fox River Socks

SHUCKING AWESOME CORN SOCKS

The feeling of putting a good pair of socks on cold feet can be a special moment in someone's day. The Fox River Sock Company has more than a hundred years of experience giving customers those little moments of joy. Their socks have gone to the moon and have reinforced many a foot fetish. Still manufactured in northern Iowa, they offer a great example of sustainable, community-focused manufacturing that confidently defies most MBA analytics. This and many other heroic brand stories were not being sung from the tops of mountains. That needed to change.

Shucking Awesome socks made from a renewable source of energy. The farm fields and rural culture of where Fox River socks is located were a large influence on the package design concepts.

PLANNING

The world's first corn sock is completely sustainable and annually renewable. To sock industry geeks, corn fiber technology was revolutionary, earth-shattering stuff. To average consumers, it was still just socks. Albeit, socks with corn in them. The goal was to launch a product that would grab shoppers' attention and intrigue them long enough to get educated on the technology's unique benefits. Capsule sent Fox River some homework to kick off the process. Two weeks later, Fox River sent back the mother load. Scattered throughout the brand history sections, tucked between fiftieth anniversaries and factory expansions, were mentions of sock monkeys, arctic treks, Olympic games, and space odysseys. Fox River was sitting on a gold mine. Its history was extraordinary but had gone unsung for more than a century.

LARGE
Style 2289
COUNTRY
QTR

MADE HERE IN THE USA

RENEWABLE. NATURAL. FOX RIVER.

RENEWABLE. NATURAL. FOX RIVER.

Fox River

Crafted Quality Since 1900

OUTDOOR

BIO-FIBER

MADE WITH SUSTAINABLE RESOURCES

ingeo

Businesses donating 1% of sales to the natural environment

MEN'S

ESTB. 1900

MADE WITH CORN

Fox River

CREATING

Capsule made it clear that Fox River should push the envelope. Fox agreed. Armed with the findings from planning sessions, Capsule created packaging and communications tying the corn sock story into Fox River's history. Thus, corn socks became more than just a product. Corn socks became a verification of Fox River's vast, quirky tradition—part of its Midwest personality. A distinct and interesting facet of a remarkable brand story that people could relate to and want to make part of their world.

IMPLEMENTING

Fox River's corn sock packaging made a big splash at the Outdoor Retailer Show. The new product line not only hauled in loads of international orders, it resurrected interest in the overall Fox River brand. By tying Fox River's history into the corn socks, audiences who thought they knew everything there was to know gave Fox River a second look.

The "Made with Corn" insignia became a product feature identifier at retail and was used as a fun give-away in tattoo form at tradeshows and events.

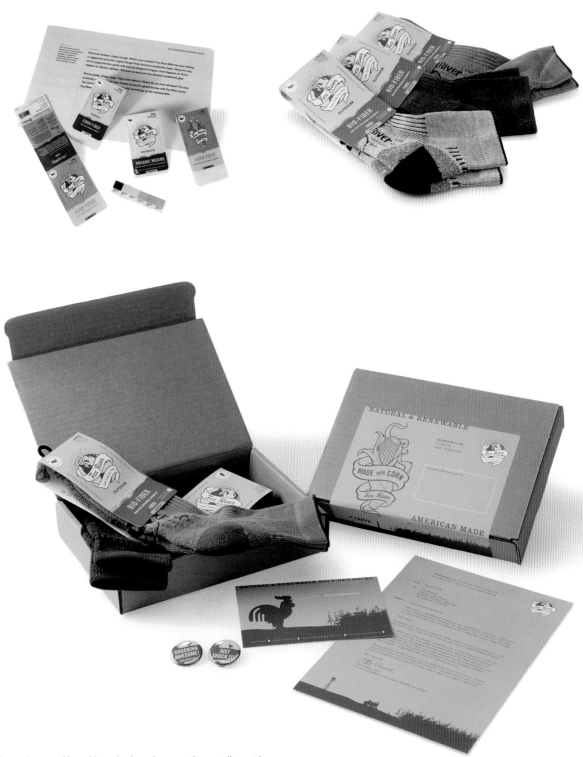

The package and brand launched at a large outdoor retail event in Salt Lake City, Utah, USA. One pair of socks was shipped to each potential buyer and if they came to the event wearing the socks, they were rewarded.

THE CLIENT: METHOD HOME

DESIGN FIRM: METHOD HOME (USA)

Method Home

OPTION OF METHOD OR MADNESS, PICK METHOD

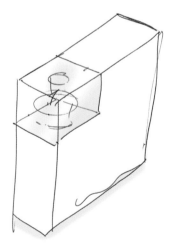

Iterative design can wander deliberately or otherwise in many directions. From pebble concepts to a Bloq, providing us with a great example of the leaps iterative design is allowed to take.

Method home is quickly becoming a household name with household items. As a business, method has founding principles with a dedication to contemporary design thinking. The rocket ship item, designed by the infamous Karim Rashid, sent method products into every designer household in every available market. It has since garnered greater appeal with the mass market, the laggards. This new crowd has picked up on how the design of something can beautify their home in use and while resting on a countertop. Now method has numerous product lines from floor cleaning and laundry detergent to hair care and body wash products.

PLANNING

The offices of method can thank this project for contributing "Don't pull a Bloq on me" to the culture and conversation. It started with a promise that method founder Eric Ryan made to their largest client, Target. In the heat of July, he said, "Sure, we can get a body wash product on the shelves by the holiday season." That was coupled with a desire to create a package that defies conformation by not standing up as most bottle designs would. This became one of those stories where planning does not seem to exist, but in reality, the experience of the team serves the role of research and strategy. There isn't enough time for thoughtful, deliberate, insightful planning; guts, brains, and experience will need to suffice.

The Bloq package stands up to any other body wash package on the market. It is a great example of a unique closure and a package with elegant ergonomics.

CREATING

The charge by Ryan is, "I want a package that won't stand up like every standard package in every bathroom." Where do you go from there? Pebbles, of course. Pebbles, or rather small rocks, don't stand up, but if you pile a few together, they make a nice organic display of product. As the design team developed this idea, it gained quick acceptance and even early praise as an elegant design solution to the challenge. However, as any design process should be iterative, this one ran into the iterative monkey known as "cost to produce." The necessary price point would likely slip right past a Target shopper. Although this wasn't apparent until the Bloq happened, someone needed to stand up for the price point. The result was what is now called "Pulling a Bloq," as the design director, Josh Handy, is now credited with doing.

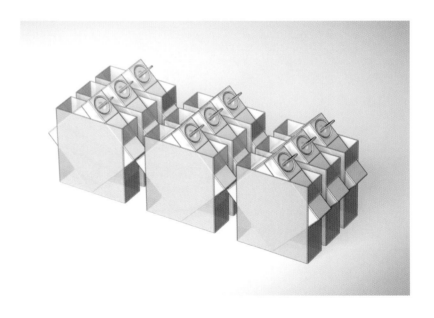

Method is not the first to do this, but it's one of the most recent to win accolades for taking hand soap and putting it on display for all houseguests to see. Much of what method has designed are products that were once hidden in a closet or beneath a sink, now on display for all to appreciate.

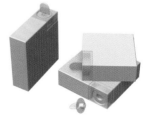

IMPLEMENTING

With the price point within sight, the implementation deadline could now be achieved. The team still had to produce the design, get it manufactured, filled, shipped, and on the shelves in what most designers would consider an unrealistic deadline. The rubber met the road and product was delivered on time, and the cool breeze at the end of this sprint relay race was product launch success both financially and emotionally. The method culture now contained another story of how their approach to product development works. Target had another selling product. And the world had another story of design improving everyday lives.

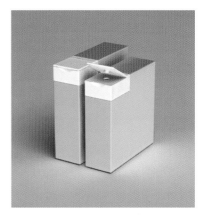

Digital renderings can convey how a closure will work as well as how each package will relate to its pair while on display. They can also be a low-cost option in comparison to physical prototypes when working on the early package concepts.

THE CLIENT: PLUM ORGANICS

DESIGN FIRM: BRAND ENGINE (USA)

Plum Organics

SQUARE AND PLUM EQUALS YUMMY

PLANNING

"Analysis paralysis." We've all heard of it and some even live it on a daily basis. Planning can be a freeway you get on and off quickly to reach your destination faster, as well as looking smarter when you arrive. Planning can also be that country dirt road that doesn't have a turnoff for nearly 100 kilometers. The talent is seeing the road ahead before you enter and knowing when to use your blinker. A robust planning process teamed with a flexible facilitator can be two positive indicators that you're on the right road. The planning team for Brand Engine makes a great match with Plum Organics. Both have a significant amount of knowledge and neither was afraid to learn something new about the baby food category. With this setup, planning for the Plum Organics line had a great chance to deliver a brand to its destination (shelves) and to look good when it got there (obvious).

The face no one could resist, packaging organic cereal that many have had trouble resisting. This package makes a promise: organic, healthy, yummy, and smart baby food. The product lives up to the promise of the package.

Stacking up a flavor selection allows you to see how the hierarchy works, using the spoon as a subtle yet essential communication device. The idea is that a photo can say much more than words, and in this case these words are whispered at a shelf where everyone else is screaming.

CREATING

The designers explored a number of concepts with the client. They refined a couple and arrived at something close to what you see. The result was a package able to convey three powerful points—the innocence of childhood, the comfort of something organic, and the feeling of food even adults would eat. All this is fine and good when you look at the package and say, "Yes it does look good, beautiful, and safe." But the creative process becomes a gold mine when the results, or rather shoppers, start showing up at the shelves.

Alternative concepts give an idea of where the package design could have gone. Each permutation provides its own feel for how the brand would come to life.

IMPLEMENTING

Baby food could be seen as a tired category with a small field of typical competitors putting out line extensions until the cows come home. The Plum Organics line approached the category, packaging, and product development from a beautiful angle. The result was a package and product parents would be happy to pull off the shelf. It delivered other unexpected results when Brand Engine discovered a significant number of adults consuming certain flavors and not hiding the fact from the researchers.

THE CLIENT: INEKE

DESIGN FIRM: HELENA SEO DESIGN (USA)

Right: Authentically blending materials like glass, metal, and plastic creates a feeling of substance with just the right sense of thoughtful style.

Ineke Perfume

THE SCENT OF STYLE AND ELEGANCE

PLANNING

Setting a flag in the sands of time to represent a new view of perfume. Companies who specialize in the science behind olfactory sensory experiences design most perfumes. Fashion models and celebrities are often the only brand names on these perfumes. The connection between the designer of the perfume and the consumer is lost. The new Ineke perfume was designed without a model, fashion brand, or other diva in mind. It was designed with the consumer in mind. The package design needed to reflect this while still capturing the elegance and exclusivity most often attached to the diva with the big name.

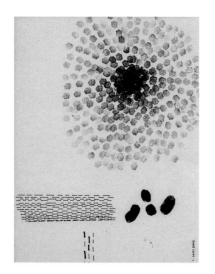

CREATING

Starting with both the visual and written language of the brand, Helena Seo walked the Ineke team through a process of listing words and collecting images. These were used to build the feeling around the perfume's story. Then individual packages were designed to help further visualize the story. After the exterior carton was done, the bottle followed suit within the design language created. There were challenges when it came to finding stock photography that would convey the right message and then having to jump to original photography to get the right feel. The design eventually came together like a three-dimensional puzzle.

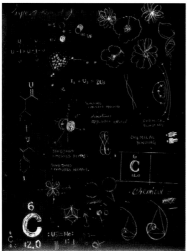

Early sketches and art can provide both inspiration and start to provide focus for where the eventual design will go.

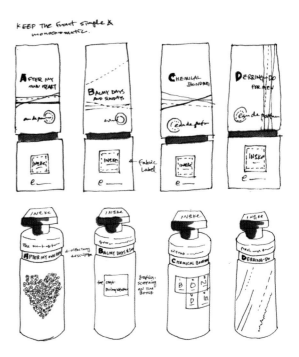

Pencil sketches in our digital age continue to be valuable when considering the feeling of an early design. With the right people viewing these sketches you can get more clear direction from your client.

IMPLEMENTING

With an exhaustive knowledge of packaging materials (glass etching, metal engraving, woven labels, etc), Ineke was able to collaboratively pull together and deliver a stunning package for perfume. The lack of a model, diva, or superstar goes unnoticed after the consumer is able to connect with the scent and make it part of her life.

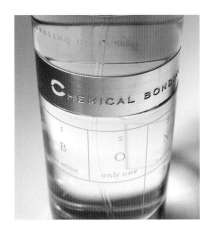

Appropriate details within a design can offer the customer something to discover as they engage with the package.

THE CLIENT: LUXELAB

DESIGN FIRM: DUSTIN ARNOLD (USA)

Right: Notice the simplicity of type and graphic elements, using the most minimalist design while still conveying the brand. Embrace the beauty of blonde and imagine what it feels like to hold this package in your hand.

LuxeLab Blonde-Aid

SMARTER THAN THE AVERAGE BLONDE

Do blondes really have more fun? If so, do they need more help being blonde? This brand identified an unmet need that any brunette would turn up a nose to: helping blondes care for their specific hair color. If there was a need to give blondes a greater advantage, this product was formulated to service that need. The package design had to gracefully convey the help the product was offering this underserved segment.

PLANNING

Planning for such a product required significant scientific discovery and experimentation before a package could even be considered. Then, after dedicating so much time to the product, the package couldn't go unnoticed. It would be like cutting off your nose to spite your face: great product, hideous package. The planning included research from LuxeLab's team as well as anything the designer could find in secondary markets. Once the product formulation was complete and a brand strategy was clear, the creative process could begin.

How a package interacts and creates a pattern in collaboration with more of the same packages can go beyond a photograph on the page. It can be a valuable tool to create a billboard effect at the point of display. The LuxeLab package achieves this in an elegant manner.

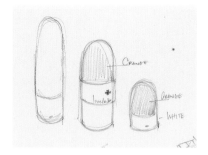

CREATING

Creating something to safely treat hair has many metaphors that work to tell the story. The designer chose to focus on medicinal metaphors surrounding the Red Cross; medical cleanliness; and elegant, simple shapes. The result, after many concepts and many more refinements, was a package design that feels healthy, blonde, and medical.

IMPLEMENTING

Getting a product to the shelf can involve a series of potholes on the long road to market. Although there are plenty of reasons for why blondes don't really need additional caring for their hair, this product has a interesting angle with its focus on blondes. And launching LuxeLab in Southern California, a market bubbling over with candidates, is a whip smart strategy. And in case you're wondering, the product works for converted blondes, too—we asked.

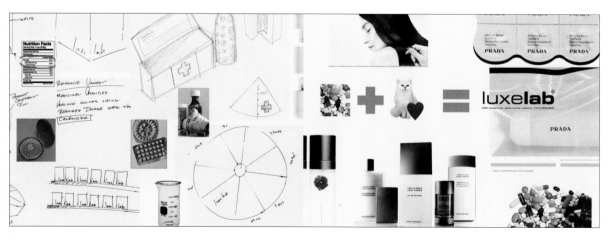

Seeing both sketches and inspirational images gives a glimpse into the minds of everyone involved in this effort. Capturing the history of anything allows us to better understand the depth of work required to bring it to life.

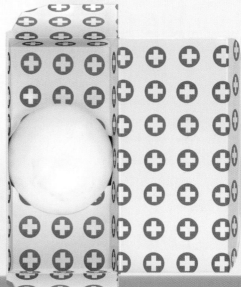

By the time a potential shopper views this package, excessive messages and clutter will have little or no effect. The clean design of the secondary packages contribute to the design and a shopper's experience with this package. For that matter, what retailer would hide this beautiful package on the bottom shelf?

| THE CLIENT: | OLD NASSUA IMPORTS |
| DESIGN FIRM: | CAPSULE (USA) |

Right: From the experience of uncapping the bottle, to pouring a shot, to actual consuming the alcohol was a designed experience. The bottle created a unique experience exclusively designed for those who could afford this super-premium vodka brand.

Double Cross Vodka

DISTILLED PERFECTION IN A SQUARE BOTTLE

From distant lands we bring liquids to markets where everyone can enjoy the fruits and grains of labor. Vodka is made from many ingredients, but the distillation and filtration process is really what distinguishes one product from another. That is, until a brand name, identity, and package are created to announce from the tallest point in Slovakia, "We are not like all the others." Old Nassau Imports sought to create a vodka product and brand with enough confidence to boast from any mountain top.

PLANNING

Taking a swim in the marketplace for vodka may seem like an adventure worth taking, but it becomes real work when you've seen your hundredth spirit bottle. The planning process for the team at Old Nassau Imports and Capsule included enough secondary and qualitative research to make an MBA proud. The use of visual language boards helped coalesce the brand language and inspire the rest of the creative process. The result was exactly what planning should accomplish: a better understanding of the risks and rewards, along with a pathway to navigate around the risks.

Visual style boards can be valuable discussion items to translate both vision to reality and visual language to written words. These boards helped the Capsule team create a bottle design to evoke the luxury brand their client desired.

CREATING

Starting with pencil sketches, images of perfume bottles, and mountaintop photos of Slovakia, the creative process had all the right inspiration. The concepts were taken to three-dimensional renderings at an early stage so Old Nassau Imports could take home a short movie and look at the presence of each bottle concept. Early decisions on bottle shape and structure led to innovative cap ideas and a variety of other fundamental bottle design elements. Then graphics were applied to the bottle, taking what was a twenty-fifth-century bottle design back a hundred years to incorporate the heritage of Slovakian culture. The result is a bottle that not only blends old and new but also creates the starkest contrast between those two worlds. This contrast conveys the idea of Double Cross in graphic and dimensional form. The bottle becomes the brand and the brand becomes the bottle.

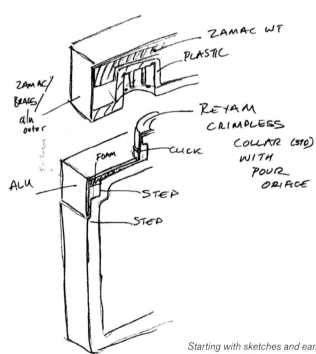

Starting with sketches and early renderings, the picture of this process starts to fill in. From a concept with a removable wristband to an explicit double cross by the bottle design, these early concepts had significant influence on where the bottle ended up.

IMPLEMENTING

Try telling your dream to someone the next morning and sometimes you're met with a curious frown. Putting the concept in front of manufacturers charged with producing the bottle, you could feel the frowns through the conference call. When challenged, the bottle suppliers who could see beyond the constraints and make this dream a reality were the same ones who landed the implementation contract. The process of refinements, implementation, and getting the bottle to the shelf requires truckloads of patience and persistence. Fortunately for everyone, the entire team had plenty of both.

Calligraphy is an old art form which offers an elegant contrast for a modern, clean bottle design. The use of a Slovakian poem on the bottle in this lettering creates an "oh, of course" feeling for the patron loyal to this vodka brand.

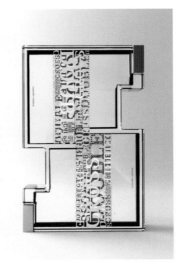

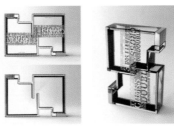

The amazing possibilities of digital renderings, which are eventually turned into short movies, can make the process of deciding on your next bottle design as rewarding as watching an academy award winner in Hollywood. These highly rendered concepts allowed the decision makers to immerse themselves in their choices.

THE CLIENT: **OUTSET**

DESIGN FIRM: **OUTSET DESIGN (USA)**

Right: A thing of beauty is effortlessly, photogenic. This package design, like a supermodel, is easy on the eyes—both in a photograph and when it goes on display at your local retailer.

Outset Chillware
COOL ENOUGH TO CHILL IN

PLANNING

Love method? Looking for the same passion for design with your grilling utensils and accessories? Hello, Outset. Planning for design in Outset has many of the same organic methods and practices. When it comes to a new product, as the idea develops, it becomes clear where the product will fit in the portfolio, market, and within consumer grilling experiences. It doesn't mean there are months spent on focus groups, surveys, or other massive quantitative research projects. It does mean, however, that strategy is mapped out based on the team's current knowledge, assumptions are made, and the brand vision comes to life in how the product and package are designed.

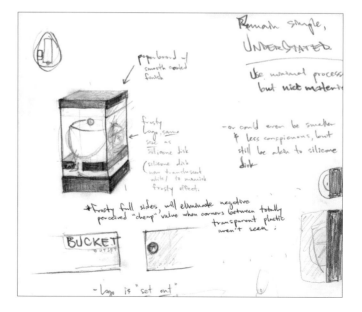

Pencil sketches can quickly lead to solid ideas. The team for Outset was also able to look back on where the package originated with these early sketches.

Everything a master griller would need—yes, everything. The package is efficient and works within the larger design language of the brand.

CREATING

The design process for the Outset team included concept work and rigorous education around what would make a great package design. The packaging design process can sometimes be crushed by a timeline closer to what it takes to cook a hot dog than what it should take to design a package. When faced with this kind of deadline, the Outset design team was able to adapt and still produce a design balancing form and function.

Deep understanding of the context of sale and use can be an essential thread to any design. The Outset packaging was designed with the context of product display in mind. The box has a bellyband that is easily removed to allow storeowners to withdraw one sample without damaging the original package. The product also merchandises like a supermodel with translucent areas allowing the shopper to see nearly all the details inside the package.

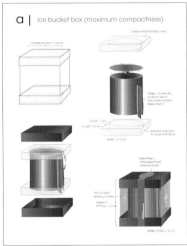

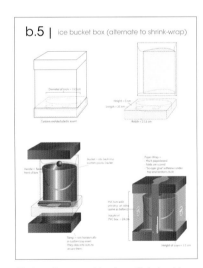

Engineering something beautiful should be as elegant as the design when you understand how it all came together. Engineering the ice bucket isn't the Brooklyn Bridge, but it still has to carry its own weight.

DESIGN FIRM: **FUSION HILL (USA)**

Making Waves and Charting a New Territory with a Unique Portfolio Design

Using a combination of research, strategy, and design, Minneapolis-based Fusion Hill strives to create some of the most innovative, thoughtful design solutions for their clients.

PLANNING

Fusion Hill attended a networking event in which marketing materials were not required or even recommended for distribution. Event attendees did not have the ability to carry portfolios or large giveaways from meeting to meeting. That left Fusion Hill in a conundrum: Come up with a way to leave a subtle impression on the potential clients who would be attending the networking event, while differentiating Fusion Hill from the competitors who would also be showcasing their wares.

"Because we were in the travel setting—namely, a cruise ship, we considered luggage tags and ID cases, but it didn't really give us the opportunity to package our story," says Kasey Worrell Hatzung, principal at Fusion Hill. "We wanted to create a product that was uniquely ours. Most other items we considered were already created and really only allowed us to 'brand' them with our logo or colors. We did consider using or giving away products that we had helped to brand or develop from other clients, like a Vera Bradley ID wallet or a food product from General Mills, but they weren't as small, didn't tell our whole story, and were often not unisex or they did not reflect everyone's taste."

In a world brimming with marketing messages, you no doubt long for a breath of fresh air. Explore Fusion Hill, and discover how we've helped clients build – and maintain – brands that make an impact.

fusion HILL

Dive In

fusion HILL

WAVE MAKERS

MN

PEPPERMINTS

FRESHEN *your* BRAND

WOMEN

We know women: their closets, their kitchens, their purses and their lifestyles. Through hundreds of in-home interviews, focus groups and trendwork, we've helped Vera Bradley, General Mills, UnitedHealth Group, Peg Perego and Drexel Heritage understand women: who they are, what they need and how they buy.

HEALTHCARE

From doctors' offices and patients' homes to hospital purchasing departments, we've immersed ourselves into the world of healthcare and created powerful results for companies like CIGNA, Medtronic, Tornier Sports Medicine and St. Jude Medical.

WOMEN

We know women: their closets, their kitchens, their purses and their lifestyles. Through hundreds of in-home interviews, focus groups and trendwork, we've helped Vera Bradley, General Mills, UnitedHealth Group, Peg Perego and Drexel Heritage understand women: who they are, what they need and how they buy.

LIKE WHAT YOU'VE SEEN SO FAR?
IT'S JUST THE TIP OF THE ICEBERG.

fusion HILL

www.fusionhill.com
612-638-5000

▲ *Whimsical and inviting, the exterior design of the Fusion Hill tin was indicative of the contents within.*

◄ *Some of the best things come in small packages. The recipients of Fusion Hill's treasure-filled tin were treated to more than a few savory mints. They were surprised to find a mini portfolio creatively constructed to fit within the confines of the compact tin container.*

CREATING

Because the event was being held on a cruise ship, the design team at Fusion Hill decided to incorporate a nautical theme into their promotional piece—a stainless steel tin of mints. They also wanted to give away something small enough to fit in a pocket, useful enough to keep and use over time, and clever enough to be memorable.

"We also thought of other candies such as gum and chocolates, but again, the mints seemed most useful and the tins would be recognizable as such, then leaving the little portfolio inside as the surprise," Hatzung says. "We found a lot of different-size tins, but we needed it to be able to house a business card and our portfolio, fit candies, and match other materials we were creating for our portfolio. Also, the portfolio inside had to be big enough to show our capabilities and samples of our work but just be a teaser."

While the Fusion Hill team discovered a lot of vendors that will print on a tin or personalize the tins and provide the mints for you, they simply weren't satisfied with what they found. "The printing samples we found were really subpar for a four-color image," Hatzung says.

Recipients were treated to a surprise when they opened the mints—a tiny accordion-folded portfolio with multiple panels that highlighted the key categories of work and industries that Fusion Hill serves, including financial, health care, consumer packaged goods, and women.

Fusion Hill had multiple renditions of the label—all fitting within a certain style. "We were looking for place-based imagery that was fresh, used our colors, but wasn't too wintry as we were sending/handing these out in early spring," Hatzung says.

At one point in the preliminary design process, the labels featured a moose in the distance. "But it felt a little too kitschy and not quite 'us,'" Hatzung explains. "We did keep the idea of the 'winds of change' with the cloud blowing. We really wanted this tin to look like a product and not just a branded Fusion Hill mint tin, so we gave it lots of personality."

fusion HILL

NORTHERN

STRATEGIC
CREATIVE
MINTS

Frost Bites

Follow Your Sense

FrostBite

▲ *Some of Fusion Hill's preliminary designs illustrate their direction of celebrating the atmosphere of the northern climes of Minnesota, where Fusion Hill is located, while playing on the minty freshness of the candies themselves.*

They branded the product "Wave Makers"—the double entendre plays off being out at sea and the idea that Fusion Hill could deliver change and impact for those ready for a new perspective. Of those attending, Fusion Hill was the only firm from Minnesota, so they wanted to play on that a bit—poking fun at themselves and their frosty climate.

Fusion Hill also chose a tin with an aluminum finish to match an oversize tin that they sent as a follow-up to prospects with their full-size portfolio included inside.

"We also needed to make sure that the mints were protected from the portfolio and for it not to feel tampered with—so we included a vellum wrap that covered the mints and added a layer between the portfolio and a business card we inserted. We then closed the tin with a clear wafer seal," Hatzung says. "Our team wore hairnets and latex gloves and put all the mint tins together in assembly-line fashion at our office."

The mints are wrapped with a little frosted vellum that says "dive in," and once you've depleted the contents and reached the bottom, there is a message that says "hungry for more?" with Fusion Hill's contact information.

IMPLEMENTING

A first "wave" of forty tins was handed out in person at the networking event. An additional 350 tins were mailed out to prospects and clients. Fusion Hill made a version for clients with customized messaging. The mailer included a clear pouch with the tins floating inside (for visual effect and protection).

"We love the personality of the artwork that uses our corporate blue and strong elements like the waves and the name Wave Makers," Hatzung says. "We like how the whole approach sets us apart from the competition and being new on the scene (for this event), heralds our location and then takes the time to introduce who we are with quick snippets and examples. We packed everything we wanted into a tiny little presentation."

Sending out the "second wave" of their portfolio to clients and prospects after the first event also proved to be very beneficial. "Because we weren't handing them out personally, we needed a unique method of transport. Our mission is always impeccable and creative presentation and packaging," Hatzung says. "We took what is a heavy-looking little tin and made it look light as air by fugitive gluing it inside a clear pillow pack. It just floated inside that pack with nothing but clear air around it."

The mailing label and stamp all fit on a 2 × 3.75-inch (5 × 9 cm) label that was adhered to the pillow pack on the back of the label so that as you looked at the package from the front you didn't see any of the mailing clutter.

"Because any printing and packaging we found from vendors was such low quality, we had our own labels printed on a durable, sticky substrate that could withstand the bumps we knew it would encounter in pockets and purses and still look great," Hatzung says.

The total run with both versions was 650 quantity, and costs for production and supplies (printing of labels, inserts, mints, and assembly) was $1,650 (£1008), with an additional $500 (£305) for postage. "This was one of our least expensive mailers by far," Hatzung says. "Our holiday mailings in past years have been closer to $10 (£6) with a similar quantity."

The overall response to the tins was very positive—in fact, many recipients requested more. They were also a great conversation starter for follow-up phone calls—people remembered receiving them and easily recalled the design firm.

"When we handed them out, people of course just thought we were giving them mints," Hatzung says. "We'd tell them there was a tiny portfolio inside, and they would look at us with surprise and start guessing what it might look like or what form it was in, and they'd just have to open them up right there. To us the idea of a portfolio and a giveaway was just the criteria of doing it at all, but people just loved it and thought it was so unique. I think the quality of the finishes, printing, layering, candies, and messages made it really stand out from other standard giveaways we saw. The ability to package so much punch and personality in such a small vehicle proved ingenious."

▲ *To entice each recipient to open the self-promotional tin, each tin was housed in a clear envelope that both enticed and engaged the recipient.*

DESIGN FIRM: LARSEN

Celebrating the Historical Passion for Design

With offices in San Francisco and Minneapolis, Larsen creates identities, marketing collateral, websites, packaging, and a plethora of other design elements that help organizations establish or enhance their presence in the marketplace.

PLANNING

Over the past thirty-four years, Larsen has developed a significant body of work and a reputation for environmental graphics—a unique medium not accommodated by many graphic design firms, and one that can be difficult to demonstrate. "To reproduce images of the work that are representative of its scale, we launched our current brochure series by designing a larger format piece (9.5 × 11.5 inches [24.1 × 29.2 cm]) that feels more like a magazine," says Tim Larsen, principal at Larsen Design. "When first handing it out, we gained an immediate increase in environmental design inquiries, mainly from clients who didn't know we had the expertise."

For Larsen, the firm's printed brochures serve as the primary component of their portfolio system. "We categorize the brochures based on wanting to present an overview of Larsen's current broad range of work (general capabilities), and to highlight specialties within our suite of services (particularly environmental graphics and identity design)," Larsen says. "On occasion, we also feature a particular industry of work from which we are interested in acquiring more business, such as retail."

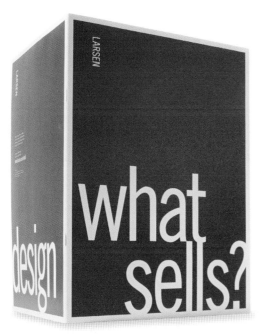

▲ With the redesign of Larsen's own identity, the company adapted a crisp, white look and feel to all of its marketing materials and expanded its arsenal of capabilities literature to include brochures specific to identity design and environmental graphics.

▲ Larsen's experience can be focused in specific industry segments, and the team was excited to promote recent work in retail and consumer products. To address the inherently louder, more assertive sales environment, this piece features large type and even bigger visuals for immediate impact.

CREATING

The firm's core portfolio was initially bound by metal rivets, so pages could easily be removed and replaced when appropriate. Since the metal scratched the brochures stacked above and below, the firm substituted white plastic rivets for the second piece in Larsen's promotional literature series—the ID brochure.

"This second component was developed based on a lesson learned: It is difficult to show a single identity design alone; identities are best displayed in quantity," Larsen says. With a compendium brochure, Larsen can demonstrate their breadth of visual solutions for identities and give the client a chance to consider a variety of directions. And since Larsen identifies itself as a consulting office, not a style office, a compendium exhibits a diversity of approaches executed by the firm's sixteen graphic designers.

One would expect a general capabilities piece to be the first brochure Larsen might develop. "With our clients, it's easier to demonstrate print collateral by showing actual finished samples," Larsen says. "They exemplify the quality of design, printing, paper, and texture for which Larsen is known. By the same token, we are better able to show our interactive design capabilities by directing prospects to URLs we've designed and developed. Therefore, the two easiest areas to promote—print and interactive—have been the last to be solved through printed literature."

Larsen created the "What Sells" retail brochure to distribute during the recent recessionary economy. "It cuts to the message and demonstrates that we have the ability to help corporations and marketing managers drive revenue to the top and bottom line," Larsen says. "Its brightly colored cover with large type and all full-page photos is a departure from the rest of the promotional literature system, primarily because B2C requires a more assertive approach than B2B."

▲ *Every month, a new project is featured in a large-format postcard, with a single thought and image on the front and a case study on the back. This direct mail is sent as a memory tickler to Larsen's client and prospect mailing list.*

IMPLEMENTING

Larsen's printed brochures are primarily given to serious prospects and clients with whom they anticipate working. "In the past, we may have sent brochures to an extensive prospect list due to its low cost, but now that we print fewer pieces and they cost more per item, we are fairly selective as to who receives them," Larsen says. "We occasionally send literature to a short list of companies in a particular industry we want to pursue, or send individual targeted packages that address news about a company that fits with our experience."

Each component within Larsen's portfolio arsenal has been designed by a different Larsen designer, with Larsen serving as creative director in every case.

The current literature system printing cost is about $18 to $20 (£11 to 12) apiece based on digital, short-run (250 pieces) printing. The unit cost of previous years' examples was $8 to $10 (£5 to 6) each, but when printed in quantities of thousands, Larsen couldn't use the brochures in a timely manner and the featured work became dated.

▲ *With its extensive portfolio of identity designs, Larsen built a card deck that could include all or some of the exemplary work based on what a client wants to see— and bound together by a rivet.*

"The goal of our promotional literature is to gain new business and referrals from existing clients, past clients, recommenders, partners, and prospects," Larsen says. "The purpose of the literature has been to exhibit our client work—rather than be a statement about design itself. In many ways, we have taken our cues for the layout of the pieces from publications like *Communication Arts* and *Graphis*." As the viewer flips though the brochure, it has a design annual feel—clean, straightforward images and minimal text. This familiar format makes it comfortable to view the work. As a result, the pieces came together easily and quickly in terms of the design process.

High-quality photography has always been a crucial element to the design (from signage to packaging to print), so Larsen has budgeted for it every year and art-directed professional studio photographers. They are then able to use these images in their Web portfolio, for case studies, and for archival purposes.

Another major decision was choosing the paper and binding method of the brochures, as Larsen wants to display top-quality materials and methods. "Our binding system has evolved from PVC to spiral to perfect binding, and more recently rivets in metal, then plastic," Larsen says. "Today, we are utilizing a match-cover style of stitching the book and folding over the cover to hide the stitches."

With the advent of the Web came significant change, however. "For many clients, printed pieces have become a supplement, and in some cases are not necessary when they can see our portfolio online," Larsen says. "Nonetheless, it's reassuring to have a leave-behind or a tangible item to mail in order to elicit a meeting. Additionally, the demographics of the final decision maker often require a variety of media for up-channel selling."

It goes without saying that every printed piece Larsen produces includes their URL so the prospect or client can locate the firm's online presence to quickly assess their abilities and access their contact information.

"An informal survey indicates people appreciate the books, which offer a chance to look at Larsen's work in depth at their leisure, and as a resource when projects arise," Larsen says. "The brochures are viewed as gifts rather than promotions because they make good reference tools that demonstrate excellence in design."

◄▼ To celebrate the company's twenty-fifth year in business, the image of a paper airplane (an adjunct element to the Larsen identity at the time) was set into motion in a flipbook that invited clients, prospects, partners, vendors, and friends to "Soar with Us."

DESIGN FIRM: OLOGIE (USA)

Setting the Stage for Success

Ologie understands what it takes to tell a good story by exploring creative avenues that will lead to smart brand solutions for their clients. Based in Columbus, Ohio, Ologie inspires a myriad of creatives, including designers, writers, researchers, planners, and strategists to develop the best outcomes for their clients.

PLANNING

Cohesiveness. It's an important element in many facets of life. Interior designers embrace it. Sports team managers strive for it. Medical specialists would be lost without it. It creates a symbiotic relationship among people or elements that defines who they are and what they do. And when an individual or firm is looking to promote themselves, creating a cohesive design for their portfolio materials is paramount. Just ask Ologie, a Brooklyn-based design firm that strives to provide a consistent message in who they are and what they do.

"When determining how to categorize our portfolio system, we separated the big buckets of information clients wanted to know," says Beverly Bethge, partner at Ologie. "We looked at how businesses talk about themselves and make themselves more digestible, so we divided our portfolio contents into three distinct categories:

- "Skill Set: What we do

- "Get Set: How we do it; our approach

- "Mind Set: How we think about it, our point of view."

◄ *Each element within the Ologie portfolio components follows a similar theme, design, and layout. Complementary yet distinct, the Skill Set, Get Set, and Mind Set elements offer a comprehensive look into Ologie's offerings.*

► *With the Get Set piece, the Ologie team thought it was important to tell clients what they're about to get into, and why this commitment of time and money is worth it. "There's a business equation on the other side," Bethge says. "The work we do is a huge catalyst for change in their organization. They need to know that. This piece gets them to see the totality of their brand, as opposed to tactics they might associate with branding, such as an ad campaign or a logo."*

Skill Set outlines exactly what Ologie does, without any jargon. "When you have key people in the business who have been at it for more than twenty years, there's a certain point of view and confidence that you can't change even if you wanted to," Bethge says. "It's how you go to work every day. If you put it out there and are honest with clients, they respond to it."

► *Mind Set is more of a character piece. It's as much an internal piece as it is an external one. If there's one document that can rally everyone in the company to deliver on-brand, this is it. "It's not a detailed process manual about how we do things," Bethge says. "It's more about how you feel about things. We're so clear on our mind-set that it took less than 10 minutes to write and was completely unedited. If a client gets through these pieces and believes in what we believe in, if they believe in the approach and think great work can come from it, if they're entertained by our style, then it's going to be great."*

CREATING

A huge part of the Ologie experience is about simplification—which is very different from being simplistic. "We simplify big, chaotic messes," Bethge says. "A lot of firms say that, but we deliver it. And our space and our collateral communicate that immediately."

The Ologie team wanted these pieces to look beautiful and make perfect sense to the user—because that's an Ologie-like experience. They also know that size matters, so the pieces are interesting sizes.

Also, in an age where every presentation is digital, Ologie still believes in leaving something tactile behind. "People like to hold something that's real," Bethge says. "We believe it makes everything more tangible. And more credible."

▲ *Each of the categories within Ologie's portfolio system means something. "To have put them into one brochure would have been too much for people to get through. And it would have been boring," Bethge says. "So we tried to give people a different way to access that information. Plus, it's like a gift, and recipients want to explore it. We're rewarding them for wanting to get to know us."*

People take action with their heart.

AND THAT REQUIRES A VERY DELIBERATE APPROACH ON YOUR PART.

ologie

FINAN
SERVIC
INTAN

But that doesn't mean financial

▲ *Three of Ologie's magazines—B2B, Greater Good, and Financial Services—all feature the work the firm has done for these industry segments. Following a distinctive design strategy, these three publications entice the reader with streamlined and engaging copy.*

IMPLEMENTING

Ologie's introductory pieces are given to prospective clients, visitors, partners, vendors, presentation attendees—many different audiences. But as the Ologie team gets to know prospective clients, and better understand their needs, they put together more customized presentations that feature case studies of situations similar to theirs.

"Clients are always fascinated by the vinyl folder with the orange *O*s all over it," Bethge says. "One client even requested something similar for their brand."

Bethge notes that advisors are always telling Ologie to specialize in a single industry. "We think that's boring. And besides, you learn so much from one industry that you can apply to another. For example, we're constantly using retail tactics in financial services," she explains.

AL
S ARE
IBLE.

ve to be.

ologie

BUSINESS-TO-BUSINESS MARKETING CAN BE COMPLEX.

Which is exactly why your story should be simple.

ologie

But Ologie's prospects and clients always ask, "How much experience do you have in my industry?" So they put together a set of magazines to send out to current and prospective clients to show their expertise in specific categories, such as B2B, financial services, nonprofit, and higher education. "The magazines share our design and photography capabilities through the layout of the pieces, but really highlight case studies through a feature-story approach," Bethge says. The magazines quickly deliver Ologie's perspective and experience with the industry. Ologie has only made one round of minor edits to two of the pieces within their portfolio system, developed three years ago.

"Whenever you look back on everything, you're bound to find something you want to change," Bethge says. "But as we look through these pieces, they still reflect exactly who we are. And we couldn't be prouder of that."

DESIGN FIRM: INTEREUROPE COMMUNICATIONS GROUP
(ICG, UNITED KINGDOM)

Separating Themselves from the Pack

From design and public relations to advertising and new media, Intereurope Communications Group (ICG) is a "one-stop shop" for clients who are passionate about strategy, design, and getting their message out there.

PLANNING

As part of its new-business drive, ICG has historically sent out various brochures to businesses to gain account wins. "However, through follow-up calls we discovered that our brochures were not gaining the attention of decision makers," says Simon Couchman, creative director at ICG. "Simply asking 'do you remember the blue brochure?' wasn't working, as marketing managers receive so much material from agencies." In addition, ICG's online presence was weak, with little content. They needed a new system that stood out from other agencies, yet wasn't so overdesigned that it weakened the creative work they were trying to show.

"Through initial research, we recognized that despite designers opting to present their company portfolios using the latest fashionable typefaces, special inks, and finishes, they were inadvertently distilling the actual work they were trying to present," Couchman says. "We therefore identified that we needed a system that was very clean and graphic, retained a strong identity, and at the same time didn't dominate the work we deliver to clients."

ICG's second step was to focus on the services that they offer and wanted to promote. They included their four distinctive services—graphic design, public relations, new media, and advertising—all under the umbrella of one company. "We therefore retained our existing corporate logo, but muted the colors to a single warm gray, and typographically we chose a classic: Helvetica Neue."

The ICG
bumper
book
of client
case
studies.

Or, how we helped our clients achieve
their communication and marketing
goals without breaking their budget.

iCg⁽ᴳ⁾

Graphic Design · Public Relations · New Media · Advertising & Marketing   www.icgonline.co.uk

◄▼ *Using the ICG stripes motif,* The ICG
Bumper Book of Client Case Studies *offers
an in-depth look at some of the projects that
have helped ICG make a name for itself.*

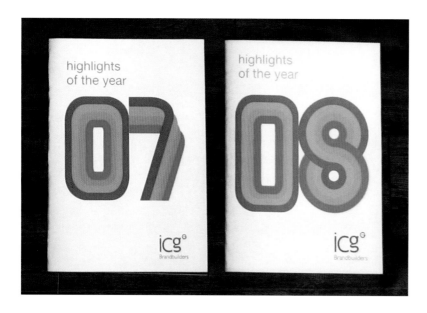

CREATING

To support and reflect the individual services, ICG introduced a set of four brightly colored stripes, which were assigned to each service. "This reflected our position as an integrated full-service agency and at the same time defined the individual services that we provide," Couchman says.

To support this striking appearance, they also started to include a device in their mailings to help people remember the portfolio items they sent out. Currently, it's a lollipop made from Blackpool Rock, a type of rock candy made in Blackpool, England. The lollipop features the ICG stripes, reflecting their location close to Blackpool itself. In addition, a sticker on the lollipop states: "Our rates take some licking…" which gives readers an immediate insight into ICG's cost structure.

"Once the core corporate brochure was agreed and developed, we then transferred the look, feel, and selected content to other promotional devices, such as our websites," Couchman says.

ICG initially considered the implementation process from a commercial perspective, asking themselves, "What do we want to sell to the marketplace?" "What messages do we want to convey to potential clients?" and "How do we effectively present this information?"

"We looked at a lot of agencies' promotional material, as well as our current brochures, and reviewed what we liked and didn't like," Couchman says. "Our house style is generally colorful, clean, uncluttered designs that communicate clearly and effectively, so we looked at using an uncluttered graphical treatment."

Influences included Farrow's designs for the Pet Shop Boys' *Introspective* album, and the Penguin book covers of the '60s. "The stripes answered our requirements," Couchman says. "Once the idea was there, it was hard to shake. We experimented with various colors and chose a vibrant selection that would stand out on people's desks and yet would work in harmony."

ICG also wanted to reflect their strategic approach and included many of the services they offer. They chose case studies with a range of strategic commercial and communication objectives, such as increasing sales. These examples would interest marketing managers and company directors.

"We presented the case studies uniformly, so that from both a copy and visual perspective they clearly explained the project or campaign challenges—as well as the creative solutions and results," Couchman says. These creative solutions were illustrated by a mix of studio-shot photography and flat spreads.

◄▲ *Each year, ICG creates an annual book reflecting on and celebrating the firm's creative accomplishments during the previous twelve months. Each month consists of one or two significant events, including projects completed, awards received, or results of a public relations campaign for a specific client. This annual book illustrates the breadth and depth of ICG.*

IMPLEMENTING

ICG's portfolio consists of a twenty-page, large-format case study brochure titled *The ICG Bumper Book of Client Case Studies* and sixteen-page pocket-size guidebooks to the firm's various individual services, as well as an activity-review mini brochure. The portfolio theme is carried out through additional promotional pieces, including a twenty-four-page public relations case study brochure, *The ICG Little Black Book of Public Relations and Copywriting*, specially manufactured holiday gifts, two blogs, and two websites.

The initial design process, including the design of the main brochure, took about a month to complete. ICG continues to update case studies and other components on a regular basis to keep materials fresh—particularly on the websites and blogs.

"The system has evolved over the last twelve months, and as the stripes are becoming more recognized, we are able to have fun pushing what we do with them a little more," Couchman says. "We had a client arrive for a meeting in the striped hat and scarf we sent out as a Christmas gift this winter. She's hoping we do gloves next."

ICG's in-house capabilities allow the firm to self-publish some of their mini guides when they need to communicate with potential clients. "For example, we have just sent out a small guide that talks about marketing during a recession," Couchman says. "These enable us to responsively communicate current issues and reflect our understanding of the challenges that companies face."

All of ICG's materials have had to be extremely cost-effective, so where possible, the ICG team undertakes work themselves, including the website build, all photography, and digital printing of the mini guides.

▲► *ICG is an award-winning full-service agency, offering clients four distinctive services, including graphic design, public relations, new media, and advertising. To promote these separate disciplines, the firm devised a set of four brightly colored stripes and assigned each service its own color (for example, orange for graphic design). The branding is simple yet effective and has been rolled out across all elements of ICG's promotional material—from stationery, business cards, and website to corporate brochures and their annual "highlights" books. It is also included on a number of promotional items, including mugs, scarves, lollipops, and even the firm's interior office décor. The simplicity of the vibrant stripes ensures consistency and creates a core brand for the agency without having to "overdesign" their own material.*

"Our strong relationships with printers enables us to have the main brochure litho-printed at a good cost," Couchman says. "We generally print around 2,000 copies of the main brochure at a time, with updates to the case studies when we reprint."

ICG also found a great supplier of the hats and scarves. The supplier can source wool in the exact colors in the system, and can produce them as ICG needs them. "Our lollipops were specially made by a local manufacturer, who even let us select our own flavor," Couchman says.

ICG distributes the elements of their portfolio differently:

- Potential clients will initially receive the brochures, along with a lollipop.

When they go to meetings, ICG's business cards and presentation continue the striped theme.

- Current clients will regularly receive the mini guides and newsletters, in addition to their day-to-day communications.

- At Christmas, ICG mails all clients their winter gift: a hat and scarf, along with the "highlights of the year" book.

"The response has been overwhelmingly positive, with an increase in new business appointments," Couchman says. "When following up prospects, the lollipop acts as a great prompt, and often we will get requests for additional lollies for clients' children. We have also received a few photos of clients on skiing holidays wearing our hats."

DESIGN FIRM: CACAO DESIGN (ITALY)

Multidimensional Portfolio Design

Founded by Masa Magnoni, Alessandro Floridia, and Mauro Pastore, Cacao Design strives to satisfy their clients' integrated communication needs. Working with clients across a myriad of industries, Cacao Design specializes in corporate identity and Web design.

PLANNING

Italian design—clothing, art, textiles, and architecture—has long been celebrated as the epitome of high-end design. Clean lines, impeccable materials, and awe-inspiring artistic renderings make Italian design elements some of the most sought after in the world. The same can be said for the portfolio brochure produced by Cacao Design. Based in Milan, Italy, Cacao Design has created a unique piece of art in their firm's recent portfolio.

"'The nonconventional brochure is an object to play with while turning over the pages," says Mauro Pastore, cofounder and creative director at Cacao Design. "This is what we always try to do when we work on our clients' brochures: change classic printed pieces of paper into designed objects. Our brochure incites an emotional response and displays the real substance of our creativity and work approach, which is to come up with unexpected solutions that speak directly to the client's heart. Enjoy your brand!"

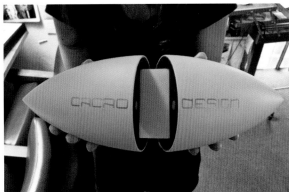

Initially, the Cacao Design team fell in love with another idea: a small-size brochure that, when closed, was about the size of a deck of playing cards with full-page photos of their work inside. "This precious little 'pit' was placed inside a big seed that reproduces our logo in 3-D, revealing the concept: cacao seed, fruit of desire, synonymous with savor and passion," Pastore says.

But as the planning process evolved, they decided to utilize a dimensional Plexiglas exterior with an etching of the firm's motto, "enjoy your brand."

CREATING

Cacao Design is very specific about their graphic choices for each project. "We pay meticulous attention to artistic detail as it relates to the brand, to create an emotional connection with the target audience before their brains process the message," Pastore says. "Words are not enough to transmit the meaning of what we do and how we do it." Their portfolio includes examples of these projects done for various clients.

What's more, the Cacao Design brochure had to present the firm's print communication projects, showcasing not only their creativity, but their attention to print and production details.

"The format in which we present our portfolio satisfies our need to demonstrate our design abilities by revealing aesthetic, smart, and functional design," Pastore says. "We chose not to use captions in our photographs but, rather, allow our clients to realize our ability to thrill, amaze, and innovate."

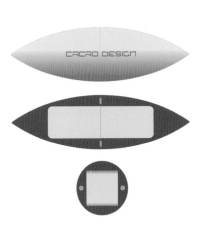

◀▲ *Cacao Design wanted to create a work of art to house their portfolio. These preliminary design ideas and prototypes incorporate Cacao's identity elements to effectively present their portfolio.*

DESIGN FIRM: NATIONAL FOREST DESIGN (USA)

Seeing the Forest through the Trees

PLANNING

What do you get when you cross high-end creative projects for such clients as Nike and Urban Outfitters with exceptional photography and illustrative copy? An outstanding portfolio for National Forest Design in Glendale, California, an award-winning, full-service creative think tank with an expertise in execution.

"We create visual languages that can last a season or a lifetime," says Justin Krietenmeyer, art director at National Forest.

National Forest's mission is to design without limits, as explained in its "concepts and executions" portfolio book: "We push and pull at the cultural fringe. We bounce our ideas off thoughts, and innovations off executions. This is what we have to offer—our combination of passion, personal commitment, fearless creativity, and innovation."

To capture this mission, the National Forest team sought to create a book that effortlessly embraced their successes in the field of design, while illustrating this "new brand of creative agency."

What's more, National Forest sought to create a portfolio book that showed the team's inherent knowledge of today's subcultures with their unparalleled expertise in graphic execution.

Each page within the National Forest portfolio book is a treasure to behold—teeming with innovative design concepts, all of which are presented in an authentic, powerful way. Filled with a wealth of case studies, the book celebrates the intrinsic values that National Forest utilizes to create their innovative concepts.

CREATING

National Forest created a portfolio book that clearly illustrates specific projects, approaches, and results featuring a variety of design styles. The ninety-page, perfect-bound portfolio book with a heavyweight bond paper dust jacket features three case studies and a handful of projects the firm recently completed.

"The National Forest book is for our clients and prospective clients, to demonstrate our capabilities as a design firm," Krietenmeyer says. "The design rationale is fairly straightforward. We have a small introduction discussing our thoughts as a design studio and its responsibilities within the world of art, marketing, and design."

The book then goes into three case studies of larger projects the firm has worked on with Nike, Element Skateboards, and Urban Outfitters. After the case studies, the book includes a handful of other projects that showcase National Forest's capabilities.

IMPLEMENTING

"Our concepts and executions book is sent out regularly to new and potential clients," Krietenmeyer says. In the book you will find a range of creative projects from an Urban Outfitters catalog, to a mural at Rudy's Barbershop in downtown Los Angeles, to a variety of action sports gear and apparel.

"We have experience with every type of design—from physical products to print ads, music festival posters, branding books, and catalogs," Krietenmeyer says. "In addition, we have taken on a number of projects from start to finish: art direction, photography, and design, so we wanted to include as much of this work in the book as possible. We sent out a couple hundred when we first got them," he says. At a cost of $45 (£27) each, National Forest probably only sends two or three a month these days—mainly to companies who are thinking of working with National.

In addition to their portfolio book, they created a demolition derby car as an art and marketing experiment. "We decided it would be interesting to purchase a car, paint it, and enter it in the demolition derby that takes place in Irwindale, California," Krietenmeyer explains. Their race team, the West Coast Rippers, ultimately raced the car and lost.

▲ *Each page within the portfolio book is strategically designed in such a way that it depicts the visual elements used in designing a project from concept to release.*

DEMOLITION DERBY   Selected Projects

A National Forest graphic experiment. After creating the race team "The West Coast
Rippers" National Forest purchased, designed, entered, and sponsored a demolition
derby car for the destructive enjoyment of all in attendance. The National Forest
demolition car competed and lost at NASCAR's world famous Irwindale Speedway
on June 17th 2006.

84

85

"We made posters, T-shirts, and pit passes. We bought a block of tickets and
invited more than 150 friends, family, and clients to come see the carnage. We
liked the idea of creating a somewhat serious collateral package for such a
wacky event," he says. "It was a fun time, even though our car lost very early on."

Every five years or so, National Forest updates their portfolio components. "As
we have only made this one book, I am not sure what we will do next time—
probably more of a printed art piece than a catalog of client projects," he says.
"The books have been received well. It is hard to tell what actually brings in the
work, but we have been busy and steadily growing as a firm."

▲ *Using the medium of a demolition derby
car, National Forest cleverly advertised and
subsequently destroyed their artistic self-
promotion—but had a blast doing it!*

Fifty Inspiring Ideas

Do you have so many deadlines that you're starting to feel like a hamster running on a wheel? Try a few of these ideas to keep the needle on your creative gauge pointing toward full.

1. TAKE A FORTY-EIGHT-HOUR COMPUTER VACATION.
   No email. No Google. No one last peek at that brochure you need to present to the client on Monday morning.

2. TRY MEDITATION.
   Filmmaker David Lynch swears his daily practice is crucial to all his creative work.

3. LEARN SOMETHING NEW THAT ISN'T DIRECTLY RELATED TO YOUR JOB.
   Sign up for a fencing class or master the art of baking puff pastries.

4. FIND A MENTOR—THEY'RE NOT JUST FOR STUDENTS.
   Look for someone whose work you admire or who simply excels in a single area where you'd like to expand your skills.

5. CHANGE THE SCENERY.
   When you feel stuck, pack up your laptop and head to the park or the corner coffee shop. An environmental shift might be enough to shake things loose.

6. FORM A SKETCHING HABIT.
   Buy a small notebook and tuck it in your bag. Then use life's spare moments—standing in line at the DMV or sitting in gridlock traffic— to draw what's around you.

7. SET A THIRTY-DAY CREATIVE CHALLENGE FOR YOURSELF.
   Maybe it's coming up with four concepts for every project that crosses your desk this month instead of three. Or temporarily giving up your blog habit and spending the found time designing a poster a week.

8. PRETEND YOU'RE NOT A GRAPHIC DESIGNER.
   How would a carpenter handle a difficult client? What would a lawyer do if he or she were snowed under with deadlines? Look for approaches and best practices to adopt from other business arenas.

9. FIND A GOAL BUDDY.
   Check in with each other once a week about your creative aspirations
   and how you're going to achieve them. It adds accountability when
   those personal goals start slipping to the bottom of your to-do list.

10. PLAY BEAT THE CLOCK.
    Is your motivation flagging at 3:00 P.M.? Set an egg timer for thirty or
    sixty minutes and challenge yourself to get as much done as possible.
    You can always revise this fast-paced work later.

11. SEARCH OUT OLD BOOKS AND MAGAZINES AT ANTIQUE
    OR JUNK SHOPS.
    Those ads and layouts might shake loose some fresh ideas.

12. DITCH THE MUSEUM AND SPEND SOME TIME
    APPRECIATING CHILDREN'S ARTWORK.
    The paintings hanging on the wall at your niece's grade school might
    offer more imaginative ideas than revisiting the Old Masters.

13. KEEP A FOUND OBJECT COLLECTION.
    Stuff anything that catches your eye—from the type on a takeout menu
    to the hierarchy on a piece of junk mail—into a box or file drawer. Then
    pull them back out when you're in brainstorming mode.

14. BRUSH UP ON PAPER AND PRINTING TECHNIQUES.
    When the right project arises, these can become innovative tools for
    communicating a concept.

15. GO ON A FACT-FINDING MISSION.
    Working on a brochure for an unfamiliar industry? Take the time to read
    up on widget-making or mortgage insurance. You might stumble on
    some context or history that illuminates the problem at hand.

16. REVIEW PAST PROJECTS FOR THE SAME CLIENT.
    Did you miss any opportunities to articulate the message? Can those be
    rolled forward into this piece?

17. STOP BEING SO SERIOUS.
    Take fifteen minutes and intentionally come up with ridiculous concepts
    for the project sitting on your desk. You might stumble on something
    useful. You'll definitely relieve some pressure.

18. GET UP AND MOVE AROUND.

Spend ten minutes away from the computer screen. Walk around the block, dust off your bookshelves, or go make silly faces at the account reps. A little physical activity might give your subconscious a chance to brew up some creative solutions.

19. ASK FOR ADVICE.

Whether you describe your problem to your cube neighbor or your mom, you're likely to get a fresh perspective. Just putting the creative dilemma into words might give rise to a few ideas.

20. DRAW SOMETHING FIFTY TIMES.

Pick any object—from the stapler on your desk to your cat—and draw it fifty times. No fair giving up halfway through. You'll force yourself to look past the obvious and stretch your idea-generating capacity.

21. BOARD GAMES ANYONE?

Stash board games at the office and break them out on slow days or when the brain drain hits on Friday afternoon. An hour of fun promotes bonding and helps put you back in touch with your sense of wonder.

22. GO SHOPPING!

Grab a fellow designer and go on a retail tour. Look for stores you don't normally shop at and take a close look at everything from hang tags and packaging to environmental graphics. Who do you think frequents this store? Do these people overlap with the target market for any of the projects sitting on your desk?

23. WORD EXERCISES.

Write 100 words about the project you're working on as fast as humanly possible. Look back at these unedited thoughts and see whether there's a key point to pull out and build on.

24. EXPERIMENT WITH DIFFERENT SOFTWARE.

Always work in Illustrator? Pop open InDesign for your next brochure. Want a real challenge? See how much fancy footwork you can do with a nondesign program like Microsoft Word.

25. BUY NEW SCHOOL SUPPLIES.

Remember what a rush it was to pick out a new Trapper Keeper? Update your desk with some fun new basics. Spring for the fancy pens or pretty magazine holders and give serious consideration to a 64-pack of Crayola crayons.

26. FIGURE OUT YOUR CREATIVE CRUTCHES; THEN THROW THEM OUT.
Falling back on a favorite font a little too often? Using a similar shape or effect in one too many layouts? Make a list of banned items and stick with it for thirty days.

27. PRETEND THAT EVERY CLIENT IS YOUR FAVORITE.
You're more likely to go the extra mile—and less likely to get irritated at suggestions.

28. REARRANGE YOUR OFFICE.
Or if that's not possible, simply reorganize the things on and in your desk. A slight change in environment can give you a creative boost.

29. WRITE YOUR DREAM PROFESSIONAL BIO.
Then work backward to see what you need to do right now to put yourself on the path to making it come true.

30. WRITE A LETTER TO YOUR CREATIVE HERO—LIVING OR DEAD.
In the letter, outline what you find so inspiring about his or her work. You might just get back in touch with what made you so excited about design in the first place.

31. PULL OUT YOUR SENIOR PORTFOLIO FROM COLLEGE.
Seeing where you started—and how far you've come—can be a powerful experience.

32. MAKE A CHANGE IN YOUR DAILY ROUTINE.
Leave the car at home next week while you take the bus or eat lunch at a hole-in-the-wall diner instead of at your desk. Breaking up your routine may introduce new influences into your life.

33. LOG OFF THE INTERNET AND HEAD FOR THE BRICKS-AND-MORTAR LIBRARY.
Peruse the stacks and flip through the books at random. Find a comfy chair and split your time between reading and observing your fellow patrons.

34. TAKE ON A FREELANCE PROJECT THAT'S COMPLETELY DIFFERENT FROM YOUR REGULAR WORK.
You'll likely bring fresh ideas back to your day job.

35. LOOK FOR INSPIRATION IN THE LEAST LIKELY PLACES.
Working on a project for men? Flip through a women's magazine or catalog to check out designs meant for the opposite sex.

36. START AN INFORMAL CRITIQUE GROUP.
Get together once a month with other creative thinkers—everyone from painters and writers to designers—to share and discuss favorite work from each person in the group.

37. CONSIDER BRINGING HANDMADE ELEMENTS INTO YOUR WORK.
What about burning or distressing paper? Can you draw the illustration yourself? What about building small props for a photo shoot?

38. MAKE CREATIVITY A HABIT.
Even when you're sitting in meetings all day, try to carve out at least an hour to touch base with a hands-on creative task—whether that's working on a rough layout or doing a sketch for your own enjoyment.

39. KEEP RANDOM LISTS.
Jot down people you admire, books you'd like to read, tech toys you want to buy, places to visit before you die, unbelievable facts—anything that captures your fancy.

40. PICK TWO PEOPLE, COUNTRIES, OR BRANDS THAT SEEM LIKE POLAR OPPOSITES.
Then spend fifteen minutes listing as many similarities between them as you can.

41. QUESTION YOUR ASSUMPTIONS.
Does this brochure have to be the same size as the last one? Is the target audience exactly the same? Is there wiggle room in the budget? Can you use illustrations instead of photos?

42. LOOK FOR INSPIRATION IN THE EVERYDAY OBJECTS AROUND YOU.

Take another look at the pencil cup on your desk. Empty it out. Turn it upside down. Look inside. Challenge yourself to discover something new about one of these humdrum items.

43. HIRE A CREATIVITY COACH.

Even if you're not in a rut, they can help you clarify your goals and push you to the next level.

44. TEACH A CLASS.

Even if it's not related to design, you'll practice explaining concepts in a way that's clear and inviting—a skill to brush up on for client.

45. KEEP YOUR OWN PERSONAL RALLY GEAR AT YOUR DESK.

When your side of the scoreboard seems to be slipping, put on a ball cap, novelty glasses, or even a pirate's eyepatch to shake things up.

46. FEELING LUCKY?

Enter a few key words related to your project into the Google search box and hit the "I'm feeling lucky" button.

47. START OVER.

Throw away your best idea and make yourself start the brainstorming process over. You might be surprised at what else you come up with.

48. DON'T LOOK AT THE CLOCK.

Stop paying attention to how much time it's taking you to come up with an idea or work out some rough spots in a design. Cover up the clocks and focus on the work—ignoring those deadline constraints for a bit.

49. FLIP OPEN A NOVEL IN THE MIDDLE AND READ ONLY THOSE TWO PAGES.

Then guess the main plot of the book and make predictions about what's going to happen to those characters. What kind of clothes do they wear? Where do they live? What kind of furniture do they have? Give your invention skills a workout.

50. USE SOMETHING FOR A PURPOSE OTHER THAN WHAT WAS INTENDED.

Draw pictures on your white tennis shoes. Create letters with chopsticks or paper clips.

CONTRI

BUTORS

"THE FIRST GREAT GIFT WE CAN BESTOW ON OTHERS IS A GOOD EXAMPLE." – THOMAS MORELL

2FRESH
London, Istanbul, Paris
www.2fresh.com

2 HATS DESIGN
USA

804 GRAPHIC DESIGN
Germany

1977 DESIGN
UK
www.19-77.com

AKARSTUDIOS
USA
www.akarstudios.com

ALOOF DESIGN
UK
www.aloofdesign.com

AND PARTNERS
USA
www.andpartnersny.com

ANDREA CUTLER DESIGN
USA

ANOTHER LIMITED REBELLION
USA
www.ALRdesign.com

BASS YAGER ASSOCIATES
USA
www.saul-bass.com

BENEFIT COSMETICA, LLC
USA
www.benefitcosmetica.com

BERGMAN ASSOCIATES
USA
www.bergassociates.com

BLOK DESIGN
Mexico
www.blokdesign.com

BOHNSACK DESIGN
USA
www.bohnsackdesign.com

B-ON CREATIVE
South Korea

BRAND ENGINE
USA
www.brandengine.com

BRANDIA CENTRAL
Portugal
www.brandcentral.com

CACAO DESIGN
Italy
www.cacaodesign.it

CAHAN & ASSOCIATES
USA
www.cahanassociates.com

CAPSULE
USA
www.capsule.us

CARLO GIOVANI/DOJO STUDIO
Brazil
www.carlogiovani.com

CARMIT DESIGN
USA
www.carmitdesign.com

CC GRAPHIC DESIGN
USA
www.ccgraphicdesignstudio.com

CDI STUDIOS
USA
www.cdistudios.com

CEMSTONE PRODUCTS COMPANY
USA
www.cemstone.com

CHANGZHI LEE
Singapore
www.leechangzhi.com

CHARGE INDUSTRIAL DESIGN
USA
www.chargedesign.com

CINCINNATI CHILDREN'S HOSPITAL MEDICAL CENTER
USA
www.cincinnatichildrens.org

CONNIE HWANG DESIGN
USA
www.conniehwangdesign.com

CREATIVE SPARK
UK
www.creativespark.co.uk

CRUSH DESIGN
UK
www.crushed.co.uk

**THE DECODER RING DESIGN
CONCERN**
USA
www.thedecoderring.com

DEERE AND COMPANY
USA
www.JohnDeere.com

DESIGN ARMY
USA
www.designarmy.com

DUSTIN EDWARD ARNOLD
USA
www.dustinarnold.com

DZIALIFORNIA
Germany
www.dzialifornia.de

**EDEN DESIGN &
COMMUNICATIONS**
The Netherlands
www.edendesign.nl

ELEMENT
USA
www.elementville.com

ELLIOTTYOUNG
UK
www.elliottyoung.co.uk

EX NIHILO
Belgium
www.exnihilo.be

FACTOR DESIGN
Germany
www.factordesign.com

FACTOR TRES COMUNICACIÓN
Mexico
www.factortres.com.mx

FLEX/THE INNOVATIONLAB
The Netherlands
www.flex.nl

FORMATION DESIGN
USA
www.vizdrink.com

FUSEPROJECT
USA
www.fuseproject.com

FUSION HILL
USA
www.fusionhill.com

GERARD DESIGN
USA
www.gerarddesign.com

GIAMPIETRO + SMITH
USA
www.studio-gs.com

GLOJI, INC.
USA
www.gloji.com

GO WELSH
USA
www.gowelsh.com

HAHN SMITH DESIGN INC.
Canada
www.hahnsmithdesign.com

HARDY DESIGN
Brazil
www.hardydesign.com.br

HARRY ALLEN & ASSOCIATES
USA
www.harryallendesign.com

HARTFORD DESIGN
USA
www.hartforddesign.com

HELENA SEO DESIGN
USA
www.helenaseo.com

**HIRSHORN ZUCKERMAN
DESIGN GROUP, INC.
(HZDG)**
USA
www.hzdg.com

**HORNALL ANDERSON
DESIGN WORKS**
USA
www.hadw.com

HOYNE DESIGN
Australia
www.hoyne.com.au

INTERBRAND
USA
www.interbrand.com

**INTEREUROPE
COMMUNICATIONS
GROUP/ICG**
UK
www.icgonline.co.uk

JASON & JASON VISUAL COMMUNICATIONS
Israel
www.jasonandjason.com

KINETIC SINGAPORE
Singapore
www.kinetic.com.sg

KOREFE
Germany
www.kolle-rebbe.ek

LARSEN
USA
www.larsen.com

LIGALUX GMBH
Germany
www.ligalux.de

LIPPINCOTT
USA
www.lippincott.com

LITTLE YELLOW DUCK
UK
www.littleyellowduck.co.uk

LLDESIGN
Italy
www.lldesign.it

LOCKSTOFF DESIGN
Germany
www.lockstoff-design.de

LUCID BRANDS
USA
www.lucidbrands.com

MEAT AND POTATOES, INC.
USA
www.meatoes.com

METHOD HOME PRODUCTS
USA
www.methodhome.com

MICHAEL OSBORNE DESIGN
USA
www.modsf.com

MILK LTD.
Greece
www.milk.com.gr

MMR STUDIO
Australia
www.mmr.com.au

MONDERER DESIGN
USA
www.monderer.com

MORROW MCKENZIE DESIGN
USA
www.morrowmckenzie.com

MUGGIE RAMADANI DESIGN STUDIO
Denmark
www.muggieramadani.com

NATIONAL FOREST DESIGN
USA
www.nationalforest.com

NIKOLAUS SCHMIDT
Austria

OCTAVO DESIGN PTY. LTD.
Australia
www.octavodesign.com.au

OLOGIE
USA
www.ologie.com

ORGANIC GRID
USA
www.organicgrid.com

OUTSET, INC.
USA
www.outsetinc.com

THE PARTNERS
UK
www.thepartners.co.uk

PEARLFISHER
UK
www.pearlfisher.com

PENTAGRAM DESIGN
UK/USA
www.pentagram.co.uk
www.pentagram.com

PRINCIPLE
USA
www.designbyprinciple.com

QUANGO, INC.
USA
www.quangoinc.com

R DESIGN
UK
www.r-email.co.uk

RAND MCNALLY
USA
www.randmcnally.com

PAUL RAND
USA
www.paul-rand.com

REAL ART DESIGN GROUP.
  INC.
USA
www.realartusa.com

RED WING SHOES
USA
www.redwingshoes.com

REUTERS
USA
www.reuters.com

RIORDAN DESIGN
Canada
www.riordondesign.com

ROME & GOLD CREATIVE
USA
www.rgcreative.com

ROOT IDEA
Hong Kong
www.rootidea.com

RULE29 CREATIVE
USA
www.rule29.com

SAGMEISTER INC.
USA
www.sagmeister.com

SEED CREATIVE
Singapore
www.seed.uk.com

SEGURA, INC.
USA
www.segura-inc.com

SPARK STUDIO PTY. LTD
Australia
www.sparkstudio.com.au

SPUNK DESIGN MACHINE
USA
www.spkdm.com

STUDIOBENBEN
USA
www.benschlitter.com

STUDIO DUMBAR
The Netherlands
www.studiodumbar.nl

SUBPLOT DESIGN, INC.
Canada
www.subplot.com

SUBTRACT STUDIO DE
CREATION
France
www.sub-tract.com

STEVEN SWINGLER
UK

TFI ENVISION
USA
www.tfienvision.com

TIHANY DESIGN
USA
www.tihanydesign.com

TURNER DUCKWORTH
UK, USA
www.turnerduckworth.com

TURNSTYLE
USA
www.turnstylestudio.com

VOICE
Australia
www.voicedesign.net

WEBB SCARLETT DEVLAM
Australia
www.wsdv.com

WILLOUGHBY DESIGN GROUP
USA
www.willoughbydesign.com

WOLFF OLINS
USA
www.wolff-olins.com

WORKTODATE
USA
www.worktodate.com

WORRELL DESIGN
USA
www.worrelldesign.com

About Maura Keller

Maura Keller is a writer and editor based in Minneapolis, Minnesota. She writes about design, marketing, promotions, and a wealth of other topics for a wide range of regional and national publications, as well as Fortune 500 employee communication materials. In addition, Maura provides copywriting and editing services for corporations, advertising firms, and creative agencies.

Her understanding of brand and marketing issues was refined during her years as a marketing communications writer for Yamamoto Moss, an award-winning brand design firm in Minneapolis.

As a writer who is "so into her work that she dreams of creating another letter in the alphabet," Maura has won awards from the Minnesota Society of Professional Journalists and several of her creative writing pieces, including her memoir and poetry, have been published in various literary journals. With a passion for literacy, she serves as vice chair for Read Indeed, a nonprofit literacy program based in Minneapolis.

About Michelle Taute

Michelle Taute is a writer and editor based in Cincinnati. She writes about graphic design for a wide range of magazines, including *HOW*, STEP *inside design*, and *Dynamic Graphics*. Her articles have also appeared in a wide variety of national magazines including *Better Homes and Gardens*, *Woman's Day Special Interest Publications*, *USA Weekend*, *Metropolis*, *Natural Home*, and *The Writer*.

Before her days as a freelancer, Taute worked on the editorial teams of an eclectic list of national magazines. Those titles include *I.D.*, *The Artist's Magazine*, *Family Tree* magazine, *Decorative Artist's Workbook*, *Popular Woodworking*—and even a stint on a short-lived Bob Ross magazine. She continues to take on content editing and project management duties for magazines and books. In addition to editorial work, she regularly handles copywriting for major consumer brands.

www.michelletaute.com

About Capsule

Capsule develops local, national, and international brands from its nerve center in the heart of Minneapolis, Minnesota, USA. Its mission is to reduce the risk of taking brands, products, and services to market through qualitative research methods, holistic brand strategy, comprehensive identity systems, memorable naming, thoughtful package and experience design, and creative writing solutions.

Capsule was founded by Brian Adducci, a designer whose brand and identity expertise is sought by international clients, and Aaron Keller, an adjunct professor of marketing at the University of St. Thomas. Their firm houses an eclectic collection of designers, managers, lawyers, writers, and researchers.

Clients include Fisher-Price, Honeywell, Red Wing Shoes, Target, Sally Hansen, Net Gear, Capital One, Medtronic, Panda Express, and Cargill.

www.capsule.com